Inequality and the 1%

Inequality
and the 1%

Danny Dorling

VERSO
London • New York

Published by Verso with a new afterword 2015
First published by Verso 2014
© Danny Dorling 2014, 2015

1 3 5 7 9 10 8 6 4 2

Verso
UK: 6 Meard Street, London W1F 0EG
US: 20 Jay Street, Suite 1010, Brooklyn, NY 11201
www.versobooks.com

Verso is the imprint of New Left Books

ISBN-13: 978-1-78478-207-8
eISBN-13: 978-1-78168-586-0 (US)
eISBN-13: 978-1-78168-994-3 (UK)

British Library Cataloguing in Publication Data
A catalogue record for this book is available from the British library

**The Library of Congress Has Cataloged the
Original Edition of this Book as Follows**

Dorling, Daniel.
  Inequality and the 1% / Danny Dorling. – 1st Edition.
        pages cm
ISBN 978-1-78168-585-3 (paperback) – ISBN 978-1-
78168-586-0 (ebk)
1. Equality–Great Britain. 2. Poverty–Great Britain.
3. Social classes–Great Britain. I. Title. II. Title:
Inequality and the one percent.
  HM821.D6697 2014
  305.50941–dc23

                    2014017678

Typeset in Sabon by MJ & N Gavan, Truro, Cornwall
Printed in the UK by CPI Group (UK) Ltd, Croydon, CR0 4YY

To Carl Lee – who knows what matters most

Contents

1

Can We Afford the Superrich?

The most important problem we are facing now, today ... is rising inequality.

Robert Shiller, recipient of the 2013
Nobel Prize in Economics[1]

Growing income and wealth inequality is recognised as the greatest social threat of our times. Robert Shiller suggests that the renewed greed of the top 1 per cent has had worse effects than even the financial crash of 2008. The top 1 per cent contribute to rising inequality, not just by taking more and more, but by suggesting that such greed is justifiable and using their enormous wealth to promote that concept. As Warren Buffett, the second richest American in 2011, put it: 'there's been class warfare going on for the last twenty years, and my class has won. We're the ones that have gotten our tax rates reduced.'[2]

For the first time in generations, there is now serious debate over the cost of the superrich. The debate rages in the US, where 66 per cent of the population in 2012 believed rich and poor were in conflict, compared to just 47 per cent in 2009. Only 43 per cent of Americans still thought that people became rich 'mainly because of their own hard work, ambition or education'.[3] Some 46 per cent of Americans believed that to be untrue, leaving 11 per cent unsure. More and more people are learning how the rich reduced their tax rates, weakened trade unions and – for a time – made the idea of avoiding tax acceptable.

To qualify to be a member of the top 1 per cent in the UK, you need a total household income, before tax, of about £160,000 a year. This estimate is for a childless couple. Should you be single, you can enter the 1 per cent with a little less; should you have children, you'll need a somewhat higher household income. These statistics and evidence of a recent contraction of inequality within the 99 per cent all come courtesy of the Institute for Fiscal Studies (IFS).[4] According to that respected body, as the very richest become richer, the rest of us are becoming more equal. However, growing equality within the 99 per cent does us little good when those at the very top keep on taking more and more.

In the UK members of the general public are now surer that the gap between rich and poor is unwarranted than ever before recorded, and they are becoming more sure of this with every year that passes. In 2010, 75 per cent of people who responded to the annual British Social Attitudes survey said that the income gap was too large. By 2012 this figure had risen to 82 per cent. Most importantly, only 14 per cent agreed that the gap was 'about right'.[5] Only one in seven people thought the rich deserved to be so rich, and most of that minority appeared to have little appreciation of just how much better off the 1 per cent were, even when compared to those just below them.[6]

In the UK, dwindling numbers believe the rich generate wealth which all the rest of us get to share, but among them are some prominent people who use their position to promote this belief. There are many multi-millionaires who financially support right-wing think tanks to argue on their behalf. An even smaller, richer group with great influence are the mega-rich owners of newspapers and television channels, but they all now face growing opposition.

Alan Denney
Occupy London, 2011

Around the world, a majority of the global protests that have occurred since January 2006 have centred on issues of economic justice. In 2006 there were just 59 large protests recorded worldwide. In just the first half of 2013 there were 112 protests of a similar size. The rate of large-scale global protest has increased almost fourfold in six years. And these protests are 'more prevalent in higher income countries'[7] – countries where most of the 1 per cent live. Why is this?

There is growing social cohesion among protestors worldwide because the vast majority of people in a majority of rich countries are now suffering as a result of growing inequalities. Since 2008, after the initial shock of the drop in the value of their stock holdings, the rich in both the US and the UK manoeuvred to become much richer. In contrast, in the UK, even before 2008, inequalities were already falling *within* the 99 per cent. But it only became clear after 2008 that there was an increasing gap between the 1 per cent and all of the rest.[8] Now even some of the most well-connected lackeys of the very rich are working for less and less reward.

The vast majority of us are becoming both more equal and often poorer than we were in 2008. In the UK the bottom 99 per cent now have more in common than has been the case for a generation. Some 99 per cent of us are increasingly 'all in it together'. It is the top 1 per cent who increasingly are not part of this new austerity norm. As the economists at the IFS explained in 2013, 'Over the past two decades ... inequality among the bottom 99 per cent has fallen: the Gini coefficient for the bottom 99 per cent was 5 per cent lower in 2011/12, at 0.30, than in 1991.'[9] By 2014 they were reporting that, once differential rates of inflation had been taken into account, the fall in real incomes between 2007/08 and 2013/14 for those near the top and bottom of the income distribution had been nearly identical.[10]

In 2011/12, the average couple without children in the UK took home £442 a week from earnings, just under £23,000 a year (see Figure 1.1). In the middle of the income distribution, people pay as much in tax as they tend to receive in benefits. The poorest tenth of households in the UK have almost no

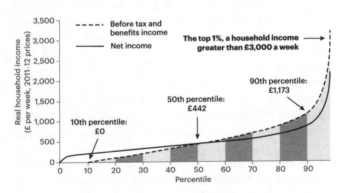

Note: All incomes are expressed in terms of equivalent amounts for a childless couple.
Source: IFS calculations using the Family Resources Survey 2011–12

Figure 1.1 Look up your weekly household earnings to find your rank

income from earnings or from a private pension (these figures include households with only pensioners). They rely entirely on the state to survive. Taking into account benefits, a couple who both qualify for state pensions will receive about £222 a week if the £1.75 pension credit they are entitled to is also claimed.[11] These are the best-off childless couples among the poorest 10 per cent of households in Britain, living on £11,500 a year. As Figure 1.1 shows, they survive on about a fifth of the weekly earnings of an average childless couple in the best-off 10 per cent.

Inequality can be measured in many ways, and this can cause confusion. Many different figures can be used. The ratio of five just quoted can be easily lowered if the private education or pension contributions paid by the richer couple are deducted, or it can be made to appear much higher if the average income of all of the top 10 per cent is used, rather than the income of the median (midpoint) couple among the top 10 per cent. Taking children into account complicates the picture further. Finally, calculating entire distribution measures of inequality, such as the Gini coefficient, tends to cause many more readers' eyes to glaze over.

Fortunately there is a strong correlation between the complex Gini coefficient of income inequality (measured after tax and benefits and adjusting for household size) and the simple measure of how much of total income the best-off 1 per cent receives each year. When the 1 per cent receives a low proportion of national income, inequality for the rest of the population is forced to be lower, because no other group can receive more than the best-off 1 per cent. Simply concentrating on the share taken by the 1 per cent is enough. It may even be one of the best measures of inequality to consider in terms of how simple a target it may be for effective social policy.[12]

Economists have measured the fortunes of the best-off 1 per cent for decades. Only recently have political activists, campaigners, and even those anarchists who most distrust economists become as interested in these statistics. In 2011

David Graeber was credited with coining the phrase 'We are the 99 per cent', and so made the best-off 1 per cent the object of opposition. And with that phrase came what appeared to be new home truths. For example, for the 99 per cent, as Graeber explains, for most people 'the fear of losing your job is far greater than the hope of finding a truly fulfilling one'.[13] However, not all of the 99 per cent are unfulfilled, and many of the 1 per cent undertake work they find dull just to remain in that income bracket – though their income often means that in the rest of life they have choices that others can only dream of, other than the choice to be normal.

Before discussing what it is to be normal, we need a better grasp of just how unusual the 1 per cent have become, and especially of how much inequality there is within the 1 per cent: far more than within the 99 per cent. A pre-tax household income for a childless couple of £160,000 a year puts you among the very poorest of the 1 per cent. By August 2013 there were 29.97 million people in employment in the UK. Average weekly pay was £473 in both the private and public sectors.[14] The average annual UK salary in 2013 was £24,596; but for the top 1 per cent their mean average was fifteen times as much: an average take-home income of £368,940.[15] That is more than twice as much as the least well-off of the 1 per cent received.

Become a member of the more well-heeled middle of the 1 per cent, and school fees are not an issue, save for the most expensive of public schools, and only then if you have several children. You are extremely unlikely to use the state sector for many services, and you may be annoyed that, as far as you are concerned, your council tax only pays for your bins to be collected. However, should you be among the least well-off of the 1 per cent, then your disposable income after paying for housing is many times less than that of the median member of the 1 per cent. The 1 per cent is not a unified group, but it is one for which a series of generalisations can be made.

The National Health Service (NHS) is only needed by those in the middle of the 1 per cent should they require emergency surgery of the kind the private sector does not provide. Be in the 1 per cent, and you may use the first-class carriages in trains when that is faster than hailing a taxi or using your chauffeur – but you may also want to drive one of your new cars yourself. Tell-tale signs such as multiple new car purchases, taking several overseas holidays a year, and other purchases generally seen as extravagances by most people – but as normal among the 1 per cent – have been used to estimate where they are most concentrated.[16]

In contrast to the 1 per cent, everyone else really does look very, and increasingly, ordinary. Take a couple without children who have a joint income before tax of £50,000. One small pay rise and they'd be members of the top 10 per cent; but they receive £110,000 less each year than the poorest of the top 1 per cent. Because it is now just the top 1 per cent who are still becoming much richer in the UK, it is within the top 10 per cent of society that growing inequality is now most clear to see – but only when the top 1 per cent are included in that top tenth.

Average household income in Britain is now just under £23,000 a year. It is a little lower than average skilled earnings. Many well-paid people tend to live with other well-paid people in the same household. The average household has one person bringing in a wage and another adding some part-time income, or a pension, but not much. The poorest tenth of households in Britain have no earnings or any other private income, and no extra income such as a non-state pension. That bottom tenth is entirely reliant on welfare payments to survive.

For the average UK family with two children, the amount needed just to survive with any decency is rising by 5 per cent a year as the costs of providing for children rise more quickly than the growth in average living costs. These costs include food, rent, heating, clothing, travel costs and all our other everyday expenses, plus the occasional treat such as the school trip that all children should be entitled to. The average family in Britain has been becoming poorer, often worrying about sums of money that are essentially spare change as far as the wealthy are concerned. We know all this because research teams now count every penny of these costs, and ask for our opinions on others' spending.

For many years, the Joseph Rowntree Foundation–sponsored Minimum Income Standards research team has charted the costs of these essentials needed to live the most basic of lives in the UK. They uncovered a 20 per cent rise in the share of all households in Britain living below the generally accepted minimal standard of living between 2008/9 and 2011/12, as living standards deteriorated.[17] These standards are derived by asking a wide range of people what they think everyone in the UK should be able to afford. Unsurprisingly, the team found that a small amount of money given to the families of poorer children has a far greater beneficial effect than when it disappears behind the cushions of the voluptuous sofas of the rich. The 1 per cent appear to have an ever-growing appetite for more money for themselves, but a large blind-spot when it comes to others' needs.

Compared to the top 1 per cent, the rest of the top 20 per cent in Britain are taking home less and less. Between 2007 and 2012, the real disposable income of the top fifth of households in Britain dropped by £4,200 a year – a 6.8 per cent fall for that group. The average fall for all households was £1,200 a year. This has reduced differences within the 99 per cent. From 2011 to 2012 median household income in the UK fell by 2.8 per cent (when taking inflation into account), but mean incomes fell by only 1.6 per cent, simply because the very rich – the top 1 per cent – did not see a fall.[18]

People in the UK are beginning to understand that the 1 per cent really are now extraordinarily rich, and very different to themselves. Most people are entirely excluded from the top 1 per cent, no matter how well they do in a career. The most expensive head teachers in Britain are paid around £112,181 per year – about 70 per cent of the annual income of the lowest-paid of the top 1 per cent.[19] The top pay of General Medical Practitioners (GPs) in the UK receives a great deal of attention. But in 2011/12 the average GP received £103,000 a year; only 2 per cent of GPs earned over £200,000, and just 160 of those earned over £250,000.[20] The remaining 520 members of this tiny group of top-earning GPs earned below a quarter of a million pounds a year. That might be far too much for someone who is essentially a public servant, but it is very low by the standards of the top 1 per cent whose ranks they have joined.

In short, almost all people who now have jobs that would traditionally place them within the best-off 1 per cent of society – head teachers of large schools, the local doctor – are now among the best-rewarded of the 99 per cent, rather than being members of a group apart. Although some mix enough with those above them to be aware of what they are missing out on, in recent years they have become increasingly more like the majority they serve than the minority who are now much richer than them. However, a tiny minority of former public servants have now joined the 1 per cent, and they often include people whose actions are not universally much admired – because they are on the take.

The figures used above that show how few doctors are members of the 1 per cent are based on GPs' income tax returns, and include all their taxable earnings. An investigation by the general practice magazine *Pulse* found that one in five of the GPs who sit on the boards of England's 211 Clinical Commissioning Groups (CCGs) – the boards that decide how NHS budgets are spent locally – also had a stake in a private healthcare firm that was providing services to their own CCG.[21] It is extremely unlikely that the GP you get an appointment with is in the top 1 per cent,[22] but we need to be aware that a few people who are paid to be GPs are also profiting greatly from the privatisation of the NHS and becoming rich enough to join the 1 per cent.

The reason we need to be acutely aware of current trends is where they might take us. In the US the top 1 per cent now receives almost 20 per cent of all income – a figure they last ascended to in 1928, the year before that most infamous stock market crash. Today, making it into the top 1 per cent in the US requires an annual income of at least $394,000. This is higher than the £160,000 in the UK because inequality in the US is greater. Getting into the top 10 per cent in the US requires an annual salary of at least $114,000 – more similar to that required to enter the UK top 10 per cent, but a little higher in real terms.[23]

The US is very unusual. In most affluent countries in the world, the best-off 1 per cent get by with far less, the top 10 per cent are much more like everyone else, and everyone else tends to be much better-off. In Japan, which is one of the most economically equitable countries in the world, the best-off receive roughly half as much as in the US – just under 10 per cent of all national income, a share very similar to what the Japanese richest 1 per cent secured in 1944; in 1945 the income share of the richest 1 per cent in Japan dropped to 6.4 per cent, and has remained within those bounds ever since – less than half the equivalent figure in the US. Losing a war, or having to pay for a war, is one of the fastest ways for a society to become more equal.[24]

Today the UK sits halfway between Japan and the US. The British top 1 per cent last secured a share of UK national income as large as they do today back in 1937. Between 1976 and 1979, less than forty years ago, their share had fallen to below 6 per cent, to what had been the Japanese post-war minimum; but these were the four years when Britain was most equal.[25] In the late 1970s the very best-off people in Britain only received a mean average income of six times the national mean – only four times after they had paid tax.

The 1970s in the UK were not just a time when income equalities were greatest for the 99 per cent – within the top 1 per cent, there was greater equality than ever before. By

1978 the very richest, the 0.01 per cent, were receiving four times what the average member of the top 1 per cent received. Today it is the richest 0.1 per cent who get four times more than the average member of the top 1 per cent, while the 0.01 per cent get even more again. As you go forward in time and up the monetary scale, the income gradient becomes steeper and steeper. As the 1 per cent have pulled away, inequalities within the 1 per cent have grown enormously.

To understand why so few of the 1 per cent feel they are taking too much, it is worth reiterating that those just tipping into the 1 per cent league today, with incomes of at least £160,000 for a couple with no children, are not likely to feel that they are particularly well-off given what they earn, between the two of them. Those who just qualify as being within the 1 per cent, at the bottom of the 1 per cent, receive only half of what the mean average household in the UK top 1 per cent earns. Those at the bottom of the top 1 per cent often feel relatively poor – but they need not, if only they were to look down a little more to the 99 per cent, to see how much they have compared to everyone else.

It is because of the growing divide between the 1 per cent and the 99 per cent that those at the bottom of the 1 per cent don't often look down. A financial chasm is opening up between them and the best-off of the rest – the best-off of the 99 per cent. It is because this chasm is now so large that those at the bottom of the 1 per cent more often look up to see how small they are in comparison to the giants above them. Above them they see what Thomas Piketty has termed 'meritocratic extremism', people who try to justify huge incomes in terms of what is required to match the wealth of those who inherit the most.[26] They are out of touch with the dwarfs of the 99 per cent. But they need to look down, because if they don't they too will soon be in trouble. And some are beginning to look to their feet and then down over the edge.

Even the worst-off couple in the top 1 per cent has eight times more than the amount a couple with two children

requires if they are to live at the UK minimum living standard –
the minimal amount of income that allows any decency. That
minimum was estimated to be £19,400 a year in 2013.[27] At an
even greater extreme, the mean average single member of the
top 1 per cent has twenty-one times the minimum necessary
subsistence income for a single person in Britain, according to
the minimum income standards described above.

It is through their actions, the influence of their corporations and the politicians they support that the top 1 per cent
in the UK fuel growing income inequality between themselves
and everyone else, leaving so many with so little because a few
think they must have so much. We know that it is because of
the huge cost of the top 1 per cent that there is more poverty
in the UK than in any more equitable rich nation.[28] Reducing
inequality will not necessarily be sufficient to reduce poverty
greatly; but poverty cannot be reduced while high levels of
inequality remain, because a large part of what it is to be poor
is being valued as near worthless.[29]

The total annual cost of the top 1 per cent is £110 billion;
this is their average of earned plus unearned income of
£368,840, shared between around 300,000 people – 1 per
cent of the UK's workforce of 30 million. That figure is much
higher than the mean of what the top 1 per cent of employees
earn a year in basic pay, which is £135,666, and it has more
than doubled in real terms since 1986.[30] This is because so
many of the 1 per cent also secure annual bonuses on top
of salary, or have other sources of income.[31] And when their
bonuses are threatened by European law they find ways of
circumventing the legislation, even with the connivance of the
UK government and tax authorities.[32]

Of those within the top 1 per cent who are receiving the
bulk of their income from earnings, we know that more than
80 per cent are men, and that, as the income share of the
1 per cent has grown, so too has the share taken by those
men within the 1 per cent. The 1 per cent are also getting
older, now mostly being between fifty and sixty-four; and the

largest, fastest-growing, and best-paid group within the 1 per cent work in finance.[33] The few that regularly appear on our TV screens are typical of the group as a whole: old, male, white and – very often – bankers.

To get a grasp of just how much money the top 1 per cent use up, a simple illustration may help. This might be how much better the money could be spent on immunising every child or ending world hunger – but the millions and billions of people who could benefit from a little sharing out of the wealth of the superrich soon render such comparisons meaningless. In a world with a population of under 8 billion, £110 billion could go a long way. But instead of thinking of the possible uses for all these monies that would most relieve suffering, let us restrict ourselves to the UK, and to a flippant but I hope helpful example.

Try to guess how many royal families you could get for the same cost as the 1 per cent. The sovereign grant in the year to 2013 was £33.3 million.[34] This is the amount of money provided by the government to the royal household in support of the queen's duties, including the maintenance of the occupied royal palaces: Buckingham Palace, St James's Palace, Clarence House, Marlborough House Mews, the residential and office areas of Kensington Palace, Windsor Castle, the buildings in the Home and Great Parks at Windsor, and Hampton Court Mews and Paddocks.

Republicans put the real cost of having an extended royal family at £202.4 million a year.[35] They include the security costs and the revenue of the Duchies of Lancaster and Cornwall. Suppose we roughly split the difference and suggest that the royals cost us less than half what the republicans claim, but three times what royalists like to report. The royal family then costs around £100 million a year to run. For the price of the richest 1 per cent in Britain, we could instead support 1,100 royal families.[36]

Of course, 1,100 royal families is a ridiculous idea, but it gives you an idea of just how much money that tiny 1 per cent of the population is receiving every year – and the superrich don't even smile and wave, rarely open buildings, never permit the public to view their palaces, and don't invite commoners to garden parties. Many people are opposed to having a royal family, partly on cost grounds. However, on those grounds they should be looking at the 1 per cent, which is well over a thousand times more expensive in aggregate than all the royals combined.

To believe that it makes sense that just a tiny proportion of people deserve such a huge slice of the cake, you have to believe that there is something very special about the 1 per cent group that justifies their income and wealth. Unfortunately many people do, even though an increasing number see the extent of their riches as unjustified. The effects of those beliefs in the worthiness of the rich are corroding the fabric of society. A majority has begun to believe that the poor have no right to live near the centres of our most expensive cities, and it becomes possible for prime ministers to claim that cutting benefits to the poorest in society is part of some moral mission.[37]

Inequality and the top 1 per cent are not the same phenomena; they are not even the same thing measured in different ways. There will always be a top 1 per cent, but there can be more or less inequality. When some of the 1 per cent use their resources to suggest that increasing inequality is good, a toxic feedback loop can result. They suggest that you only have to earn more to go up the ladder. That is not true. You can only go up the ladder if someone else comes down it (see the illustration on page 15). The number in the top 1 per cent is fixed. Few people are prepared to accept a fall in income except on retirement, and in the UK and the US the top 1 per cent have recently shown themselves to be the most able group at ensuring their incomes continue to rise in defiance of the economic crisis.

We have seen this before. There was rising poverty in an era of escalating inequality that preceded the First World War, and before the Wall Street Crash in 1929, which caused shock waves to reverberate across all the rich countries of the world.

'Sacrifice' by James Francis Horrabin

Today, similar levels of excess to those seen in the 1930s among the rich are only found in a few very unequal countries – places that have forgotten their past. The US, Canada and the UK lead the rich world's inequality league table. The countries of the rest of Europe and Japan show that the opposite is possible. In places like Switzerland, the best-off 1 per cent receive only half the proportion of income they receive in the UK. It is possible to have many bankers but not to pay them so much; and Swiss bankers don't appear as accident-prone as their US and UK counterparts, despite their much lower average remuneration.

Although the rich can fuel a particular kind of wealth-creation – one of ever more wealth for themselves – there is no perpetual-motion machine causing the top 1 per cent to become richer and richer and take an even greater share year on year, with their salary reviews and property value escalators.[38] There is no iron law dictating that everyone else must step down in times of austerity, with those at the bottom drowning.

The superrich bubble has burst many times in many places over the course of world history. The bubble bursts when a country loses a war, as the invading forces have no interest in maintaining the wealth of the leaders of those they were fighting; but it can also be deflated slowly, by public consent, as occurred in the UK between 1918 and 1978,[39] and as is still taking place in countries as diverse as the Netherlands, Switzerland and Japan. Sometimes a chain of events means that the bubble bursts in many places at the same time. This happened a century ago, during the First World War. The rich had been allowed to become too rich. They were the only people with the money to finance a fight that went on far longer and was far costlier than the warring governments had expected. Governments were forced to super-tax the wealthy. A surtax, or super-tax, was introduced in 1909, and its level was raised rapidly during the First World War.

A poster from the People's Budget 1908

By 1918 super-tax was bringing in 12 per cent of all income tax.[40] Then, during the Second World War, when monies were needed quickly again, the UK top rate of income tax rose rapidly, reaching 99.25 per cent by 1945, and did not fall below 90 per cent until the late 1970s.[41] Perhaps surprisingly, the main effect of a super-tax was not to raise revenue. What it did was to curtail the greed of most of those near the top of the income hierarchy, deterring them from seeking large pay increases and bonuses. Pay at the top rose far more slowly than pay at the bottom for the whole period from 1918 to 1978. Britain became more equal. In 1966 the Beatles famously complained about the tax man taking such a high proportion of their earnings, and spreading those monies – which had initially come from the thousands of record-buying teenagers – back into society. High taxes did not appear to curtail the Beatles' success, but the pop stars' public anger at not being able to make even more money than they were doing was just the tip of the iceberg of private angst among some of the very richest people in British society, who were coming to believe that they were hard done by.

The superrich bubble began to grow again from the 1970s onwards, as the 1 per cent slowly regained the upper hand over the 99 per cent below them. It happened partly by accident and partly by design.[42] As inflation slowed, debts of all kinds did not shrink as fast as they had before; the richest of the 1 per cent grew richer, and the power of the international bond markets it controlled subsumed that of democratically elected politicians.[43] From the Beatles' lyrical complaints (in 'Taxman') through to a newspaper magnate's influence on his journalists' reporting, the wealthy getting wealthier again was increasingly portrayed as 'only fair'. When portrayed as equitable, the bubble of their wealth only grows and grows, but it cannot keep growing forever.

What is it that eventually breaks the bubble? What causes the wealth of the superrich to implode? The simple answer is that the price of the rich becomes too high, the bubble grows too large, and eventually there are too few people left with enough assets to service it. What appeared to be a perpetual-motion machine is revealed as a chimera. International bond markets fail, share prices crash, the value of gold falls towards its industrial worth (as a good conductor of electricity), property prices crash towards what people can realistically pay. Beliefs in the scientific wisdom of orthodox economics are shattered, and revealed as a stupid hoax.[44] The bubble bursts in many ways.

The price of the richest 1 per cent is easy to calculate: it is how much extra they cost above what would be an equal share. If the top 1 per cent take 20 per cent, then their additional price is 19 per cent of the entire economy. It is normally a huge amount. The price rarely falls below 5 per cent of the entire national income, so let us call that the necessary cost of the top 1 per cent under capitalism. When the top 1 per cent take 15 per cent, as they do now in the UK, then an extra 10p in every pound earned in Britain unnecessarily goes to the people who already earn the most.

It is hard to assess precisely when that price of the superrich becomes too burdensome to be sustained any longer. There will always be a price. There will always be a small group who receive substantially more; but, after taxes have been taken, that price has ranged from 3 per cent of the economy of the UK in 1978 to almost 24 per cent in 1913.[45] Today their take is around 15 per cent, and most people know it is too high. But how might a fall in the price of the 1 per cent be achieved?

In a few affluent countries, such as the Netherlands and Switzerland, the best-off 1 per cent have never been cheaper, have never had a smaller share of national income than they have today. After taxes, their additional income may cost as little as 2 or 3 per cent of national GDP. In contrast, the same group of people in the US are each costing the nation more than ten times as much. In 1916, in countries like Sweden and the Netherlands, the richest 1 per cent were taking more than a quarter of the total national income. By 2011 in Sweden they were taking 7 per cent, and in the Netherlands less than 6 per cent. The take of the richest 1 per cent in Sweden fell to as low as 4 per cent in 1981. So, for Swedes, the top 1 per cent taking 7 per cent is high – it is, after all, still seven times the average income. But it is less than half the 15 per cent which the best-off 1 per cent were taking in the UK around 2007, and just a third of what the richest 1 per cent in the US are now taking.[46]

In countries like the Netherlands and Switzerland, the relative incomes of the rich have never been lower than they are today. In Sweden and France, they are not far off their lowest shares. Only in a few rich countries, like the UK and the US, have the richest succeeded in taking more and more, year on year (see Figure 1.2).

What matters most is that the wealth of the richest 1 per cent has a great impact on the rest of us. In the UK today, the poorest couple could double their annual income and the median households could be 10 per cent better off if the richest

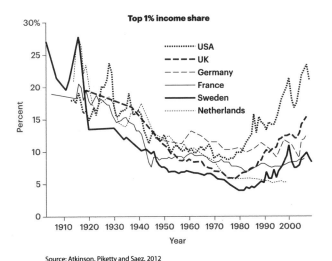

Source: Atkinson, Piketty and Saez, 2012

Figure 1.2 Where the 1 per cent have taken the most and the least

1 per cent took just five times the average income rather than fifteen times, and the excess was shared out more equally. Some might argue that the 1 per cent pay their way in tax. In a highly unequal country where the richest 1 per cent take a huge amount of the income, they will often inevitably end up paying a greater share of the income tax. In the UK it is widely reported that the top 1 per cent pay between 25 per cent and 33 per cent of all income tax received by government. Before the 2008 crash it was nearer a quarter; now it is nearer a third.

A spokesperson for the Treasury recently insisted: 'The government has taken action to protect those on low incomes from the challenging economic circumstances we face: 2.7 million people have been taken out of income tax altogether as a result of increases to the personal allowance.'[47] The truth is that most people have so little money that their income is insufficient to pay much direct tax. Despite this, the poor often end up paying the most tax relative to their measly incomes, due to indirect consumption taxes; but still their taxes are only a small proportion of what the government needs.

Often the reporting suggests that the rich do us a favour by paying tax. Rarely is it pointed out that they take too much income, or that the government currently collects only 26 per cent of its revenue through direct income tax. Value Added Tax and National Insurance account for 35 per cent of government revenue. Today one of the most closely comparable countries to the UK in terms of income and taxation inequalities is Russia, where the best-off tenth of the population now take sixteen times the annual income of the worst-off tenth, compared to around fifteen times in the UK.[48] But rich Russians still flee to the UK because they are even better off here, benefiting from lower UK taxes on the rich and especially on their residential property.[49]

In the UK a similar degree of inequality to that now seen in Russia has been attained but it was attained at a slower rate, so it is easier to present current high inequality as natural. Nevertheless, in 2013 it was revealed that the richest person in the UK was the Russian billionaire Alisher Usmanov, whose fortune was estimated at £13.3 billion.[50] Twenty-five years ago the list had been topped by Queen Elizabeth, whose wealth was then estimated at £5.2 billion.[51] Although we could afford to run 1,100 royal families for the annual income cost of the best-off 1 per cent, we could not afford to have 1,100 royal families as rich in wealth. That would require almost £6 trillion. UK total net worth in 2012 was estimated to be only £6.8 trillion.[52] However, this figure jumped by half a trillion pounds in just one year – the twelve months to August 2013.[53]

The rise in UK national wealth was put down to the increased property values – but we know which property rose most in value, both in absolute and percentage terms: the wealth of the superrich and the value of their land and property in London. If inequalities in the value of property continue to rise at current rates, the wealth of the 1 per cent would approach 1,100 times the wealth of the royal family. But is this really possible? Where will they get that huge amount of extra money from?

When the divide between the 1 per cent and the 99 per cent has widened while countries have become poorer overall, the consequences have been dire. As the richest become richer and richer, everyone else suffers as a result. During the last four years, the divisions in the economic and social interests of the 99 per cent of people, in both the US and UK, have started to narrow rapidly.

Without the support of the upper middle class, it becomes harder for the elite to rule, to secure the election of their favoured politicians, to control public opinion, to remain elite. This happens when members of the upper middle class realise that they have more in common with those beneath them than with the top 1 per cent. A new solidarity develops. Dissent rises and is not subdued. The top 1 per cent have 53 per cent of the total personal tradable wealth in the UK, the next 4 per cent have 10 per cent of the wealth, and the next 45 per cent have 31 per cent. The remaining 50 per cent of the population

If UK Land Were Divided Like UK Wealth (excluding main residence)

THE NEXT 45% WOULD OWN THIS

50% WOULD OWN THIS

THE NEXT 4% WOULD OWN THIS

THE RICHEST 1% WOULD OWN THIS

Source: Office for National Statistics surveys of assets 2006–08, updated by and incorporating data from *The Sunday Times* Rich List of 2010

Figure 1.3 Liquid Wealth in the UK: inequalities in worth of disposable assets

have only 6 per cent of the total wealth between them all (see Figure 1.3).[54]

The top 1 per cent today have an enormous amount of money. They own newspapers and TV channels, and they spread myths to offset the growing consensus among the 99 per cent; stories about benefit scroungers are designed to rally people to their side.[55] They spread myths of generating jobs through their 'wealth creation'. They are treated with deference in newspapers and on TV and radio news programmes, just as clerics used to be treated a century ago. Business 'dragons' are presented as benevolent creatures, not destructive, scaly reptiles. The BBC Radio 4 *Today* programme has a business slot fronted by a former city executive, in which CEOs are rarely criticised.

If the National Minimum Wage had kept pace with FTSE 100 CEO salaries since 1999, it would now stand at £18.89 per hour, instead of £6.19 per hour.[56] For some reason, however, BBC reporters rarely ask CEOs why the gap between their pay and the pay of the poorest staff in their organisations has grown into such a gulf in so short a time. The unstated implication is that the lowest-paid staff are lucky to have any job at all, and only have what they have thanks to the benevolence and fine *leadership* skills of the 1 per cent.

If the top 1 per cent actually created more jobs as they became wealthier, then ordinary people would be surrounded by employment opportunities in both the US and the UK. Instead it is in Germany, where the wealthiest 1 per cent receives half as much, in pay and bonuses, as their counterparts in the US, that unemployment is at a twenty-year low. Even in Germany, there is no minimum wage and many of the new jobs are insecure; but in countries that control their top 1 per cent, that group works more effectively for the good of all, or at least creates less trouble and a little less misery.

The fact that both the UK and US are far less equal than almost all other affluent nations, and that inequality in both has in the past been significantly less, is not as widely recognised as it needs to be. We also need to begin to recognise how the top 1 per cent get away with taking so much, what effect a very rich 1 per cent has on society in general, and how 99 per cent of people are persuaded into accepting so much less.

The top 1 per cent differentiates itself from the rest in many ways. Inequality is more than just economics – it is the culture that divides and makes social mobility so painful, both for those dropping down the income and wealth scales and for those going up. Therefore the rest of this book is structured not in terms of economic outcomes, but according to how the top 1 per cent school their children and what happens to the rest of our children; how they are rewarded for work, and the effect on everyone else's employment; how their amassing of more and more wealth affects the cost of all our homes; and how so many aspects of our health are related to the extent of inequality.

This book concentrates especially on how the top 1 per cent impact upon the lives of the remaining 99 per cent. It has already been widely demonstrated that growing inequality and poverty have terrible effects on the health and well-being of the rest of society. What is not so well understood is how, as the inequalities grow, politicians who are members of the 1 per cent are forced to break promises such as that of not introducing university tuition fees – as Mr Clegg had promised – because they do not wish to acknowledge the alternative of stopping the 1 per cent taking so much.

A much greater promise than 'no tuition fees' has been broken by the leader of the Conservative Party. That promise was made in 2006. Some political leaders within the 1 per cent have become very good at promising to reduce inequality just before they gain power, but then increase it. Foremost in the race to the heights of hypocrisy is the prime minister: 'We need to think of poverty in relative terms – the fact that some people lack those things which others in society take for granted … In the next twenty-five years, I want my party to be in the vanguard of the fight against poverty.'[57]

In the United States, after one-and-a-half terms in office, President Obama admitted that, even under his tenure, 95 per cent of income gains between 2009 and 2012 had been won by the 1 per cent.[58] He has now left himself only two years in which to reverse that trend, in which to try at least to keep a small part of the promise he made to those who voted for him so enthusiastically. But even if he fails he may tell himself, and others, that he did not.

In May 1988 the then prime minister, Margaret Thatcher, told the House of Commons: 'Everyone in the nation has benefited from increased prosperity – everyone.'[59] That, of course, was untrue. But some were more grateful than others. Twenty-five years later, when she died, it became clear that the very wealthy twins, Sir David Barclay and Sir Frederick Barclay, owners of the *Daily Telegraph* and *Sunday Telegraph*, had allowed her to stay in London's Ritz hotel for nothing – presumably out of gratitude.

To this day, it remains unclear who had been paying for Mrs Thatcher's £6 million home in Chester Square, Belgravia – although it appears not to have been her or her family.[60] Among the top 0.01 per cent are people who fervently believe that inequality is good, that the poor deserve nothing more than to be poor because they do not have it in them to be any better, and that the rich are worth their riches. Most of the top 1 per cent appear not quite as deranged and driven, but they are a hard group to survey, let alone tax, so it is time we took a closer look at life at the top and its effects on us all.

2

Childhood

There is a damaging 'poverty of aspiration' in Britain that lies not in the working classes but among our political elites. Yet what UK society needs, more than anything else in the contemporary moment, is greater equality and less social and economic distance between its citizens.

Diane Reay, Professor of Education,
University of Cambridge, 2012[1]

We have an educational system that is designed to polarise people. It creates an elite that often has little respect for the majority of the population, thinks that it should earn extraordinarily more than everyone else, and defines many of the jobs of others as so contemptible as apparently to justify their living in relative poverty. The ideology that underlies elitism is imparted in childhood. For the elite, especially in the most unequal countries where the educational systems help to maintain the status quo, other people's children can be greatly denigrated.

The country where the richest 1 per cent takes the most is also the rich country where sixteen- to twenty-four-year-olds are most likely to be innumerate – the United States of America.[2] England is home to the third-most innumerate cohort of young adults in the rich world. In Finland and Japan, two of the world's most equitable rich countries, young adults are the most numerate. The top four countries by young adult numeracy also include the Netherlands and Korea, where equality levels are high, but not the highest (see Figure 2.1). These coincidences appear to be related in at least three ways.

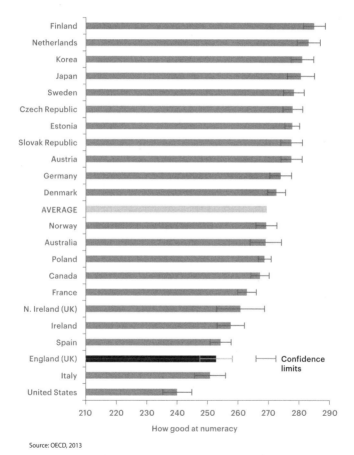

Source: OECD, 2013

Figure 2.1 Mean proficiency in numeracy at ages 16–24, OECD Countries 2013

Firstly, when the rich take as much as they take in the US and the UK there is less left to spend on the rest, and the education of the poor suffers. The easiest way to increase the value of private education is to reduce the quality of state education by simply spending less on it, just as reducing the quality of the NHS increases the benefits of private health-care without having to do anything in particular to improve private healthcare. When the rich say they want lower taxes, they are also saying they want to pay less for other people's schools and hospitals.

Secondly, how we educate and bring up our children more generally matters because, for example, when many people are innumerate it is easier to convince a large number that they or their children might one day be among the 1 per cent – despite the fact that the number of people in the 1 per cent is fixed. Many others in these unequal situations assume that they do not ever 'deserve' to be in that top 1 per cent because they are simply too stupid, as demonstrated by their exam results. The myth that the people at the top of the economic pile are super-intelligent is widespread.

Thirdly, when the top 1 per cent dominates society, as it does in the US and the UK today, it is able to shape what we call education to work more in its favour, to become less about learning and more about ranking. Children are repeatedly tested and channelled towards what they are told is their allotted place along the continuum, to be the 'best' they can, which is usually not a lot in the opinion of that 1 per cent, if not also of their teachers. To overvalue the 1 per cent is to devalue the rest.

As the divisions within our society grow, the main aim of teachers becomes no longer to educate the child for life, but increasingly just to try to keep their school out of trouble. They must teach children how to pass tests rather than how to learn. The whole enterprise has become distorted in the name of supposedly upholding accountability. But some teachers do not have to concentrate on crowd control as much as others. Schools in Britain vary more than in almost any other comparable country, because children in Britain, and especially England, are more segregated into different types of school.

Private 'prep' schools for younger children in England have average class sizes of thirteen children – half the average size of state primaries, and far fewer per teacher than the crowded primary schools of cities with growing populations. This is because so much more money is spent per child in the English private sector, which results in less being spent on state schools because there is less pressure from the very affluent for their improvement. They do not want to be taxed more to provide schools they avoid using. Only nine countries out of thirty-five surveyed by the OECD had larger class sizes than those in the UK, and they were mostly much poorer countries. Private schools and the bodies that promote them use these statistics to encourage the few who have the money to have a choice not to use state education.[3]

It is the very richest, the 1 per cent, who most solidly support segregated education, who almost all use only private schools – usually the most expensive of all private schools. They are followed by another 6 per cent of the population who find paying the private school fees far harder, but feel they must do so because of how wide the private/state division in England has become. State education suffers in the UK and, largely as a consequence, is not seen as being as good as elsewhere in Europe – where almost everyone uses it. In the UK and US, when people complain, some key supporters of the 1 per cent suggest privatising all schools.

Maintaining an Unfair Advantage

> I believe that the only way to make a major improvement in our educational system is through privatization ... Vouchers are not an end in themselves; they are a means to make a transition from a government to a market system.
>
> Milton Friedman, *Washington Post*, 19 February 1995[4]

Attitudes towards education once held by only a small elite have today come to be presented as common sense. Many members of the 1 per cent who wish to see their share of income rise like to portray current state schools as the problem, and they suggest that those schools are the reason why others end up being paid so little, and why average incomes have dropped. They have convinced many people of this. They often pretend there was once a golden age of state schooling when the grammar school gave working-class children a chance. Some may even believe this was true – but grammar schools were a relic of a more unequal age.

People currently buy access to 'top' education for a reason – to gain an unfair advantage. The UK government's own Social Mobility and Child Poverty Commission has undertaken research that found that, three years after graduation, 'male graduates from a managerial background who attended a private school are around 10 percentage points more likely to enter the highest status occupations'.[5] By 'managerial background', the authors of this study meant having a parent who was a manager, and they equated status with pay.

The private school advantage can be found to influence later careers 'despite the same prior academic attainment, subject choices and university'. The Commission found that it was a disadvantage to have had state education, to come from an area where fewer went to university, or to be female or black. The highest-paid jobs are given mostly to particular kinds of graduates, not just because of what they have achieved, but also because of what schools they have been to, their sex, their ethnicity – even which town they lived in prior to getting into university.

It is not even true that people with the same high-grade A levels are academically equal. Two studies released in 2013 under the Freedom of Information Act revealed that children who went to state schools did better at university than their private school counterparts who had the same A level results: 'All other factors being held constant, students from independent schools tend to do less well than students from comprehensive schools.'[6] This finding is hardly surprising, as private schools are more sought after if they help their pupils to achieve unexpectedly high grades, rather than helping them to be more self-sufficient in their ability to learn in the future.

If your private school is more exclusive, you can then charge higher fees and make a greater profit (or, at least, pay the head teacher more). Earlier research had suggested that it was only in Oxford and Cambridge that children arriving from comprehensive schools might feel intimidated to the extent that their studies suffered, so that private school pupils there had an instant advantage. Given that just four very private schools, confusingly called 'public' – namely Eton, Westminster, St Paul's Boys and St Paul's Girls – and one highly selective state sixth form college, Hills Road in Cambridge, send more children to those two universities than 2,000 other secondary schools, this finding is hardly surprising.[7]

It is often claimed that the national debate on higher education is dominated by an interest in entry to Oxford and Cambridge universities; but, for many in the 1 per cent – the only people with the financial means to hope to secure places for their children in those few feeder schools – this really matters. The most prestigious one hundred schools (out of many thousands) in Britain, 84 per cent of them private, secure 30 per cent of all Oxbridge places.[8] In June 2013 the Office for Fair Access 'argued that access to the elite universities in England has hardly improved in recent years despite lots of pressure from government and numerous initiatives, including fee waivers, scholarships and bursaries'.[9] In 2014 when they checked again, they found no improvement, and noted that in 'one highly selective university, rich students were *16 times* more likely to attend than poor students'.[10] The name of the university was not revealed.

It is hardly surprising that, as the rich in Britain become richer and private school fees increase, with all that money being spent on trying to secure a string of A grades from a very small number of children, overall access is not becoming more equitable, and remains extremely unfair. As Stefan Collini, of the University of Cambridge, explained when commenting on the latest international education statistics, 'countries committed to high-quality comprehensives, such as Finland, yet again come out on top. A stratified and class-segregated school system is not the answer: it's the problem.'[11]

The secretary of state for education, Michael Gove, has never made it clear that he is opposed to widespread selection and greater privatisation – especially by stealth, with the creation of free schools that might be sponsored by a company, and private companies taking over former comprehensive schools when they are forced to become academies. His wife, the journalist Sarah Vine, may write on the problems with the private sector; but while her views appear to mirror his on the issue of different pupils having very different potential, she is more honest than he is about what drives many rich parents to choose private schools:

> The private sector ... is built on very different principles. Its agenda is a fundamentally selective one, based not only on ability to pay, but also on pupil potential. And it is also, let's face it, about snobbery. Of course the parents of private school children are paying for the best teachers and facilities. But let's be honest: they're also paying for their child to mix with the right kind of kids.[12]

Note that teachers who actively support private education, and all the attitudes it promotes, are described as 'the best teachers'.

In more equitable countries, like Finland, almost all children are seen as 'the right kinds of kids', and almost all become those kinds of adolescents. This does not mean that they become somewhat arrogant and overconfident boys and girls, used to wearing suits and ties or formal dresses and old-fashioned gym-wear from a very early age – it means they become normal, that they can easily mix with others, and you cannot tell simply from their appearance, let alone from the moment they open their mouths, whether they come from a rich or poor background.

In the UK, increasing numbers of young people try to hide their class backgrounds by means of how they dress and behave. Television, among much else, makes young people far more aware than their grandparents were of how they might be perceived; but they cannot escape the effects of being segregated as children. You do not learn how to mix by not mixing.

The UK's education system is beginning to look more like that of the US than like the schools and universities of other countries in Europe. Many American private universities now spend just a sixth of their fee income on teaching. These private providers take more than a fifth of fees in profit, and spend even more on marketing.[13] Marketing can be effective. The parents who send their children to those private universities no doubt believe they have some of the 'best teachers'. It will have been the job of the marketing department to persuade them of that. The most prestigious private schools in the UK also have marketing departments, which are absent from almost all state schools – although academies are beginning to compete in this marketplace of style over substance.

Privatisation is most advanced in the university sector. Since 2010/11, fully private universities in Britain, most of them new, have had access to tax-payers' money, and are free to make a profit. That first year, over £40 million pounds was accessed by such private bodies, £9 million in grants; but this will seem like chicken feed in comparison to what is planned in the way of subsidies to the private education market. Pundits now talk of the 'subprime student loan',[14] because what is being purchased through borrowing is often not worth the initial fee, let alone the interest on that fee. Students should ask how much of their student fee is spent on university marketing, to entice the young people who come after them into paying such high fees. But what can they do?

There is an answer: don't reach so hard for the top, and don't believe the marketing hype. This attitude is already being adopted. For four of the last five years, the numbers of children enrolled in private fee-paying schools in the UK have fallen, by 2013 the number was standing at only just over 500,000. Part of the reason for the fall is that the average annual private school fee is now £14,000; and part of the reason for this high price is that numbers are dropping. Average annual fees for boarding school stand at £27,612 – almost £29,000 for boarding sixth-formers. Nevertheless, the number of pupils in those schools fell by 1.4 per cent in the year to 2013, to 66,605.[15] The numbers attending boarding schools are also dropping – not only because of cost, but also because of increasing fear of what boarding does to children: 'the ex-boarder is a master of emotional disguise'.[16] Many of the 1 per cent are ex-boarders. But, while private school enrolment is falling, there is – as yet – no great drop in university attendance, because there appears to be no alternative, especially if you wish to be socially mobile.

Social Mobility

> We should stick with orthodox comprehensives, phase out grammars, do the same to faith schools, and promote the good local school over supposed 'choice'. And we should do everything in our power to pull parents away from fee-paying places, starting with an end to their charitable status, and an insistence that the intakes of all Russell Group universities should reflect the proportions of school students in state and private education – and, come to think of it, those who've been to comprehensives and grammars.
>
> John Harris[17]

Social mobility is lowest where local 'choice' in education superficially appears highest. The Manchester local authority of Trafford has the highest level of educational social segregation.

This is due to secondary moderns and grammar schools having been retained there, as well as private school provision being high. When confronted with the evidence that government education policy was reducing social mobility in such areas, 'A spokesman for the Department for Education said they did not wish to comment on the report.'[18] Others, such as John Harris (quoted above), have been more robust in explaining what might better serve the interest of the 99 per cent.

Most people in Britain – well over nine out of ten people – attend state schools. Of those people, as adults, 99 per cent have friendship groups that only include people who went to state schools.[19] Thus, although privately educated children will probably have friends from state schools, they will only be from a very narrow slice of those schools. Rather than socially preparing children for the wider world, a private education is likely to restrict the breadth and depth of their social contacts later in life. One possible reason why parents choose private schools is that they fear the state sector. Many parents do not know that it is children coming from the poorest addresses who do worse, not those who go to the supposedly poorest schools.[20]

The country that many educationalists look to for good lessons is Finland, where 99.2 per cent of school education is state funded. In Finland there is no inspection of teachers or league tables; pupils are not set or streamed; and in four international surveys since 2000, 'Finnish comprehensive school students have scored above students in all the other participating countries in science and problem-solving skills, and came either first or second in reading and mathematics. These results were achieved despite the amount of homework assigned in Finnish schools being relatively low and an absence of private tuition.'[21] What John Harris describes could be as good as what Finland has.

There are people who do not want you to know that there is a better way. Sometimes it is easy to see the motive. When the tobacco industry began to spread doubt about the health hazards of smoking, it inadvertently created a new area of research into learning – an area of study concerning 'how ignorance is made, maintained and manipulated by powerful institutions to suit their own ends'.[22] Should you believe that the employment market is set to polarise further, that there will only ever be a small space at the top, then you might think it is kindest that most children never understand this, because they will never have any power or much money. What good would it do for all children to think that they should have the same chances, if most must lose?

Pocket Money

> I mean, your society's broken, so who should we blame?
> Should we blame the rich, powerful people who caused it? No
> let's blame the people with no power and no money and these
> immigrants who don't even have the vote, yeah it must be their
> fucking fault.
>
> Iain Banks, final interview[23]

Who are the people with no power and no money? Many of them are children. The 1 per cent and 99 per cent are not just groups of adults. According to one survey, most children in Hull receive only 5p when they put their teeth under the pillow. In contrast, across all of London, the tooth fairy's largest averages over £5 per tooth. Given inequalities across the capital, in parts of London she may well be delivering £50 notes on some streets and 50p or 5p pieces in others.[24] In Glasgow the average deposit by the tooth fairy is reported to be 11p. Such salacious stories can dull us to the extent of inequality. They can make inequality appear normal. And similar inequalities are reflected in children's pocket money.

When I was first given pocket money, in the 1970s, the UK's richest 1 per cent only received four times the average income, after they had paid their tax. Unemployment benefit was much nearer to a very low working income than it is today. Despite the dole being so generous, almost no parents were out of work. Better welfare benefits did not lead to more people on the dole. Pocket money was very limited, but common after a certain age. Forty years later what you get, if you get anything, depends far more on the income of your parents, or parent. Children are acutely aware of the relative differences in their social circumstances. Children are much less able than adults to select whom they mix with. Adults decide which children are put into which school class.

One in six children in Britain received no pocket money in 2013. But, for those who did, the average was £6.50 a week, or 93p a day.[25] The variation in children's income is huge. Pocket money in Britain was just a pound a week in the 1980s. By 1997 the average had risen to £1.67 a week; and in 2007 it had risen rapidly to its highest-ever recorded average (for those receiving it) of £8.01 a week, before falling by a quarter following the 2008 crash.

To understand how rising income inequality can hurt a society, it helps to think about pocket money and schools. Imagine a school-of-inequality, where the average pocket money received each day is a fraction above the current 93p national average – at, say, £1 per child each day, or £7 a week. To make things easy, there are exactly one hundred children in the school. But they don't each receive the same pocket money. In this fictional school, the inequality in distribution of pocket money is as great as the inequalities in income in the United States today. In the US the richest 1 per cent take 20 per cent of all income. That same inequality within a school of one hundred children would mean one child receiving 20 per cent of the combined pocket money that all the children in the school receive every day – or £140 a week!

This example might seem ridiculous, but it is simply a reflection of how unequal income is in the US – and of where we in the UK are heading. Next, try to imagine what that rich child might think about the other children, and how the other children might treat that richest child. Seen from the point of view of children, the injustice of gross inequality is clear. A child cannot easily pretend to have done anything to have 'deserved' so much. They are described as 'spoilt', using words and judgement that for some reason we don't apply to rich adults.

The other 99 children in the school-of-inequality will each, on average, receive just a fraction above 80p a day, or £5.60 a week for the overall average to still be a £1 a day. At this rate it would take an average child a year to receive what the 1 per cent child receives in just a couple of weeks. The richest child might be ostracised, unless he hides his income and behaves like the other children. If the school pocket money reflects parental income distribution, then hardly any children will receive the average amount of 80p a day for the 99 per cent. A few will receive much more than 80p, but most will receive much less. Averages can be very deceptive. In the school-of-inequality, when the richest kid is excluded, the daily £1 average falls to 80p. Separating the children into three numerically equal sets, according to how much pocket money they receive, will mean that the top set receives on average pocket money of £2.50, the middle set receives on average 40p each a day, and the lowest set consists of children who mostly receive no pocket money.

There would be a large overlap between that bottom class and the children in the school getting their lunches for free. In 2005 about one in six children in Britain received free meals at school because their parents were so poor. That figure is rising rapidly as poverty deepens, and soon as many as one in three will have received a free lunch at school in Britain because their parents were very poor at some time in the previous six years.[26]

How does the inequity of parental income make children feel? Surveys have been taken of how many children in Britain believe they get the correct amount of pocket money. In 2012 an online survey of children aged between eight and fifteen found a minority thought they were not getting enough; but in a repeat survey in 2013, 53 per cent of the responders thought they did not get enough. This was despite the fact that this group, which excluded those without internet access, were getting an average of five times as much as their parents' generation had received as children – or about twice as much in real terms.[27]

These feelings of deprivation have arisen because pupils compare what they get with their friends. And it turns out it is in London that such comparisons are most important. When surveyed there, 56 per cent of children thought such comparisons were important. It is in London that the highest incomes are found and overall income inequality is greatest. And it is in London that you can find the nearest thing to a school containing a mix of children that is financially representative of the national composition.

In reality, even the most mixed of schools will still have missing chunks from both the top and bottom of the income scale. British children are highly segregated by income right from birth, and through all their school days. In a survey by the Halifax bank, boys thought it was more important than girls did to know how much their friends were receiving in pocket money. Boys were also more likely to think they did not get enough and – very probably as a result of their comparing and complaining more – it was boys who received, on average, 5.5 per cent more pocket money than girls. The gender pay divide begins early. A second 2013 pocket money survey, carried out on behalf of the Pocket Money Savings website, confirmed that boys received more, but suggested that the differential rose to 16 per cent once pocket money was associated with carrying out chores in the home.

By 2013, children in Britain were apparently being paid, on average, £1.21 for tidying their bedrooms, £1.24 for doing their homework, 78p for washing up – and £2 for 'good behaviour'.[28] At that price, a child quickly works out that it is worth behaving badly to encourage their parents to then bribe them to behave well! Pay them to tidy their bedrooms, and children may be learning that something is not worth doing if they are not paid to do it.

Children learn both from their parents and from making comparisons with other children. If their parents are well off enough to be able to start paying them to do the washing up, they will come to expect to be paid for doing it. If one child hears that another is paid just for 'behaving well', then – what are they to think?

Potential

40–45 per cent or more of US Fortune 500 CEOs, billionaires, federal judges and Senators attended elite universities whose median standardized test scores are above ~99th percentile for the overall US population: i.e. ~1 per cent of the population make up ~50 per cent of the elite group running the country … However, even within this 1 per cent there are huge differences between the brains and character of a Zuckerberg and an average senator.

Dominic Cummings, advisor to Michael Gove, 2013[29]

If greed is presented as normal, then you are being taught to be greedy. If a few children at the top are continually given the implicit message that they deserve the most, they will come to expect the most. In Britain the children of those at the top attend private schools, and each has more than three times as much spent on their education than the rest (see Figure 2.2). For the exclusive 1 per cent, much more is spent on their school education than that.[30]

In the UK more money is spent on private education than almost anywhere else on the planet. Recently almost all of the richest 1 per cent, and about half of very affluent children (the next 9 per cent) were privately educated, while only around 1 per cent of the 90 per cent below them ever went to private school. In OECD nations that have more equality, this private/public school inequality is largely avoided. In addition, and probably not unrelated to this acute divide, in 2012 the number of teenagers staying on in school in the UK

HOW EVERY £100 SPENT ON SECONDARY EDUCATION IN THE UK IS DISTRIBUTED

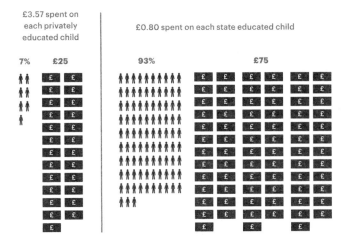

£3.57 spent on each privately educated child

£0.80 spent on each state educated child

7% £25 93% £75

THE BEST-OFF 7% OF CHILDREN IN BRITAIN HAVE THREE TIMES AS MUCH SPENT ON THEIR SCHOOLS THAN THE AVERAGE CHILD OF THE OTHER 93%

Source: Diane Reay, 2012

Figure 2.2 Educational Spending on Secondary School Children in Britain

after age sixteen fell for the first time in a decade, and the proportion of sixteen- to eighteen-year-olds 'not in education, employment or training' rose by 8 per cent in that same year.[31] These youngsters were previously classified as 'Status Zer0 [sic]', but since 1999 designated by the acronym NEETs. Neither title is edifying.[32]

Less is being spent on the education of the majority, who are consequently more likely to drop out earlier. The private schools, attended by the richest children in Britain, thus promise a very high chance of later enrolment in our 'top' universities. These universities were recently labelled by one educational commentator 'finishing schools for gilded youth, as bestowers of glittering prizes'.[33] Careful research has shown that dividing children up within schools tends to set them all back on average by a month, although it may give a small advantage to those put in the 'top sets'.[34] Growing educational divisions are a huge social problem in economically unequal countries. They are often only promoted because they might confer a slight benefit on those at the very top – but those arguing for division have the power and money of many of the 1 per cent behind them.

Even among the 'top' universities, divisions are growing and the numbers attending the less-favoured of the elite Russell Group universities – Birmingham, Leeds, Liverpool, Manchester, Nottingham, Sheffield, Southampton and Warwick – fell between 2011 and 2012. A year later, it was reported that these divisions between the 'top' universities were widening, just as income inequality in the UK was continuing to rise.[35]

Despite the fact that only 7 per cent of children attended private schools, some 70 per cent of judges went to such establishments, as did the majority of the members of almost all other 'top' professions, from the lowest-paid London journalist to the highest-paid CEO. On any given day, a fifth of children in Britain qualify for free school meals – but this is true of only one in every hundred children who later attend either Oxford or Cambridge universities.[36] Part of the reason that there is such concern over which university children go to is what happens to them and their income after that. Among the top UK employers paying salaries that might one day put a young person in the top 1 per cent, some 60 per cent only visit twenty or fewer universities to recruit from. And they visit some of those universities far more eagerly than others – especially Cambridge, London (UCL and LSE), Manchester, Nottingham and Oxford.[37]

The following is a list of the firms and government businesses involved in such recruiting. These high-salary employers disproportionately draw graduates from those universities that service the top 1 per cent in society. Universities in the UK are increasingly viewed as stepping stones into top companies:[38]

Accenture, Airbus, Aldi, Allen & Overy, Apple, Arcadia Group, Army, Arup, Asda, AstraZeneca, Atkins, BAE Systems, Bain & Company, Baker & McKenzie, Balfour Beatty, Bank of America Merrill Lynch, Bank of England, Barclays, Barclays Capital, BBC, Bloomberg, Boots, Boston Consulting Group, BP, BT, Cancer Research, Centrica, Citi, Civil Service, Clifford Chance, Co-operative Group, Credit Suisse, Deloitte, Deutsche Bank, Diageo, DLA Piper, Dstl, E.ON, EDF Energy, Ernst & Young, ExxonMobil, Foreign & Commonwealth Office, Freshfields Bruckhaus Deringer, GlaxoSmithKline, Goldman Sachs, Google, Grant Thornton, Herbert Smith, Hogan Lovells, HSBC, IBM, J.P. Morgan, Jaguar Landrover, John Lewis, KPMG, Kraft, L'Oréal, Lidl, Linklaters, Lloyds Banking Group, Local Government, Marks & Spencer, Mars, McDonald's Restaurants, McKinsey & Company, MI5, Microsoft, Ministry of Defence, Morgan Stanley, National Grid, Nestlé, Network Rail, NHS, nucleargraduates, Oliver Wyman, Oxfam, Penguin, Police, Procter & Gamble, PwC, RAF, Rolls-Royce, Royal Bank of Scotland, Royal Navy, RWE npower, Saatchi & Saatchi, Sainsbury's, Santander, Savills, Shell, Simmons & Simmons, Sky, Slaughter and May, Sony, Teach First, Tesco, Transport for London, UBS, Unilever, and WPP.[39]

When the 1 per cent have held so much sway over our society for so many decades, the effect can be that otherwise sensible people begin to believe that it is fair if the poorest are only given a minimum of resources, and just enough education for their children, so that if one of them should turn out unexpectedly to have 'potential', then it can be realised. Here is how this view is put by the director of the leading British progressive think tank, the Institute for Public Policy Research (IPPR). Note that all he is doing is reflecting what has now become common wisdom:

> At the other end of the scale, individuals require a sufficient income to live free of stigma or shame, and should receive public services, such as education, that are distributed in such a way that each can fulfil their potential and enjoy equal

standing with their peers. Market inequalities are necessary for
economic efficiency and freedom of choice, but within ranges
constrained by these factors.[40]

'Potential' is the give-away word that implies the inevitabil-
ity of large disparities in ability, and consequently in income.
It is presumed that, if certain minimum levels of educational
services are provided, then the few more able among the lower
orders can be talent-spotted, as a young footballer might be,
if provided with a chance to show off on a level playing field.
Begin to believe that only a few are truly remarkably gifted,
and you can begin to create justifications for the remarkable
geographical concentration of multi-millionaires in Britain
(see Figure 2.3).

The word 'potential' appears in the motto of Save the
Children's 2012 report on child poverty: 'We save children's
lives. We fight for their rights. We help them fulfil their potential.'[41] But how does the charity know what each child's
potential is? 'We don't presume a limit to their potential'
would be a better ending for their motto. The only studies
there have been which suggested that some children differ
from others in aptitude for some aspects of context-free logic
('geekiness') find that the association is inherent rather than
inherited, so that any predisposition to find abstract reasoning
easier is not passed down generationally.[42]

It is remarkable – in the early twenty-first century, in one of
the most advanced and fortunate nations on earth – to have
to acknowledge that some people really do believe that some
of us are actually of 'better stock' than others. They don't
say this out loud, of course. Animal breeding metaphors are
hardly acceptable as a way to talk about fellow citizens. But
they find other ways of saying the same thing – for example,
by equating talent and capability to one's wealth. The usually
unspoken underlying rhetorical question is: Well, how else did
you or your parents get to be wealthy?

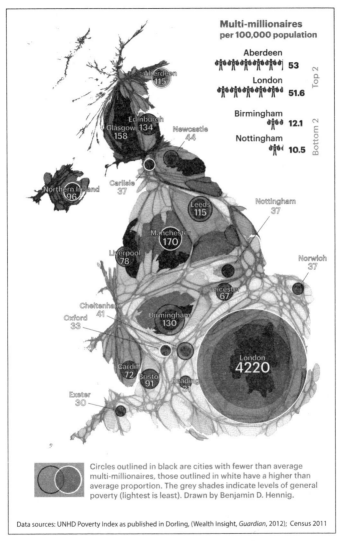

Multi-millionaires
per 100,000 population

Aberdeen 53 — Top 2
London 51.6 — Top 2

Birmingham 12.1 — Bottom 2
Nottingham 10.5 — Bottom 2

Aberdeen 115
Edinburgh
Glasgow 134
Newcastle 44
Northern Ireland 96
Carlisle 37
Leeds 115
Nottingham 37
Manchester 170
Liverpool 78
Norwich 37
Leicester 67
Cheltenham 41
Oxford 33
Birmingham 130
Cardiff 72
Bristol 91
Reading 91
Exeter 30
London 4220

Circles outlined in black are cities with fewer than average multi-millionaires, those outlined in white have a higher than average proportion. The grey shades indicate levels of general poverty (lightest is least). Drawn by Benjamin D. Hennig.

Data sources: UNHD Poverty Index as published in Dorling, (Wealth Insight, *Guardian*, 2012); Census 2011

Figure 2.3 Mapping the abstract metrics: poverty and wealth 2012

The assumption which has become the mainstream elite view is that all children are limited and only a few are potentially talented, and that talent is then reflected by wealth. Such a view leads to criticism of calls to reduce income and wealth inequalities. The director of the IPPR puts the establishment message more subtly in a section of his paper headed 'Refashioning Equality', when he says he wishes to *challenge* 'a focus on abstract metrics of material equality with a commitment to valuing the expressive and cultural dimensions of life, recognising that one's position in society only makes sense in relation to others, and improving everyday experience over the pursuit of abstract utopia'.[43] He is presumably trying to explain that what is good enough for the masses may not be good enough for people who can write as obscurely as he can. The concept of 'the 1 per cent' is an abstract metric, but a very useful one which can also be used to consider the expressive and cultural dimensions of life, including theories of childhood and education.

There are many people who believe that it is, or should be, the 'fittest' who get to the top.[44] These people believe that we are largely ruled by our betters, and that that is good for us.[45] They think that almost all of the 1 per cent are very clever – much cleverer than most people – and that within the 1 per cent there are some exceptional geniuses.[46] However, many of the 1 per cent are, in fact, not part of an especially talented bunch, and even those who are talented may not be that special.

A remarkable number of those who rule us believe they do so because they are special. That is less surprising when you realise that most went to schools and universities where they were repeatedly told they were all special – although most are at least clever enough to realise that the majority outside their circle might not take kindly to being told this. Dominic Cummings is not like most of those who have got into the top echelons.[47] He has a tendency to say what he believes. He wrote the words used at the start of this section in a thesis made widely available when he was advisor to the secretary of state for education, Michael Gove.[48] In that thesis he also suggested that 70 per cent of a child's attainment is determined by his or her genes.

Following the human genome project, it has been possible to conduct various whole-genome association studies to assess how much the entire genetic code might be affecting the chance of particular outcomes without having to know which parts of the code matter most. Studies in children have shown that over 20 per cent but under 50 per cent of their differences in the ability to do abstract logic or IQ tests might be accounted for by tiny variations in a very large group of genes, but not by individual genes. It is not possible to carry out equivalent comparisons on thousands of individual environmental factors.[49] Twin, family and adoption studies show that being brought up by someone with a high IQ does not particularly boost your ability in IQ tests.[50] Some would point out that the most intelligent teachers are not necessarily the best teachers.[51] None of this implies that the children of people who have been able to acquire a lot of wealth will necessarily be gifted.[52]

In educational research it is now the norm to develop 'approaches to teaching and learning that do not rely on determinist beliefs about ability'.[53] Children can be taught to be good at tests and to get better at them, and children who start off with more advantages in life tend to see those advantages multiplied, especially in more unequal societies.[54] Children who do not do well at tests can be demoralised by the system, and that increases the likelihood of future failure.[55] They are less likely to talk themselves up – or 'self-enhance', as such boosterism is called in psychology. Thinking you are great is more common among the rich, but also more common in more unequal countries where the population at large has to begin to mimic the self-enhancing behaviours of those above them just to get by (see Figure 2.4).

Having a high opinion of yourself – believing you are part of a deserving minority who has got to the top and that there

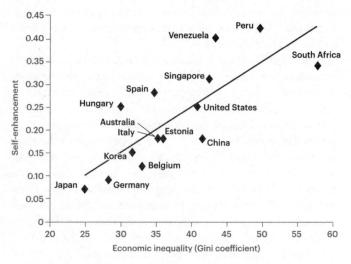

Note: The data points for Australia and Italy are very close and overlap on the graph.
Source: Loughan, Kuppens et al., 2011

Figure 2.4 Individual average self-enhancement verses economic inequality in fifteen nations

are only a few others like you – is a trait that is much more common in more unequal countries. A comparison of attitudes in fifteen nations which did not include the UK found that 'people in societies with more income inequality tend to view themselves as superior to others, and people in societies with less income inequality tend to see themselves as more similar to their peers'.[56] The study implied that high self-esteem and self-enhancement might be an accurate, justified attitude, but that it is often viewed by others as signalling an arrogant and unwarranted sense of superiority. Overvaluing yourself implies undervaluing others.

In a major speech in November 2013, London mayor Boris Johnson told his audience: 'Whatever you may think of the value of IQ tests, it is surely relevant to a conversation about equality that as many as 16 per cent of our species have an

IQ below 85, while about 2 per cent have an IQ above 130.'[57] A numerate audience would have known that exactly 50 per cent of the population have an IQ above or below 100, and the ratios at all other IQ values can be found in a table. IQ is defined so that 16 per cent always score below 85: no other result is permitted.

Genetic determinism is an attractive idea to many in the 1 per cent. It is used as a defence by those who support their wealth as justifiable – although their superior inherited abilities apparently make them unable to manage satisfactorily on much less money. Whatever the truth about how much the ability to do well at IQ tests is inherent, what is obvious is that it should be no justification for receiving more money.

There is no evidence that people with high IQs are more likely to be in the top 1 per cent by income. Worldwide, the vast majority of those who score highest on such tests will be very poor. In richer countries, people with high IQs might find solving obscure mathematical puzzles easier than most others. They may also be less worldly-wise, less adept in other ways – and as they are not greedier than average, there is no reason why they should be much richer.

If genetics do play a part in determining who is in the wealthiest 1 per cent, it will be in the fact that this small segment of society contains more people with genes inclining them to be acquisitive, to hoard, and to be less concerned about others. These are what psychologists call 'individualistic traits', rather than the norm of being more pro-social, with positive, helpful and friendly attitudes to other people, not grandiose or conceited.

Steve Jones, emeritus professor of genetics at University College London, puts the case against the favoured few succinctly. In chastising Dominic Cummings, he noted: 'For geneticists, the more we learn about DNA, the more important the environment appears. The lesson from the double helix is that we need more and better teachers, rather than wringing our hands about the unkindness of fate. A few lessons about elementary biology might be a good place to start.'[58] We now worry about the extinction of rare species, and the loss of their genes, and see apparent genetic variation within our species as more and more important (see the illustration below). Hereditary rights appear to be back in fashion. We do not question dynasties in particular professions as much as we did when we were more equal, and today many more people argue against inheritance tax than the number of people likely to be subject to it. As the middle class shrinks, it becomes easier for the rich to argue that they deserve to pass more of their wealth to their children, who, in turn, deserve to receive it.

Much more is inherited than money. Think about what kinds of subjects the children of the 1 per cent are educated in, and what careers they are steered towards. Only a tiny fraction of the 1 per cent consists of talented singers, sport stars or entertainers. From a 2004 analysis of tax returns in the US,[59] the proportion of the population that was both in the top 1 per cent of taxpayers and worked in the arts, media

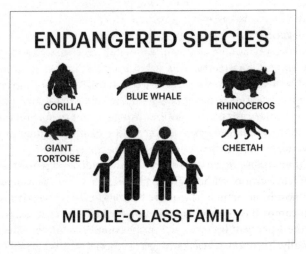

Resistance to the impoverishment of the majority, USA, 2013

or sports was just 0.031 per cent. For every two showbiz or sports celebrity members of the top 1 per cent, there were three estate agents, four lawyers, twelve people working in finance, and twenty-six executives and top managers who were not directly working in finance. Most of the very rich are people who have control over their own pay – not those whom the rest of us think of as very able, but often people who are entrusted with large amounts of other people's money.

It is a myth that within the top 1 per cent there is a disproportionate number of geniuses. Instead, there is a disproportionate number of financiers, bankers and bosses, especially in the US and UK. Somehow the idea of 1 per cent of the population being particularly clever has become mixed up with the idea of there always being 1 per cent at the top. It is in the interests of those who have the most to promote the idea that they deserve their riches because they are very special – but that promotional effort emanates in particular from just two Anglophone countries. Could that be because there are over 4,000 households in the UK and US combined with a minimum wealth not including property of $100,000,000 each? This means that there are more superrich families in these two countries than in the next eight most superrich-containing countries combined (see Figure 2.5).[60]

Today, as the superrich crowd into the UK, buying multiple homes in London, at exactly the same time as more money than ever before is being spent on the school fees and university education of the children of the 1 per cent, millions of children at the bottom of the 99 per cent are falling into poverty, or seeing their poverty deepen. Some 40 per cent of children in the UK now go to university, while another 40 per cent leave school without five good GCSEs – now considered the most basic of qualifications. The 20 per cent between those two camps has been squeezed even further in recent years.[61] As the 1 per cent becomes richer, the country polarises educationally. In contrast, year on year from 1918 through to 1978, the UK became progressively (and educationally) more equal,

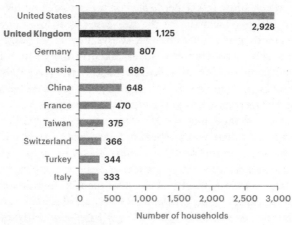

Source: Boston Consulting Group, 2012

Figure 2.5 Number of $100 million households in the world, by country, 2011

at that time when those at the top took less and less, and eventually, after comprehensivisation, most children attended the same type of school.

Over that same 1918–78 period, British culture admitted more and more people from normal backgrounds to the highest levels of society. Increasing numbers of MPs came from the working classes. Regional accents began to be permitted on radio and TV – only slowly at first, but then increasingly often. And actors began to star on TV and in the theatre who had backgrounds not unlike those of most of their audience. However, actress Julie Walters recently explained: 'I look at almost all the up-and-coming names and they're from the posh schools ... Don't get me wrong ... they're wonderful. It's just a shame those working-class kids aren't coming through. When I started, thirty years ago, it was the complete opposite.'[62]

The idea of progressive improvement generation after generation is now a distant memory. It implied not just improvement in overall standards, but also standards rising most at the bottom, for those groups of children who had been made to leave school at the youngest of ages in the past. Today, those who will learn the least at school will tend to be those who have the fewest books at home, and whose parents cannot afford access to a computer and the internet. In 2013 the children's commissioner attributed what was happening in the UK to cuts and austerity: 'Families with children will lose more of their income than families without children. However, lone parents will lose the most out of everyone.'[63] And the main reason for rising poverty in childhood was that so many parents were paid such low wages (see Figure 2.6).

As the poor become poorer, the rich tend to become more selfish. In 2012 Debra Leigh Scott, an American university lecturer, wrote a blog about what was happening in the US that illustrated what the UK might become if the 1 per cent continue to take more and more. One observation stood out: 'I often see it on late-model, expensive cars near my town. It says, "Cut School Taxes." These drivers/voters/taxpayers have given up on the schools, or they have kids who have graduated,

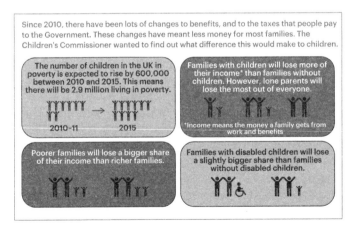

Figure 2.6 What differences will changes to taxes and benefits have on children?

and/or they're being selfish.'[64] How did Americans get to the point where some of the old not only think they should not be paying taxes to school youngsters, but also want others to know they think that? And how long might it be before the first bumper sticker appears in the UK demanding, 'Lower our taxes. Cut the education budget'?

3

Work

Excessive financialization – which helps explain Britain's dubious status as the second-most-unequal country, after the United States, among the world's most advanced economies – also helps explain the soaring inequality.

Joseph Stiglitz[1]

Growing inequality is the result of market failure. So say increasing numbers of economists,[2] including Kim Weeden of Cornell University and David Grusky of Stanford. This duo recently explained how the power of people at the bottom of the income distribution has been smashed in recent decades, while the power of those at the top has accelerated away.[3] They also showed that the better-off have secured high salaries largely by 'licensing' their work, so that only a small number of people are said to be qualified enough to carry it out.

Since 1979, two-thirds of all the gains in income made by the top tenth of earners in the UK have been taken by the top 1 per cent alone. In the UK these are far more likely to be bankers than in the US because, compared to their respective national economies, the City of London is much bigger than Wall Street.[4] This matters because financiers have started to use qualifications as a means to try to legitimise their take, including securing masters of business administration degrees (MBAs).

It is the young who tend to dominate in low-paid, unlicensed jobs. In 1993 7 per cent of employed young women between sixteen and twenty-four worked in low-paid, low-skilled jobs in the UK, but by 2013 that had increased to 21 per cent. For young men in these 'elementary occupations', the figure increased from 14 per cent to 25 per cent in the same period.[5] On hearing of these statistics one MP, Teresa Pearce, responded: 'This saddens me but does not surprise me. I see this among my own constituents, with young women sometimes working two jobs just to try and pay the rent.'[6]

In contrast to the majority of workers, those people employed in licensed occupations are paid more partly because the numbers that can enter them are restricted. The medical and legal professions, as well as academic and many other professions, have all increased demand for their services and increased the qualifications required to provide those services, thus driving up their wages. But in most of these occupations only a very few people are paid enough to qualify to be members of the 1 per cent.

The way qualifications now act as a barrier to gaining a well-paid job has fuelled rising inequality and helped to legitimise the 1 per cent. The earnings of graduates have risen much faster than those of non-graduates, even as the supply of graduates has increased from just 3.4 per cent in 1950, of which 77 per cent were men, to over half of young adults today, of which a majority are now women.[7] Just having a single university degree, however, is no longer a guarantee of a good job – or even of getting work at all. Increasingly, graduates need multiple qualifications.

Most of the increased income of the top 1 per cent has been achieved through personal negotiations over increasing their pay and bonuses. This has been found to be the case for both top financiers and top managers, especially chief executive officers (CEOs). The huge rise in business schools has led to qualifications for managers going from being ornamental to being essential. Growing inequality is not an unfortunate by-product of highly efficient competitive markets, but the end product of subtle rises in protectionism. In effect, the upper-middle and upper classes have become unionised through professional bodies such as the British Medical Association and the British Bankers' Association.

The UK has followed recent US trends. By 2012 the best-off tenth in the US were taking over half of all personal income for the first time – almost certainly the highest share they have ever received.[8] By one estimate, the top 1 per cent saw its take rise to 22.5 per cent of the national total of personal income – not quite half of the top tenth, and not yet quite as high as the share it was taking in 1928, the year before the Wall Street Crash,[9] but very close to that previous inequality record (see Figure 3.1).

When the historical abnormality of today's highest incomes is pointed out some still suggest that its recipients must be worth so much pay – presumably because other people have become relatively worthless. However, as another economist, John Kay, put it in the *Financial Times* in 2012,

> Complex modern production is undertaken in teams, and the make-up of an effective team is largely fixed by the nature of the production process. It is difficult, perhaps impossible, to attribute output meaningfully to any particular member. Individual rewards are largely determined by custom and hierarchy, and through a political process involving bargaining between shareholders and employees and among different groups of workers.[10]

John Kay was not alone in 2012 and he has been joined by many likeminded voices since. In 2013 Daniel Boffey in the *Observer* reported how the incomes of the 1 per cent were moving away from the rest of the 10 per cent and how 'a financial adviser and private wealth manager ... was photographed last week spending £330,000 on a 30l bottle of

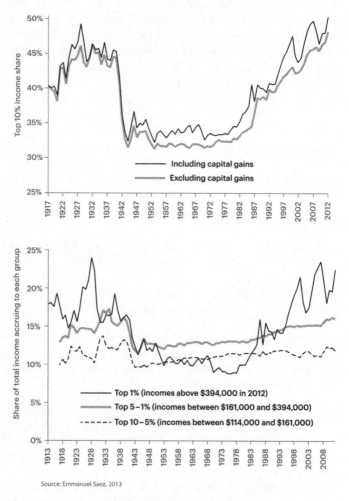

Source: Emmanuel Saez, 2013

Figure 3.1 Top incomes in the USA, 1913–2013: 1 per cent, next 4 per cent, and rest of the 10 per cent

champagne at the Monaco grand prix'.[11] In 2014 David Horsey in the *Los Angeles Times* explained how wrong it was that a school teacher in California makes almost the same working for a year as the CEO of Oracle Corporation makes in an hour.[12] A week before David's article the World Bank had issued guidance stating that without a great reduction in inequality no amount of economic growth would reduce poverty.[13]

The Making of a Perfect Storm

> Some people continue to defend trickle-down theories which assume that economic growth, encouraged by a free market, will inevitably succeed in bringing about greater justice and inclusiveness in the world. This opinion, which has never been confirmed by the facts, expresses a crude and naive trust in the goodness of those wielding economic power and in the sacralized workings of the prevailing economic system. Meanwhile the excluded are still waiting.
>
> Pope Francis, 2013[14]

Oxfam, the leading UK-based poverty charity, has published detailed research on how Britain is brewing up a 'perfect storm' of social harm and unrest through growing income inequality.[15] Buried deep in their report, the Oxfam researchers summarise how, according to the leading World Bank economist Branko Milanovic, 'the real cause of the crisis lies in huge inequalities in income distribution that generated much larger investable funds than could be profitably employed'.[16] By the end of 2013 even the pope was echoing the World Bank and leading poverty researchers.

Oxfam explains how the International Monetary Fund has now also reached the same conclusion as the World Bank,[17] suggesting that 'any success in reducing income inequality could therefore be very useful in reducing the likelihood of future crises'.[18] Oxfam deplores the fact that so far the opposite is currently happening – that, between 2007 to 2011, the ratio of FTSE 100 chief executives' earnings to average wages rose from 92:1 to 102:1,[19] and Oxfam appeared disgusted that this occurred even as real wages fell, all storing up further trouble for the future.[20] They explained that a concern with ratios is not the politics of envy, but simply indicates a desire for justice.

In the space of just the four years to 2011, each of the UK's 100 top-paid FTSE CEOs had their wages increased by the amount of what ten average people are paid per year. Collectively, they took 1,000 people's annual pay just in their additional annual bonuses – which were on top of the sum equalling 9,200 times average pay which, between them, they took, in effect, as their basic salaries. Apart from any other complaints we might have, these huge wage packets do not appear to make them better bosses. Instead, extreme pay means that stranger and more maladjusted people end up becoming selected for the top jobs.

As a writer on neuroscience noted recently, 'One of the most damaging ideas to come out of the recent furore surrounding bankers' bonuses is that we're all just jealous of the rich. But recent evidence from neuroscientists points instead towards a deeply rooted instinct for equality.'[21] We have a deeply rooted instinct that great inequality is unjust.[22] But not all of us have preserved such instincts, and those perhaps temporarily lacking them are disproportionately found within the 1 per cent.[23]

A 2001 study, 'In Search of Homo Economicus', concluded that economists' assumption that most individuals are largely self-interested was untrue. In fact, most individuals care about fairness and objectivity.[24] It is not just the behavioural scientists who are confirming this. In 2012 economists determined that the 'bliss point' – the income level at which people are most satisfied – is, in Western Europe at least, an annual income of around $30,000. After that, rising pay produces little measurable increase in personal happiness.[25]

The evidence is mounting. Experimental psychologists describe people who are well adjusted and have positive, helpful and friendly attitudes to other people as 'pro-social'. In 2011 some of those psychologists demonstrated that, for the majority of pro-social people, getting more than they deserve reduces their sense of well-being. It is only the small, narcissistic, individualistic minority who enjoy getting much more than others.[26] The very rich are much less likely to be pro-socially inclined.[27] We may be making a mistake when we blame them for being greedy. Many of them may not be able to help it. The very rich desperately need the help of the better-adjusted majority.

Coincidently, estimates of the proportion of the population who suffer from narcissistic personality disorder suggest that it stands at only 1 per cent – the majority of whom are men. The textbook definition of this mental health problem is that its sufferers' 'sense of self-importance is generally extrava-gant, and they demand attention and admiration. Concern or empathy for others is typically absent. They often appear arrogant, exploitative, and entitled.'[28] Does that remind you of anyone?

Thankfully a mere 5 per cent of people in the UK strongly agree that large differences in wealth are necessary for Britain to be prosperous.[29] The UK has fourteen times as many highly paid bankers as does what is apparently the next most prof-ligate country – Germany. Germany has a larger population and higher national wealth, but only 7 per cent of the number of similarly high-paid bankers in the UK. In 2011 some 2,436 bankers in the UK took home the equivalent of over 1 million euros in pay and bonuses. A third of them worked for Barclays Bank.[30] The number of those high-paid bankers in Germany in 2011 was 170, in France it was 162, while in many other European countries it was zero.

In 2013 the *Times* reported the news that the UK paid its bankers so much as 'Britain's Dominance in the Highest Paid Areas of Banking' – as if it were a triumph.[31] On the one hand,

Verso/Leo Hollis
The City of London: expanding its horizon

they have a point, as it is not easy being a top banker: you have to believe, after all, that you are worth very much more than everyone else. Perhaps higher-than-average testosterone levels help, but the UK's men are unlikely to have a much higher than average level of that hormone; and there are artificial stimulants too. A few months before the *Times* told us how lucky we were to have so many extraordinarily well-paid bankers in our midst, the *Sunday Times* had reported that it had been bankers using cocaine who had got us into this terrible mess.[32]

When they were later interviewed about the 2008 crash, UK bankers said they had become 'over-confident' and 'took more risks', leading to the meltdown. The biggest gamblers of all, in the US, took the most cocaine. People like Bernie Madoff, once described as a financial genius and then lampooned in the tabloids, worked from an office described as 'the north pole' – because it contained so much white powder.[33]

Cocaine is the drug of the 1 per cent and of inequality. The singer Robbie Williams once quipped that cocaine is God's way of telling you you've got too much money. Unsurprisingly, the highest levels of cocaine use per head in Europe are to be found in the UK.[34] Cocaine is also the only drug whose use has increased since 1996, but only among the rich. Use in general, and especially among the young, has dropped since 2008 – but has fallen less among older users, and, one suspects, not at all among top bankers.[35]

In 2012 a City of London banker explained that his colleagues' addictions often stretched to things other than drugs. In revelations that emerged during the trial of UBS trader Kweku Adoboli, it was revealed that there were 'absolutely thousands of undiagnosed gambling addicts in the City. The difference is that the odds are slightly more in your favour than if you're gambling in a Ladbrokes, and so there are many more people who can be successful gambling addicts.'[36] A year later, the crack cocaine purchases of the chairman of the Co-op Bank were revealed, along with those of many others among the 1 per cent – pop stars, athletes, and anyone else who needed a little something to keep on keeping on.

Financial journalist and author Michael Lewis recalled his time in the 1980s with a Wall Street investment bank (possibly in their London branch) as follows:

> I was telling people what to do with their money, but it was bullshit. Wall Street floats on bullshit. At the bottom of it is the belief that someone can tell you what's going up and what's going down. They can't. I knew what I was saying was without value. And yet they were throwing money at me to say it. It was mad. I began to think, If the market can miss-value me this way, what else can it miss-value?[37]

Before Lewis's revelations became public Professor Mark Stein, from Leicester University's School of Management, described how a 'culture of mania' – complete with the classic

psychiatric-textbook features of denial, omnipotence, trium-
phalism and over-activity – created the conditions for the
credit crisis of 2008.[38] All this is now well known, and the
majority of the population appear to accept that the bankers
were out of control, and caused the financial crisis. But the
1 per cent has subsequently behaved as if the 99 per cent are
fools, and persuaded the current government to place the
blame for Britain's economic crisis at the door of the previous
government's spending.

Look with optimism and you see countless signs that we're
decreasingly impressed by greed. In the private sector, the
demotions of Barclays 'fat cat' bankers Rich Richie and Bob
Diamond were milestones.[39] In May 2013, when Diamond
said he was 'never in it for the money', his words were greeted
with incredulity. The press reported how, as well as having a
lavish home in London, he owned a £24 million penthouse
apartment in New York, concealed under the name of a
Russian-sounding company.[40]

Top bankers appear to be strangers to shame. In April
2013 the former HBOS chief executive, James Crosby, was
forced by events to relinquish his knighthood and a third of
his £580,000-a-year pension.[41] This was over a year after
Fred Goodwin, chief executive of RBS, had been stripped of
his knighthood.[42] None of this prevented an employee of the
government-rescued Royal Bank of Scotland being outraged
at the offer of a £4 million annual pay package, because he
knew that someone doing a comparable job in another bank
was being paid £6 million, as revealed by the chair of RBS at
the end of 2013.[43] By spring 2014, even senior Conservative
MPs were calling for some controls to be imposed on these
spiralling rewards and for the rigid application of the EU
bonus cap.[44]

Such greed has caused the public to become increasingly
weary and angry. They now rate bankers along with politicians
and journalists as by far the most likely of fifteen professional
groups not to tell the truth.[45] In January 2014 the New Year

Honours list included a majority of women for the first time – and bankers were conspicuous by their absence.

Apart from the now publicly funded top bank bosses, there are only a few in the 1 per cent who are paid through taxes or a licence fee. But there has been acute public anger following revelations about the top-pay arrangements of BBC mandarins, and perks such as the publicly funded Sky TV subscriptions for wealthy high court judges. One judge complained: 'next will be our cars, drinks, entertaining and flowers. We must resist this.'[46] But they will probably lose their chauffeurs, and much of the rest. All these perks are now under threat, including the idea that the private school fees of the children of senior members of the armed forces should be paid for by the state.

And it is not just the publicly funded brigadiers, some bankers and a few of the judges. Many UK television celebrities and broadcasters have also taken pay cuts. Jeremy Paxman took a 20 per cent cut, and other celebrities who are said to be paid less now than in 2010 include Bruce Forsyth, Graham Norton and Gary Lineker.[47] The current director-general of the BBC is paid much less than his predecessors. Below the level of the best-off of the 1 per cent, life has become tougher. A few of those at the top are beginning to believe again what Adam Smith knew way back in the eighteenth century: we are not all that different from each other.

Starting from the Bottom

> The difference of natural talents in different men is, in reality, much less than we are aware of; and the very different genius which appears to distinguish men of different professions, when grown up to maturity, is not upon many occasions so much the cause, as the effect of the division of labour. The difference between the most dissimilar characters, between a philosopher and a common street porter, for example, seems to arise not so much from nature, as from habit, custom, and

education. When they came into the world, and for the first six or eight years of their existence, they were perhaps, very much alike.

Adam Smith, *The Wealth of Nations* (1776)[48]

Despite the greed of those at the top of the heap, many still find fault first with the unfortunates struggling at the bottom. Young people who cannot find employment typically appear among these innocent targets. Foremost among those casting aspersions on the young is David Cameron. The Conservative prime minister said in 2013: 'Today it is still possible to leave school, sign on, find a flat, start claiming housing benefit and opt for a life on benefits.'[49] In fact, people almost never opt for poverty. As Adam Smith noted more than two centuries ago, although some may be more prone to selfish habit we are all very much alike at the start – it is the circumstances we find ourselves in that turn us into bullies, or the bullied.

Unemployment is highest among young people simply because they are the most vulnerable when the job market shrinks. You can keep a firm or a branch of the civil service going for some time using only older employees. Rather than sack people or deny those at the top the pay rises to which they feel entitled, you just refrain from hiring new staff when people leave or retire, and expect those remaining to take on extra work – often for no extra pay. In the short term that is easier, but in the long term such behaviour is unproductive. Being overworked is miserable, and being unemployed is miserable – two miseries which could cancel each other out and (as an added bonus) give any organisation an infusion of new blood.

Until most allowances were cancelled, in 2010, there was an exceptionally high uptake of Educational Maintenance Allowances by those choosing to study rather than claim dole. Young people in Britain wanted to learn rather than languish on benefits. Almost all young people would choose work over the dole – almost any work. You have to be completely out of touch not to know this; but many in the Coalition government

Industrial Worker Magazine, 1911
How the pyramid works

are from one of the most out-of-touch groups – Britain's 1 per cent. Two-thirds of the cabinet are millionaires; most of the rest are in the 1 per cent by virtue of their gross household incomes.[50]

Ross Fergusson of the Open University, and a member of the International Centre for Comparative Criminological Research, explained UK youth employment policy in 2013 as being the policy of the 1 per cent: 'Unashamed by a record of youth non-participation worse than that of almost all twenty-nine OECD countries, the Coalition now proposes to withdraw most of the last remaining welfare rights of young people, including those who are likely to be worst affected by recent changes.'[51] Apparently the rich need a lot of money to persuade them to work – but the Coalition wants young people to take any job going, no matter how unsuitable or insecure it might be, even if it is based on a 'zero hours' contract, and no matter how bad the future prospects in that line of work.

There are, of course, worse fates than being out of work in the UK. Of all the countries in Europe, recent OECD statistics suggest that Estonia has had the greatest increase in poverty among eighteen- to twenty-four-year-olds, followed by Spain – and then the UK. The UK ranks above even Ireland in terms of the proportion of young people without work.[52] But the Coalition assumes that, as there are still young people coming to Britain and taking jobs, many of those who are already here are being too choosy. In reality, as entrepreneur Nick Hanauer so memorably put it, 'If it were true that lower tax rates and more wealth for the wealthy would lead to more job creation, then today we would be drowning in jobs.'[53]

Early in 2014 the Equality Trust calculated that an extra 1.75 million living-wage jobs – enough good jobs for all the unemployed young people in Britain – could have been created if the richest one hundred people in Britain had not seen their wealth increase in just one year by a total of £25 billion, and those monies had instead been diverted into employment.[54] One way of realising this, of course, would have been to increase the taxation of the very rich, and to use those taxes for job creation; but it would be even more efficient for that money never to flow through the pockets of the very rich in the first place – for firms to pay their 'top' employees less and employ more younger people alongside them.[55]

In England and Wales alone, it has been calculated that 40 per cent of sixteen- to twenty-four-year-olds 'are failing to make the most of their abilities in the workplace, with nearly 1.3 million not working at all and another 1.2 million who are underemployed or overqualified'.[56] Between 2012 and 2013 the wealth of the richest one hundred people in Britain rose by 11 per cent – just a little less than the 13 per cent increase in the wealth of the richest 0.7 per cent of people on the planet. For the 2.5 million young adults who are unemployed or underemployed in Britain, the monies required to finance the kinds of jobs they could do are instead being sucked up by a tiny elite of one hundred individuals who cannot possibly need it. In the UK the effect is staggering, but what is happening worldwide is almost impossible to imagine.

In just one year, between 2012 and 2013, the richest people on the planet increased their wealth by 13 per cent, from $87.5 trillion to $99 trillion. The 32 million richest individuals (0.7 per cent of all people) came to hold 41 per cent of the total wealth of the world, while the poorest two-thirds of the planet's inhabitants saw their wealth drop from 3.3 per cent to 3.0 per cent, all of them owning property or having resources worth much less than $10,000 each. In Figure 3.2, the numbers to the sides of the two pyramids indicate total wealth of each segment of the world's population. All the time, as the rich take more, the number of good jobs available to the poor falls.

Not Enough Work for the Young

The chronic gap between the incomes of the richest and poorest citizens is seen as the risk that is most likely to cause serious damage globally in the coming decade.

World Economic Forum, 16 January 2014 [57]

The World Economic Forum, a body of some 700 global experts, ranks growing inequality as the greatest risk to the economic health of the world. Climate change comes second, and the high and rising levels of unemployment third. These experts are no radical leftists, but the harm being caused by the very richest taking so much is now so pitifully obvious that, from pop stars and popes through to right-wing media pundits, people of all walks of life are beginning to revise their opinions accordingly.[58]

A recent report from US scientists, utilising tools developed by NASA, stated that environmental collapse 'can be avoided and population can reach equilibrium if the per capita rate

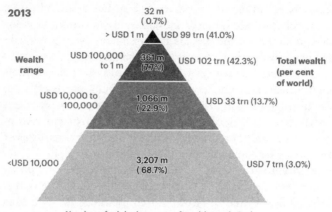

Source: *Global Wealth Report 2013*, Credit Suisse and Oxfam

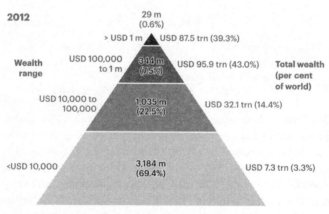

Note: Figures rounded to sum to exactly 100 per cent in 2012.
Source: James Davies, Rodrigo Lluberas and Anthony Shorrocks, *Credit Suisse Global Wealth Databook 2012*

Figure 3.2 World wealth parade, 2013 and 2012

of depletion of nature is reduced to a sustainable level, and if resources are distributed in a reasonably equitable fashion'. The same researchers are clear about where the greatest risks to the necessary reduction in inequality being achieved come from: 'Elites and their supporters, who opposed making these changes, could point to the long sustainable trajectory "so far" in support of doing nothing.'[59] You cannot wait for those much richer than you to act; and if the disparity between us and them continues to widen, there are many far broader reasons to be concerned than pure self-interest.

Pollution is the product of the rich far more than of the poor. In the UK the average carbon emissions of the richest tenth of households are three times greater per capita than those of the poorest tenth, their emissions from car use are eight times higher, and from international flights nine times greater. Moreover, the study that these figures came from did not include estimates for flights taken by the 1 per cent, or the carbon pollution caused by heating and maintaining second homes.[60] In India the best-off 1 per cent pollute at about twice the rate of the rest of the top 10 per cent by income.[61] In the UK the rich are richer, and pollute even more. Those with most concern for the environment – the young – have the least resources to waste.

In the four years from 2008 to 2012, the incomes of people in their twenties in Britain fell by around 3 per cent a year, each year, reaching 12 per cent below 2007 levels in real terms by the end of the period. Few complained about the low wages, because a fifth of UK residents under twenty-five were out of work by the start of 2014. Of those in work, most were working part-time or on zero-hours contracts, or were on probation, or otherwise without any security. Many were even working for free as interns, under the guise of training or 'work experience'. Employers are getting work done for free by people who, in a properly functioning market, would be paid.

Fewer and fewer firms will employ young adults – a quarter now offer no openings to the young at all. In reporting all this

The divide between rich and poor could not be clearer

in 2013, the master of Hertford College, Oxford, Will Hutton, was forced to conclude: 'We are governed by charlatans.' And he asked his readers: 'Who cares for the condition of Britain or its people?'[62] The implication was that the 1 per cent did not. By the end of 2013 we already knew that there were some 1.46 million people who said they worked part-time because they could not find full-time work. This was the highest figure since records began in 1992. The rise in part-time work helped push up the national count of employees to 30 million, and helped the dole queue fall to just under 2.5 million.[63] But fewer people had adequate pay and used the qualifications and skills they had acquired.

The UK Labour Force Survey reveals that today almost one-third of working men who are in part-time employment are there because they cannot find a full-time job; for women that proportion is just over one-eighth. Too many people are underemployed, while many others are doing unsatisfactory jobs. When in 2013 she interviewed people who had been persuaded to take part in so-called back-to-work schemes, the journalist Mary O'Hara found that many were 'left ... wondering how their elected politicians could be so ignorant of need – and be so cruel'.[64]

George Osborne unveiled a new and cynically titled 'Help to Work' scheme in autumn 2013. The UK initiative was modelled on one in Denmark, but cost four times less per jobseeker. In Denmark there is more money available to help people find work, because the rich take less.[65] For the same reason, employers can afford a larger workforce. In contrast to the Danish schemes, Osborne's intervention was deeply unpopular. The *Mirror* headline read: 'Forced Labour: Conservative Party to Force the Jobless to Work for Nothing or Lose Their Dole: The Long-Term Unemployed Are to be Sent Out to Cook for OAPs or Pick Up Litter in the Meanest Welfare Shake-Up Ever'.[66] Forcing people to work for nothing puts the UK in danger of breaking international laws on slavery.

Lauding Help to Work, millionaire Mr Osborne told the Tory Party conference in Manchester that autumn: 'No one will get something for nothing.'[67] But, as a trust fund baby, he has been getting something for nothing all his life. The new regime, with unpaid community work placements, was due to start in April 2014. The similarities with a community service order issued by a court for committing a crime were obvious. Martin Sime, the chief executive of the Scottish Council for Voluntary Organisations, commented: 'We don't need this twenty-first-century version of the workhouse' – not least because it demeans community work. Giving out the message that cooking for elderly people is a punishment says a lot about the people who thought up the 'Help to Work' policy.

Many people try to explain to the 1 per cent that their policies are causing harm. Dr Mary Brown, a freelance education consultant, explained: 'At the moment, many people do this sort of work for nothing, or for an insultingly low wage. It's insulting them even further to suggest their activities are regarded as on the same level as a punishment regime for the work-shy.'[68] But too many of today's 1 per cent have been brought up to think they know what is best for those beneath them. And, like the worst of their Victorian antecedents, some think it helps the poor to have money taken away from them.

Removing benefit payments from young people, or any other group, has a knock-on effect on local economies. Benefits involve transfer payments from the state to local businesses and landlords, via benefits claimants, with some returning to the state again in VAT, business rates and council taxes. The government gets some money back in the end, but in the meantime it stimulates economic activity. It is a form of investment. These cuts are not really about saving money – they are about the 1 per cent's view of the way the state should operate.

Few of the 1 per cent work in the public sector without also having private means. Many do not need to work at all, but many have firm views about how other people ought to behave – views not constrained by mixing much with those less prosperous than themselves. The education secretary, Michael Gove, helped illustrate this in September 2013 when he commented that people attending food banks had made the wrong choices in life. Despite his humble origins, Gove's salary, combined with his wife's earnings, now take his family into the 1 per cent income bracket.[69]

In June 2013, Conservative peer and welfare reform minister, Lord David Freud, who retired early from banking with a fortune, insisted that the recent sharp increase in the numbers of people resorting to food handouts to feed their families was not necessarily linked to benefits sanctions or delays. He suggested that more people were taking charity food because more food banks existed.[70] Lord Freud's social status has always placed him among the wealthiest. In such circumstances, a '1 per cent group think' emerges, typified by an arrogance that easily dismisses any contradictory evidence.

In October 2013 the Red Cross produced a sixty-eight-page report to explain why it was now collecting food for starving people on the streets of Britain, and in many other parts of austerity-hit Europe:[71] 'We now see a quiet desperation spreading among Europeans, resulting in depression, resignation and loss of hope for their future.'[72] In France 75 per cent of those who ask the Red Cross for food handouts do so because if they paid for the food they could not pay their rent. Rising poverty in Germany has led 5.5 million middle-class Germans to become poorer; in contrast, only a tenth of that number – half a million – stepped up a class and became richer in the same period. Socially you are ten times more likely to fall than rise, even in Germany. The Red Cross report ended with the International Labour Organization's estimate that the risk of social unrest had increased by 12 per cent across the continent within just one year.

When people do not have work, or the work they have is paid too poorly, then, when benefits are being slashed, they come to rely on handouts from charities to survive. In Britain, the use of food banks tripled in the twelve months prior to

MAS Youth Maryland
The food bank

September 2013. By the autumn, some 120,000 children were coming to rely on these food handouts. That was on top of the free school dinners and any breakfast club meals they received. In October 2013 the prime minister's official poverty tsar said he wanted to know whether Mr Cameron was 'burying his head in the sand and hoping he could get through to the election'.[73] Many of the 1 per cent, like David Cameron, are ignoring the issue of rising hunger. If they think about it at all it may make them uncomfortable – although some appear to blame the poor for being hungry.

In December 2013, despite mounting evidence of a growing food poverty crisis in the UK, ministers maintained that there was 'no robust evidence' of a link between sweeping welfare reforms and a rise in the use of food banks. Recently released government statistics had revealed a surge since the recession in the number of English hospital admissions with a diagnosis of malnutrition – up from 3,161 in 2008/09 to 5,499 in 2012/13.[74]

In the same month, the government was exposed as deliberately delaying publication of research it had commissioned into the phenomenon. In a letter to the *British Medical Journal*, seven academics from the Medical Research Council, experts in Public Health, drew the obvious inference: 'Because the Government has delayed the publication of research it commissioned into the rise of emergency food aid in the UK, we can only speculate that the cause is related to the rising cost of living and increasingly austere welfare reforms.'[75] The price of food in Britain rose during 2013 because keeping it low was not a priority.

When the 1 per cent takes more there is less for the rest. In the UK the cuts required to preserve the position and wealth of the 1 per cent are taking £19 billion a year out of the economy. Almost none of the planned cuts will be noticed by the 1 per cent. The alternative to many of the cuts is to tax the 1 per cent more, along with a few others at the top of society, at the same rate as the 1 per cent are taxed in more equitable countries. However, instead of raising taxes, the Coalition government has cut top taxes to 45 per cent. In contrast, when Margaret Thatcher introduced a mini version of austerity in the early 1980s, she raised 50p more from taxation for every 50p she cut in government spending. Cameron raised taxes by 17p for every 83p Osborne cut, and he raised them mostly through VAT – a regressive tax that takes a higher proportion of your income the poorer you are – rather than through the income tax on the rich.

It is in poor or corrupt countries that taxes for the rich are lowest. Income tax rates on the richest are just 10 per cent in Bulgaria and Kazakhstan, and 13 per cent in Russia. In contrast, top tax rates exceed or equal 75 per cent in France, 57 per cent in Sweden, 55 per cent in Denmark, 52 per cent in Spain, and 50 per cent in Japan, the Netherlands, Austria and Belgium. In the last three countries the top tax rate kicks in at earnings of below the equivalent of £50,000.[76] In contrast, in Britain, the lowered 45 per cent top rate does not kick in until your income reaches £150,000, and is only applied to income above that threshold.

People pay tax if they are made to. When there was a 50 per cent tax band in the UK, over 80 per cent of people earning between £500,000 and £10 million paid what they owed.[77] The slightly higher 50 per cent tax rate did not deter the large majority of those who were eligible to pay it from doing so. Some declared income in a different year in order to avoid it legally, but most high-earners will pay the taxes levied on them. Higher taxes do not result in less being levied. That is one of the nastier lies of a few of the 1 per cent – those who hate taxes the most.

Figure 3.3 shows that it is not until people with annual incomes of over £10 million are considered that the beginnings of tax evasion become obvious, and the proportion paying at a rate of over 40 per cent falls to 72 per cent. Before that point, usually at least four out of five higher-earners pay income tax at the correct rate. For those earning below

£150,000, no one pays tax at above the 45p rate because it is not levied at that rate. For those earning above that but less than £250,000 a year, only a minority pay their overall tax at a rate over 40 per cent, because only the very highest earners in that group would be expected to.

Just under a quarter of the £19 billion in public spending cuts comes from incapacity benefit for the disabled, this is a massive reduction in funds which once kept its recipients just

Proportion paying their tax at a rate of:

	Under 10%	10% to 20%	20% to 30%	30% to 40%	Above 40%	TOTAL
£100k to £150k	1	8	24	67	0	100
£150k to £250k	2	3	13	77	6	100
£250k to £500k	2	2	5	18	73	100
£500k to £1m	2	2	4	11	81	100
£1m to £5m	3	2	5	10	80	100
£5m to £10m	4	3	4	8	81	100
Over £10m	6	3	8	12	72	100

Annual income before tax

Note: Percentages do not always appear to sum to exactly 100 because of rounding.

Source: House of Commons Library, 2013

Figure 3.3 Average Income Tax Rate paid by higher-rate tax payers in the UK 2012

out of poverty; a similar amount reflects cuts in tax credits that once kept many working families out of poverty. Only 2.5 per cent of the total is made up of cuts to housing benefit – but because this £490 million is being taken from people who are almost always impoverished, cutting it will still cause great harm.

The absolute immiseration of the poorest will have little immediate impact on those, mostly in the 1 per cent, who make the cuts. Neither will it affect many of the services the richest use, nor the areas where the vast majority of the 1 per cent live: 'Much of the south and east of England outside London escapes comparatively lightly.'[78] And which is the local authority area least affected, per head, by the cuts? It's the City of London. Why did that authority need to be protected the most from austerity? Most people in the UK think the rich have too much influence over where the country is headed, but not as many as in the US and other large, if often poorer, countries – where the excesses of the very affluent may be more obvious (see Figure 3.4).

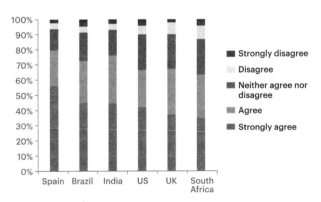

Source: Oxfam's own polling. Respondents were asked whether they agreed with the statement 'The rich have too much influence over where this country is headed'.

Figure 3.4 Attitudes to inequalities in wealth and power in six countries, 2014

Low and Falling Pay

> To keep our wages coming in, we have at all times to be polite
> and welcoming to the very rich, hiding our disgust behind our
> hand as we open the door to plutocrat X or prince Y and say:
> 'Ah, sir, how very good it is to see you again. I have prepared a
> warm bath and a hot concubine just as you like them. Pay no
> attention to the talk of revolution in the kitchen.'
>
> Ian Jack, 2013[79]

In 2010 and 2011, to keep their jobs, millions of workers
accepted pay cuts or took shorter hours. Between those two
years, average public sector pay fell from £16.60 to £15.80
per hour, and for private sector work it fell from £15.10 to
£13.60. In 2012 and 2013 wages fell again in real terms. By
2013 the average employee in Britain was earning 15 per
cent less than he or she would have done if the normal pay
increases most workers experienced prior to 2008 had continued. The total annual pay packet for the bottom 95 per cent
of UK workers had been reduced by £52 billion since 2008.[80]

Thousands of unemployed people are now compelled
to work without pay. The companies employing them are
allowed to keep the number of wageless workers toiling for
them secret. Even charities, such as the Salvation Army, are
involved.[81]

In May 2013 a judge ruled that the Department for Work
and Pensions should reveal the names of employers using this
coerced, unpaid labour. The department replied that it was
'very disappointed' with the judge, and might appeal to the
high court, or simply block the move with a ministerial veto.[82]
They saw such secrecy about the names of firms colluding
with government in making people work for no pay as part of
'winning the global race' – a world-view seeing life as competition, not cooperation.

The odious phrase 'winning the global race' could only
have been coined by the products of the kind of school that
impresses on its pupils the overwhelming importance of always

coming first. The words 'to the bottom' can often be profitably added after 'race'.[83] Such language hides the real intention, which is to drive down employment rights and wages. For the lowest wages in the rich world you have to look to the US, where the best-off among the poorest tenth of paid workers take home only $387 a week to live on – just $55 a day, and 3 per cent less in real terms than they earned in 2000.[84] This is unsurprising, because the 1 per cent takes an increasingly large slice of the cake in the US, and more than in any other large, rich country. The 1 per cent cannot allow the bottom 10 per cent to be paid decently if they themselves are to remain so disproportionately rich.

It is wrong to imagine, as is sometimes argued, that the polarisation of society serves a positive economic purpose. Economists based in Hamburg, Göttingen and Harvard have recently studied trends in nine high-income countries, revealing that, as those at the very top take more, national economic growth becomes more sluggish. It is not just that there is less to go round when the richest leave less for everyone else; the chest fills more slowly when the 1 per cent take more, and when many are forced to work for nothing.[85]

Some seventy-five years ago, economic historian R. H. Tawney had made the same point about inequality: 'Innocent laymen are disposed to believe that these monstrosities, though morally repulsive, are economically advantageous, and that, even were they not, the practical difficulties of abolishing them are too great to be overcome.'[86] Innocent laymen became less innocent after the Second World War, and for forty years there was increasing equality; but between 1978 and 2008, more and more of us forgot what happens if you do not carefully monitor the greed of the greediest. Increasingly, becoming a more popular theory throughout the 1970s and attracting a consensus by 2003, mainstream opinion among economists was that a growing economy raises all boats. They believed that redistribution was incentive-dulling. Robert Lucas, Nobel Prize winner, epitomised the pre-2008 orthodoxy when he wrote in 2003 that, 'of the tendencies that are harmful to sound economics, the most seductive and ... poisonous is to focus on questions of distribution'.[87] Within ten years he was being quoted in the *Economist* as a fool. But it was not all his fault; greater inequality distorts and dulls the mind.

Extreme inequality degrades everyone's behaviour. The more complacent elements of the middle class are currently rediscovering their objective status as employees and superior servants. Those below them do not believe their grandparents when they tell them that they had it better, in a world that was a more pleasant place to live. Their great-grandparents are usually no longer around to tell them how such a world was won.

Many books are now being written to explain that there are areas of our lives where crude markets are inefficient, and where competition causes harm. Michael Sandel's *What Money Can't Buy* is a good example. Other current titles, such as Chystia Freeland's *Plutocrats*, explain what it is like to be superrich; or how it is to live life more precariously, as Guy Standing's *The Precariat* makes clear; or what it feels like to be at the bottom, as Owen Jones describes in *Chavs*; or the top as Jones describes in *The Establishment: And How They Get Away With It*.

In the US the growing precariat majority – those whose lives are economically precarious – has come to be called the 'task rabbit economy'. Task rabbits are people who bid for very short-term jobs on the internet. To win the bid, the task rabbit must be willing to bid below what they think others will put in as their lowest bid. The job might be to clean a garage, paint an apartment or buy groceries. The firm that matches up these temporary servants and their not-too-fussy masters, and carries out criminal record checks on them, is called Taskrabbit.com. Rabbits receive star ratings based on what previous masters thought of them.[88] Task rabbits are frontrunners in a race to the bottom.

If task rabbits are an extreme case, 'temps' are the new

normal. Temps range from casual day labourers to university teaching assistants hired for ten months, or ten days. Many of the 1 per cent revel in a world in which the increasingly fragmented 99 per cent have ever-decreasing bargaining power. Nowhere in Europe is such revelry clearer to see than in the place which is home to most of the UK 1 per cent: London. And as a result of declining solidarity in the richest large city in all of Europe, 28 per cent of Londoners are now living in poverty. They are unable to live a simple, decent life, unable to afford many routine, unexceptional items.[89] But they are there mostly to work, or to find work.

A majority (57 per cent) of the Londoners who live in poverty are in families with at least one wage earner, but their wages are now insufficient for them to survive with dignity. More people in poverty in London now rent privately than live in social housing. A quarter of all Londoners rely on housing benefit. As a result, although London has seen the greatest mean average increase in salaries and wages in recent years of any European city, it is also the most economically divided and remains the 'poverty capital' of England.

London is leading the rest of the UK into accepting growing and now gross inequality as almost inevitable. London is the 'unpaid intern capital' of Europe. But it is also home to a new resistance that began in the US among the young, the unpaid and the underpaid.

No other UK city has as many squatters as London has. Protests are most common here, and the age of the people involved is getting younger and younger. It is the young who have lost the most in recent years, and it is they who are beginning to show their resentment through resistance. That resistance is spreading, and is expressed in many ways, from street demonstrations to the graffiti and other art of the Occupy movement.

London is where financial deregulation began, in the 1980s. It is London that benefited most, and it is in London that those with some of the greatest debts now reside. London is

Leepower

In it together? Occupy London 2011

home to most of the 1 per cent, most of the rest of whom live just a short distance away from the capital. London's financial markets were constrained between 1929 and 1978, just as they were in the US, when the 1 per cent was forced to become more normal (see Figure 3.5). Since those constraints were lifted, on both sides of the Atlantic, the very rich have become richer and everyone else's lives more precarious.

The City of London's 'Big Bang' took place in 1986, with extensive government deregulation of the UK's financial markets. Top-paid employees have secured a doubling of their income since then, only to trail way behind the 'top' bankers and similar members of the 1 per cent who have received so much more than the average top-paid employee. The gap between their respective annual incomes now averages nearly a quarter of a million pounds.[90]

A salary escalator has been created by the assessment of remuneration through the comparison of top pay in any institution with a group of other institutions which just happen, on average, to pay more. Keeping up with the poshest of Joneses

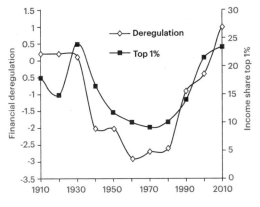

Source: Financial Deregulation, nber.org/papers/w14644.pdf; Income
share: Piketty and Saez (2003, 2012)

Figure 3.5 Financial deregulation in inequality, USA
1910–2010

in this way comes with a huge and growing price tag. At last, this is beginning to be widely understood. It may be that even many of the cosmopolitan elite are starting to understand just how extreme and harmful the inequalities have become.

London is now the most overpaid city in the world, considering the circumstances of the national population. In 2014 the UK minister for cities, Greg Clark, produced a report in which he and his co-author claimed that London was not so unusual. They presented data showing the proportion of the national population living within the capital cities of a number of countries and the share of national GDP received by the people of that city. On the basis of that data, the greediest city on their list was Moscow although it only looks rich in comparison to the poverty in much of the rest of Russia. But second, despite its similarly high internal levels of poverty, was London, where residents of the capital received, on average, 1.7 times as much in income as the national average. It is an example of how inequality makes us stupid that the minister thought he was presenting a case for London's normality, when in fact he was doing the opposite. At the lower end of the list was Vienna, whose citizens were apparently 1.3 times as productive as the average for Austria; Stockholm, where the equivalent figure stood at 1.2; and Tokyo and Seoul, each with a figure of 1.1.[91] Of course, almost all that extra London money flows into the pockets of the city's richest residents.

Most of the population of the UK never see the mansions of the rich, or know how much their everyday lives differ from what is normal. Press coverage of celebrities often strains to make them appear 'just like you and me'. Nigella Lawson was filmed as if she was cooking in her own kitchen – the existence of the 'team cupcake' supporting her and her husband's lavish lifestyle was only fully revealed through a court case involving several of her servants.[92]

The existence of, and inequalities within, the servant class are instructive here. A century ago income inequality was even higher than it is today. Incomes varied twenty-five-fold just

Verso/Leo Hollis

Kensington: one of the richest neighbourhoods in London

between the servants of a grand stately home. The highest-paid member of the household, the steward, might be paid 27p a day; a valet half that; a lady's maid less than half again; a kitchen maid half of her wage; and a postilion, the very lowest, received just a penny a day.[93] These figures relate to 1913, the year when the top 1 per cent in the UK took more than they ever had before, or ever would thereafter (see Figure 3.6).

There are still a few who behave with crass indifference to the feelings of others, an attitude that epitomised the British gentry in that year just before the First World War – appearing not to care, for example, how much a meal might cost in a time when many are going hungry; or requiring a servant to pack their clothes every time they are washed as if they have been newly bought and packaged. One well-known British businessman, who has appeared regularly on the TV

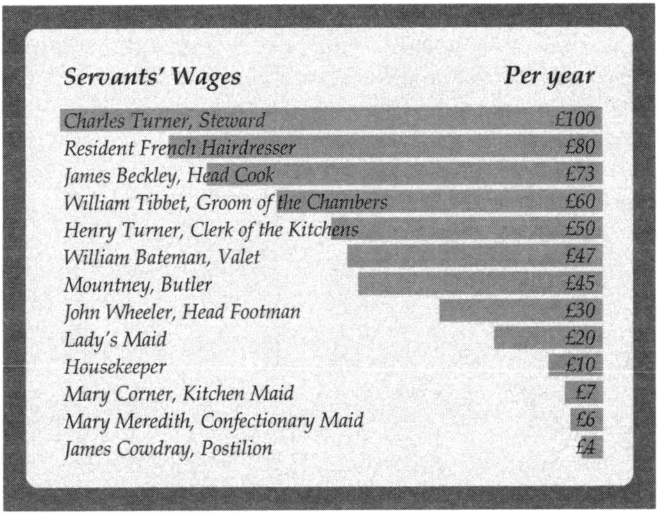

Servants' Wages	Per year
Charles Turner, Steward	£100
Resident French Hairdresser	£80
James Beckley, Head Cook	£73
William Tibbet, Groom of the Chambers	£60
Henry Turner, Clerk of the Kitchens	£50
William Bateman, Valet	£47
Mountney, Butler	£45
John Wheeler, Head Footman	£30
Lady's Maid	£20
Housekeeper	£10
Mary Corner, Kitchen Maid	£7
Mary Meredith, Confectionary Maid	£6
James Cowdray, Postilion	£4

Source: Blenheim Palace, 2013

Figure 3.6 Income inequality between the servants within a stately home, 1913

programme *Dragons' Den*, is reported to sign restaurant bills without looking at the total, and to have hired a personal butler to fold and pack away his shirts, placing layers of tissue paper between them.[94] Apparently this butler used to work for the royal family, and he wanted people to know that. This is a form of madness.

As Clive James astutely put it in 2009,

> We've reached a turning point. A madness has gone out of fashion: the madness of behaving as if only too much can be enough. There will always be another madness, but not that one. From now on a man will have to be as dumb as a petro-dollar potentate to think that anyone will respect him for sitting on a gold toilet in a private jumbo jet. Excess wealth is gone like the codpiece. The free market will continue but any respect for the idea of free money is all over.[95]

It takes a little time for everyone to get the message, but after the crash of 2008 it began to shine clearer than ever, at least to many of the 99 per cent. Some even began to pity the rich for how stupid they often appear, bereft of a plausible rationale for their riches.

4

Wealth

The idea that capital income is 'unearned' is beneath contempt. You earn the returns on an investment by working, delaying gratification and saving. The argument that an inheritance is 'unearned' (so that we can take what we like in Inheritance Tax) is just as weak: someone earned the money.

Mathew Sinclair, TaxPayers' Alliance, 2013[1]

Between 1 and 2 per cent of people are not naturally empathic.[2] This small group find it enormously difficult to understand how other people feel or to appreciate a different point of view. Others have a little empathy but are still highly individualistic.[3] It is hard to become rich if you are not primarily looking out for yourself. Those who amass fortunes manage to do so partly because they don't like sharing and see themselves as special, as more careful with money, as being worth more than others. They tend to see others, and sharing, as 'just weak'.

The richest people in the world have a revealing acronym to describe themselves – HNWI – high-net-worth individuals. These are people who have a spare million US dollars' worth of wealth, not including their primary residence or their pension. Worldwide, there were estimated to be 12 million such people in 2012, with a mean 'investable' wealth of $3.85

million each. It is worth looking at where the world's richest live, what they have, and the huge inequalities even within this tiny group.

Most of the world's 12 million superrich possess 'only' a little over $1 million in disposable wealth. In the two years after the 2008 credit crunch their numbers and mean wealth fell slightly, but by 2012 both were again rising. The majority of the world's HNWIs live in the US, Japan or Germany. London is preferred as a second home, so many are not officially resident in the UK. Around 465,000 HNWIs live in the UK,[4] making up about 1 per cent of all British adults and accounting for just under 4 per cent of the world's superrich.

Globally, the top 1 per cent of HNWIs, with at least £30 million in disposable assets, are known as 'Ultras' (UHNWI). In 2012 there were 111,000 of these people in the world, but they held over a third of all the wealth of the 12 million superrich – or, on average, just under $150 million each. By the end of 2013 the richest 300 people in the world held $3.7 trillion, or about $12 billion each,[5] and their collective wealth rose the most in that year – by 16.5 per cent.[6] The idea that they had earned that money is highly questionable.

London has become home to more UHNWIs than any other city on the planet. With somewhat spurious precision, the estate agent Frank Knight recently reported that there were now some 4,224 UHNWI families living in London alone in 2014, and that they expected some 5,000 families with liquid assets exceeding $30 million to be calling the city their (sometime) home by 2024. The attraction is not just in London's history, nightlife or convenient time zone – it is chiefly the country's lax tax regime. As Pippa Malmgren, one-time economic adviser to George Bush, puts it: 'The crackdown on tax havens in Switzerland has removed these old options for new capital. As a result, there has been a huge influx of global capital into the UK.'[7]

Famously, the best-off segment of the UHNWIs, numbering just eighty-five people worldwide, held almost half the wealth of the richest 300 by January 2013 – some $1.7 trillion dollars, which was the same as was held by the poorest half of the world's population, or some 3.6 billion people. When Ricardo Fuentes, head of research at Oxfam, released the killer fact that eighty-five people now held the same amount of wealth as half of all humanity, the statistic went viral. Oxfam's international website had more hits in one day than ever before. All around the world, many appear more interested in inequality now than they have ever been.[8]

Inequality worldwide is far greater than inequality within any single country – but in some countries internal inequality continues to grow rapidly. There is perhaps no country where this trend is more pronounced than in the United Kingdom, where the poorest continue to see their benefits and wages fall while the world's superrich trickle in at the top. For every superrich individual at the very top, there are over 700,000 people who have now become poorer at the bottom, so that the wealth of the richest one hundred people in the UK now equates to that of the poorest 30 per cent of all UK households, and that ratio is worsening.[9] From among those one hundred people, the five richest families now own more wealth between them than the poorest 20 per cent.[10]

While the wealth of the HNWIs has remained stable, the wealth of the UHNWIs has grown by an annual 10.9 per cent in recent years, and that of the 85 richest people on earth by a little more than that, tipping them into international pariah status by 2014 and ensuring that by March of that year just the 67 richest of them then held as much wealth as the poorest half of all humanity.[11] The wealth of mid-tier millionaires has grown by 'only' 10.2 per cent a year recently, while the wealth of what analysts call the 'millionaire next door' – someone with less than $5 million – increased the least, by 'only' 9.3 per cent a year. All the rich are doing very nicely, but since 2011 the divisions within the richest have been widening.[12]

Governments worldwide are beginning to target the superrich as a potential source of revenue. In his autumn statement

*HNWIs = High Net Worth Individuals, people who have a spare $1 million in easily disposable assets, not their main home or pension

Number of HNWIs* (thousands)

HNWI population growth, 2011–12

Country	2011	2012	Growth
US	3,068	3,436	12.0%
Japan	1,822	1,902	4.4%
Germany	951	1,015	6.7%
China	562	643	14.3%
UK	441	465	5.4%
France	404	430	6.4%
Canada	280	298	6.5%
Switzerland	252	282	12.0%
Australia	180	207	15.1%
Italy	168	176	4.5%
Brazil	165	165	0.2%
South Korea	144	160	10.9%

Note: Percentage growth rates will not match column totals due to rounding.
Source: Capgemini Lorenz Curve Analysis, 2013

Figure 4.1 People with over $US1 million spare by country, 2011–12

of 2013, the UK chancellor, George Osborne, announced that for the first time capital gains tax would apply to the property of non-residents in the UK. Even before that, in the year to 2012, the London auction houses Christie's and Sotheby's reported a 56.5 per cent increase in the value of old masters put up for sale.[13] The very richest in Britain are now at something of a loss over where to put their money. But they are very good at hiding it.[14]

In the UK we have no real idea how much the truly wealthy own – just a series of estimates, none of which are reliable. What we do know is that, to get into the 1 per cent, defined in terms of income, you need a household income, as a couple, of about £160,000 – a little more if you have children, a little less if you are single. What we do not know is what the entry bar is to joining the 1 per cent in terms of wealth.[15] The best estimate we have is the Capgemini and Royal Bank of Canada 2013 World Wealth Report, which suggests that roughly 1 per cent of the population of the UK has a million dollars' worth of cash to spare – money not tied up in a primary residence or pension plan. But we do not know much about the less liquid assets of the wealthiest 1 per cent.

This segment of society has been described by Ken Roberts in his 2001 book on class as 'the best organised and most class conscious of all the classes'[16] – a statement which conceals the fact that this is also the class with the highest degree of inequality within it. What looks like class collusion may simply be the outcome of the thousands of independent but selfish actions of the very rich. They do not have to be organised to look organised.

The nearer you get to those at the top, the less organised they seem. Sit at high table next to the master of one of the richer Oxbridge colleges, and you may realise he is having trouble staying vertical due to the pre-dinner drinks; but to the masses of undergraduates below him, he looks as if he is in charge – which is all he needs to do in order to be retain his position. In the 1990s John Scott described the network of London clubs used by some of the 1 per cent.[17] But I suspect Scott's London clubs were more about drinking, and escaping neglected wives, than about maintaining upper-class solidarity.

What keeps those who rule in power is not just a common culture, but the much wider belief that there is no alternative. The members of the international ruling class are highly dysfunctional – think Nigella Lawson and Charles Saatchi multiplied many times. What makes them so powerful is that

Verso/Leo Hollis

A club on Pall Mall: home to the elite for two centuries

they can rule despite constant inebriation, divorces, narcissism and neuroses.

Of course, members of the House of Lords with shared 'business interests' act together to get a corrupt healthcare bill through parliament. But when they do so, they are like drones in a beehive, they look as if they know what they are doing; but they are merely following their programming and behaving as expected. Occasionally we discover a Mont Pelerin Society or Bilderberg Group, and we think these are just the tip of the iceberg, and beneath the waters lies a vast conspiracy – but such explicit collusion is in fact the exception. The rich rule because their money rules; their own participation is relatively marginal. Receiving huge sums of money leads almost all people to behave in ways that a similar person would not behave if they were living in a more equal society.

Once a culture is established, it includes mechanisms for its own perpetuation. For example, women are better at passing exams at school than men. On average, girls reach all their developmental markers earlier than boys: from walking and talking to learning to write. Women also live longer. But patriarchy ensures that women cannot organise themselves to realise their potential. As a result, men continue to run the system as stupidly as ever. It is not that they are more able – it is almost as if the culture is in control, and changing the direction of culture is far harder than just winning hearts and minds.[18]

Today the UK Office for National Statistics (ONS) estimates that, to be in the top 10 per cent of households, you have to have total assets, including illiquid assets, of almost £1 million, while entry into the 1 per cent requires assets of £2.8 million. But the statisticians say little about how much wealth people have beyond that,[19] and the cut-off point is highly unreliable. After the cut-off, things become murkier still (see Figure 4.2 – based on figures originally released by official bodies, though possibly in error). The ONS appears to have no idea how much wealth the 1 per cent hold. They know far

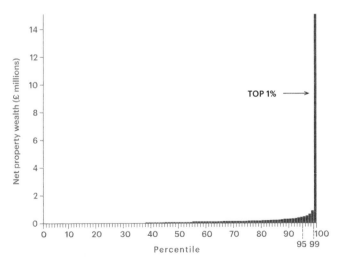

Source: George Monbiot and ONS, 2013

Figure 4.2 Property wealth in the UK: net positive equity by wealth percentile

more about the wealth of the other 99 per cent in society, even though it is tiny on a per capita basis in comparison.

Seeing Others as Human

> I also wish you'd listen when your child asks you to look at the pirate hat they've made, instead of scrolling through your emails on your iPhone. I wish you'd get down and play the games with them instead of chatting to other parents. Because when you look back at the photos from your party, you won't be in them. Instead, it will be me holding your child's hand and unwrapping their gifts with them. You won't remember my name; you won't remember the party, either.
>
> Children's entertainer[20]

In Dubai a 2.4-kilometre-high, 400-storey vertical city in the sky is planned, with internal lifts carefully segregated so as to separate the servants and workers from the residents.[21] The front and back stairs of a London town house used to have the same purpose. As *Forbes* magazine put it, before the crash: 'If you want to know where the world's hottest economies are ... skip the GDP reports, employment statistics and consumer spending trends. All you need to do is answer one question: Where are the fastest elevators?'[22]

By contrast, in the US growing horizontal segregation has become normal, and causes severe commuting inefficiencies. In recent years, in twenty-seven of the thirty largest US cities, residential segregation by income has increased: rich areas have become richer, poor areas poorer. Simultaneously, neighbourhoods in many places have become more alike. Those with comparable incomes huddle together in ever more similar housing. Only a few of the largest cities – such as Boston, Chicago and Philadelphia – are left with any mixed neighbourhoods.[23]

When people do not mix, it is easier to believe that not everyone is equally human. How can they be the same if their

Michiel 2005
Dubai: a city for the superrich

monetary value is so different? One outcome of growing inequality is rising mistrust. Conspiracy theories proliferate among the poor that those in charge are deliberately seeking to keep them down because they do not see the poor as being of the same species.[24] At the extreme, in the US, some 12 million citizens tell public pollsters that they 'believe that shape-shifting reptilian people control our world by taking on human form and gaining political power to manipulate our societies'.[25] These beliefs that the very rich are part of a conspiracy of control are also widely held in some of the poorest areas of the UK. Beliefs in the 'illuminati' or in a less sinister 'club of the rich' who just marry and socialise together and look down on the masses are commonplace in pubs and gyms in working-class neighbourhoods, and particularly among young men who have otherwise 'been de-valued as useful members of society [and] find value for themselves locally', developing a meaningful identity in the face of adversity.[26] Inequality both creates and magnifies ignorance.

Theories of the inherent inferiority of the poor circulate among the elite. Often those theories are bolstered by an upbringing full of hints that privileged children are superior and born to lead. Consider how the world must seem through the eyes of a young scion of a wealthy family. As a boy, you attended a school in a suit and tie, maybe even a frock coat. You are aware that your 'education' cost an 'awful lot' – a fortune if you boarded. You might not know just how expensive it was by most people's standards. How can you make sense of your situation other than by believing that you are somehow special, and that all this extra attention was in some way warranted? Your school might even help you firm up that belief by making you take an exam that only the truly gifted (they say) could pass.

To see how intricately wealth, power and education are linked consider one particular King's Scholarship Examination Question, set by what is often labelled the most prestigious 'public' school in the UK, Eton College, in 2011:[27]

> The year is 2040. There have been riots in the streets of London after Britain has run out of petrol because of an oil crisis in the Middle East. Protesters have attacked public buildings. Several policemen have died. Consequently, the Government has deployed the Army to curb the protests. After two days the protests have been stopped but twenty-five protesters have been killed by the Army. You are the Prime Minister. Write the script for a speech to be broadcast to the nation in which you explain why employing the Army against violent protesters was the only option available to you and one which was both necessary and moral.

Eton College has now removed the web link to that 2011 exam paper, but a commentator under the original story helpfully noted:

> When you clicked through to look at the question you found a quote from Machiavelli's *The Prince* and some 25 marks

available. Five marks for summarising the quote, five marks for noting any reservations you might have about sending in the Army, and fifteen for putting this authoritarian policy into practice. So 80 per cent of the marks are for absorbing and applying an authoritarian philosophy, and 20 per cent are for critical thinking.

As this commenter said, 'That's training, not education.'[28]

It is not hard to train people to treat others badly, especially if you can persuade your young recruits not to consider others as fully human. As inequality rises, growing numbers of people turn a blind eye to the suffering of others, while they become increasingly concerned about themselves and how they are seen. That is why charity fundraising events involving the superrich are public spectacles, with the press often invited along.

In the same year that the Eton exam paper came to light, Westminster School was ridiculed for holding an auction for unpaid internships. These included a chance to work in the investment office of the private bank Coutts, or a week with the master jeweller Fabergé, or with retail communications agency Portas, or with a premier investment services advisory firm established by a man who has 'more than 14 years experience in private banking and wealth management'.[29] Parents bid huge sums of money so that their children could work unpaid; the connections they would gain were clearly seen as worthwhile.

Private banking is associated with the bulk of large-scale tax evasion. The world's leading tax justice campaigners in 2012 reported: 'Our analysis refocuses attention on the critical, often unsavoury role that global private banks play. A detailed analysis of the top 50 international private banks reveals that at the end of 2010 [they] collectively managed more than $12.1 trillion in cross-border invested assets from private clients, including ... trusts and foundations.'[30] The tax justice study found that, as a result of this private bank-aided tax evasion, nearly a third of all private financial wealth in the world is owned by just 0.001 per cent of the population – some 91,000 people. Almost all of the rest is owned by the next 0.14 per cent. Almost everything else, excluding the homes people live in, is owned by the global 1 per cent. Even if you include all residential property, the global 1 per cent hold half the wealth of the planet – some $110 trillion, or sixty-five times the wealth of the poorest half of humanity.[31]

So what do the very richest desire? Within the richest 1 per cent, the top 0.01 per cent have a series of goals. The *Wealth Report 2012*, a survey of HNWIs, found:

- 16 per cent already own a ski chalet, 12 per cent are interested in owning one;
- 40 per cent already own beachfront property, 23 per cent are interested;
- 20 per cent invest in sports teams, 16 per cent are interested;
- The US and UK are the most popular locations for a second home – Singapore is the fifth most popular;

Verso/Leo Hollis

Beachside paradise in Florida: second homes for the superrich

- London and New York are the most important cities to the HNWI;
- 27 per cent believe 'availability of luxury housing' is a necessary attribute for a city to be 'considered globally important'.[32]

Of those six goals, four explicitly concern homes, or at least property. But to secure such goals requires some work and training. According to the *New York Times*, awaydays for the children of the extremely rich are now arranged that cover 'topics as various as financial literacy, prenuptial agreements and managing family dynamics [and] are offered by large financial institutions like Citi Private Bank, business schools and organizations for wealthy families like the Family Office Exchange and the Institute for Private Investors'.[33] These are events in which wealthy children can get together and feel comfortable with their wealth, and learn how to hold on to their family money – including protecting it from their spouses. Some top private banks now include psychologists as part of their private client banking package. Included in their advice is a suggestion that you meet with your parents at your country club, not their home (it is less emotive). You need spare assets of at least $50 million to gain such advice.[34]

It is worth noting that state security services are particularly active in the countries that the 1 per cent prefers. Singapore is notorious for its security apparatus, the United States has its US Patriot Act (the Uniting and Strengthening America by Providing Appropriate Tools Required to Intercept and Obstruct Terrorism Act), and the UK has more CCTV cameras per person than any other large state – the highest estimate currently being one for every eleven people in the country.[35] The superrich want enhanced levels of security. Simultaneously, the children of the 1 per cent are becoming ever more dependent on their parents' wealth. Family expectations reduce the freedom of the very rich and their mental security. They need to take out prenuptial agreements if they

marry someone economically less well-off: honest relation-
ships become impossible to maintain under conditions of
great inequality. Within the 1 per cent, the use of trust funds
to maintain the family wealth, rather than having to rely on
salaries – and keeping much of this wealth secret – is common.
This sort of extreme deviousness separates many of the 1 per
cent from everyone else.

In the UK a scheme exempting privately owned artworks
from inheritance and capital gains tax if they are open to
public access has been described as 'a racket'.[36] Owners of
stately homes are about to become, for the first time, eligible for lottery money to help them with repairs and upkeep,
increasing the value of their property assets,[37] providing there
is 'greater public access' – which the public would presumably
pay them for.[38] This money for stately homes was announced
at the same time as it was reported that the Building Schools
for the Future programme would end. That programme had
been hugely successful in improving the quality of state school
buildings, and thus of public education.[39] It is not that there
is too little money to build schools, but, rather, that a choice
must be made about where the money should go: state schools
or stately homes.

Housing Paupers and Princes

> The Coalition have been digging the moat around the citadel of
> good fortune as fast as they have been pulling up the ladder of
> opportunity ... we cannot all be rich. Either the wealthy need
> to share what they've got, or the poor need to live with a lot
> less than they've been promised.
>
> Theo Middleton, Squatters Action for Secure Homes, 2013[40]

The wealthy have been getting much wealthier in recent years,
and in the UK this is mostly to do with home ownership.
During 2013, housing prices in London rose by over £50,000
for an average flat or house, bringing the cost of a typical

London home up to £450,000. If this rate of change continues, the £0.5 million price barrier will be breached during 2014. Prices in London in early 2014 were rising more than twice as quickly as in the country as a whole.[41] These are now prices that almost no one but the very affluent can afford.

House and flat prices in London have risen especially high and especially quickly not so much because members of the 1 per cent from overseas have been buying in recent years – although that has made a difference – but because extremely rich members of the 2 per cent of people who are landlords have been buying so quickly and so bullishly. The very richest of landlords will have bought the most – all of them members of the 1 per cent. Such purchasers buy in cash, using the rent of their existing tenants to purchase yet more homes to rent out. Across Britain as a whole, the average cost of a home in a city rose from 5.6 to 5.8 times the average salary between 2012 and 2013. In the most expensive city, Oxford, it rose from 9.8 times to 11.25 times – reaching over £340,000 – in that year alone,[42] partly because landlords were buying up so many of the available homes, accelerating price rises and reducing open market supply.

In January 2014, the *Financial Times* released an analysis showing that, over the course of just the previous five years, the equity of mortgage holders in Britain had fallen by £169 billion, while that of landlords had risen by a massive £245 billion. The estate agent Savills and the *Financial Times* found that UK landlords' total equity had more than doubled, from £384 billion a decade before to £818 billion at the time of publication (2014). The large fall in the combined equity of homeowners with mortgages reflected the fact that buyers were now borrowing more.[43]

In March 2014 the *Financial Times* published a letter explaining that there was a problem with the 1 per cent building luxury homes in the capital – since a very large proportion of the owners are non-domiciled, often living only part of the year in those homes:

If London's current building capacity is focused on satisfy-
ing foreign buyers, then the supply challenge for the domestic
market is made bleaker. Overseas demand flooding the London
market pushes up land prices – which pushes up development
costs, making domestic-focused sites less viable, and therefore
less likely to happen. On top of the cyclical risks created by the
housing market, foreign demand comes with foreign exchange
risk – another source of volatility for a development market
which ill needs it.[44]

When the *Financial Times* begins to publish warning after
warning about the unfettered free market, it is time to listen.

The *Financial Times* was breaking ranks by revealing just
how rich landlords were becoming, and how dangerous the
glut of new overseas monies was. The *Times* will publish letters
explaining that landlords have an average age of fifty-three,
and 'benefit from significant tax breaks, and cheap mortgages,
due to the unearned wealth already accumulated from house-
price inflation',[45] but as yet that newspaper will not denounce
this state of affairs in its editorial pages. Other mainstream
newspapers simply present rising prices as a bonanza, and
suggest increasingly bizarre ways in which those who can
afford neither to buy nor to rent can be housed in the capital.
In October 2013, the *Daily Mail* reported that shipping containers were being stacked up in car parks in North London
to be used as housing. Planning permission had been granted
for two car parks to be used as temporary shipping-container
housing estates. Approvingly, the *Mail* commented: 'It is
thought each of the homes could save taxpayers £25,000 each
year by taking people off housing and other related benefits.'[46]

At the same time, the *Daily Mail* ignores the taxes that are
not paid by many landlords, or by many of the world's wealthiest individuals who live in London in very large homes. These
include Russian oligarchs, Saudi royalty, and US financiers,
who are among the global cohort estimated to be avoiding
$32 trillion in taxation[47] – enough to buy a billion shipping
container homes!

Below the fabulously wealthy are the superrich who own the bulk of expensive UK property. The *Sunday Times* estimates that there are at least a thousand Russian millionaires who now live full-time in London. Most of them value their anonymity, but a few wish it to be known just how much London property they hold, much of it kept empty.[48] And beneath the millionaires and multi-millionaires are those whose rental property affords them profits of £200,000 or more each year, who are borrowing even more to buy more, and who are hoping to join the new London Russian aristocracy through future growth of their assets – paid for by the rent of their tenants.

In 2013 a rich British man and his wife bought their seventh house in London – a four-storey, £1.35 million Georgian townhouse – for their twenty-seven-year-old son, Nicky, whose computer games firm and football agency were being dissolved five years after their launch. This would be just another story of the rich buying up more property than they can use if it were not that Nicky's father was former prime minister Tony Blair.[49] For those not as rich as the Blairs, but not poor, it is an uncomfortable fact that a whole generation is now growing up with a financial interest in their parents' early death, so that they can inherit a deposit for a mortgage. The richest fifth in Britain, as homeowners, have benefited from lower mortgage rates, with their average housing costs falling from just over £500 a month in 2008 to just over £400 in 2011. Meanwhile, average housing costs have risen for every other quintile due to rising rents – generating more money that is paid to the best-off.[50]

Since 2011 the savings of the rich, especially of the 1 per cent richest among the best-off fifth, have continued to grow as most people with modest wealth have seen their savings deteriorate. The total amount being saved by the richest fifth in society grew each month between 2008 to 2011, rising by 'an extra £400 million a month'[51] at the end of that period. But for the majority in society, saving has become less and less possible. By December 2013, there had been the largest fall in average overall savings ever recorded over a five-year period,[52] while the most affluent continued to squirrel money away. This has had a particularly disastrous impact on the bottom half of society. A whole generation is growing up asking where the money is, why they have to pay to study, and why there are so few good jobs – let alone homes they can afford.

The housing situation for people of average and modest means has deteriorated rapidly. The private landlords who have bought up so much council housing do not maintain it at the former standards – not unless it is in a very rich area. If tenants complain, a landlord is likely to carry out what the charity Shelter calls 'retaliatory eviction'.[53] Private landlords also fill housing less efficiently. A few years ago, the waiting list for social housing in Britain contained a few hundred thousand families. It now numbers 3 million people. In 2013 the number of millionaire homes in the UK increased by a third in just one year. Someone, somewhere (usually in London) now becomes a property millionaire every seven minutes. In the homes of multi-millionaire properties, an area the size of the average doormat is now estimated to be worth £3,500.

Verso/Leo Hollis

The polarising property market of London

Few who have not bought their own homes have any significant wealth, except what they might be saving for a deposit on a home. Even some who are buying their own homes find that they have no wealth. By summer 2013, it was estimated that 'nearly 800,000 of those with a mortgage [were] in negative equity'.[54] That number will grow rapidly if more people borrow huge amounts to buy homes in the near future, and if house prices fall when interest rates rise. Growing wealth inequality leads to an increasingly less efficient use of our existing housing stock, and rapidly increases housing prices as a result, because less efficient use reduces supply.[55] This forces up rents, forcing even those on a living wage into effective poverty.

In a contradiction that is only apparent to those who see both sides of life in the city, the great concentration of wealth in London coexists with the highest concentrations of poverty in the country. London has the most people aged between forty-four and sixty-four who have at least £1 million of wealth: just over a fifth of that age group in the capital are paper millionaires. At the same time, just under a fifth of that group have almost no wealth at all. As a result, and as London Assembly member Darren Johnston explained to his constituents in September 2013, 'investors, rather than occupiers, buy the homes, leaving most Londoners with little choice but a lifetime of insecure renting'.[56]

By the official definition, more than twice as many children in London live in poor households (40 per cent) than are poor nationally (20 per cent). London has the highest proportion of poor households to be found in any region of the UK, including Northern Ireland. The rather staid Office for National Statistics itself describes the situation in the capital as 'hollowed out', because so few families are now average in that city – far more are rich and far more are poor.[57]

Recently the Joseph Rowntree Foundation concluded: 'The key driver of urban wage inequality or employment polarisation is affluence.' The very rich are employing more people on very low pay to service them in various ways – to clean for them, to look after their children, to cook and chauffer for them – whether directly or by going out more often to eat in restaurants, use taxis, and so on. The Work Foundation researchers who conducted one study found that income inequality was highest in London but similar in Reading and Bracknell, Guildford and Aldershot, and Luton and Watford – and also, by one measure, in Manchester and Warrington, as well as Wigan.[58]

A small number of northern towns are included among the most unequal either because they contain rich enclaves, such as Didsbury in Manchester, or have outlier suburbs that are affluent, or are what the Liberal Democrat Lord Oakeshott referred to in 2012 as 'the nicer parts of the north'.[59] The term 'urban' is most often used by euphemising commentators to describe those parts of the north where more housing is unused – although the amount that is empty within the heart of London has also risen in recent years.[60]

How many homes are empty or underused? It is hard to obtain accurate statistics for England. In the whole of Scotland, there are 2.5 million dwellings, of which only 2.4 million are occupied. Of the empty 111,000, 66 per cent are simply vacant, while 34 per cent are officially listed as second homes. A further 950,000 occupied homes in Scotland contain only one adult.[61] At the other extreme, in Kensington and Chelsea, the residential population fell between 2001 and 2011 as an increasing share of the most expensive property was held empty.

There is a huge problem with housing in the UK because people buy and hold on to housing as an investment. In doing this, they are copying (in very small measure) the property portfolios of the 1 per cent. Most people try as hard as they can to get a mortgage and to buy, because they think that doing so will make them safer in the long term. Renting, including even long-term-tenancy social housing, is now universally regarded as insecure. If the 1 per cent hold on to their property and work hard to prevent it being taxed, that has a great influence

Social housing, Salford

on the behaviour of the rest of us. We cannot see that only a tiny number of people – the 1 per cent – can really get rich at the expense of the rest: it is simply impossible for many of us to do what they do, because the rest of us don't have enough for all of us to plunder.

Recent research by economists Andrew Oswald and David Blanchflower has shown that, when the rate of home-ownership rises, people end up with longer commutes to work. This is partly because they hold on to their home for longer even if they switch jobs. Unemployment also rises, as it becomes harder to move to where there is work, and it is harder for some new businesses to start because the necessity of moving becomes a bar to recruitment. In short, the owner-occupier housing market is bad for the labour market.[62]

Unfortunately the current private rental market is not necessarily good for family life. According to the Institute for Fiscal Studies, UK government cuts and employment trends mean that, by 2020, a quarter of all children (3.4 million) will be living in poverty. The rise in poverty now expected will reverse all of the reductions that took place under Labour between 2000 and 2010. The Coalition government's official target is that less than a tenth – about 1.3 million – should be poor by that date.[63] Sometimes targets are meaningless. The current government's actions, typified by George Osborne's 2014 budget of give-aways for the rich, are designed to increase poverty among the majority; and as poverty rises more families will have to rent. Osborne's budget was explicitly targeted at what he called the 'makers, doers and savers'. He changed the rules on pension annuities so that the few with large private pension pots could use the money instead to buy property to give them extra retirement income – presumably properties for the 'strivers and shirkers' to rent and, if lucky, live in.[64]

Private renting is not necessarily good for households with children. Today almost a quarter of all households in England with children live in rented homes (see Figure 4.3). It was half that proportion just ten years ago. Only a third of these households have lived in the same home for three years. Children are now far more often moved between schools and friends every year. Often they have almost no friends as a result. They might not settle in their new school, and the consequences are disjointed teaching, a greater risk of illness and lower rates of attendance.[65]

When social policy is determined by members of the 1 per cent, their lack of knowledge can result in perverse outcomes. Those who have the least – those with vulnerabilities such as unemployment, poor housing, a lack of qualifications, mental or physical illness and disability, low income and material deprivation – are often punished the most. The most recent changes in benefit rules have had terrible effects. As the Children's Society and the National Society for the Prevention

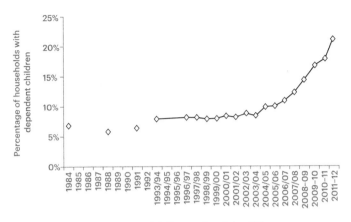

Source: Social Mobility and Child Poverty Commission, 2013

Figure 4.3 Households with children in private renting, percentage in England 1984–2012

of Cruelty to Children explained in 2012, 'Overall, the negative impact is perversely greater for families with more vulnerabilities. Families with four or more vulnerabilities lose around 8 per cent of their net income from the changes, compared to less than 5 per cent for families with no vulnerabilities'[66] (see Figure 4.4). Those families with the most vulnerabilities are almost always renting, and often, as they find it harder and harder to get through life, they are paying ever more of what little income and benefits they receive to a landlord.

The most vulnerable families in Britain – those with five or more vulnerabilities – stand to lose £3,000 a year in income by 2015, although subsequent events mean it will be more in real terms.[67] It is also projected that, because of the cuts being driven by the interests of the 1 per cent, there will be many more families falling into the vulnerable group in the near future. Some 100,000 more workless families will be created as the 'wealth creators' fail to be 'job creators'.[68] If you are trying to imagine how the proportion of children living in homes owned by a landlord can rise even further, consider this trend.

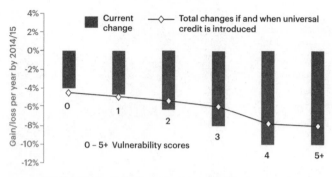

Note: The most vulnerable families score five or more vulnerabilities.

Source: Howard Reed, 2012

Figure 4.4 Tax and Benefit changes by vulnerability in the UK, impact, 2010 to 2015

Just as key members of the richest 1 per cent, when in power, work so hard to cut benefits for the poorest groups, their supporters also work hard to influence public opinion by suggesting that these are benefits we simply cannot afford. They have recently been highly successful, especially in capping housing benefit and other benefits related to housing, such as grants to refit housing for wheelchair use. Support for public spending on the disabled fell rapidly with the onset of the crash, as the Conservatives blamed Labour's spending for the rise in public debt, rather than the bank bail-out costs. A large section of the press feasted on 'benefit scroungers', but was strangely quiet about tax avoidance.

In 1998, 74 per cent of people in Britain wanted to see more spending on benefits for disabled people. But as the Tory rhetoric of 'high-spending Labour' strengthened, this proportion fell to 63 per cent in 2008, and then to only 53 per cent by 2011. This fundamental long-term change in attitudes towards welfare and benefit recipients reflects the success of a long-term campaign of vilification against welfare recipients, including those traditionally seen as the most 'deserving' of the poor.[69] Today it is easy for right-wing councillors to suggest

License under Creative Commons

Abandoned houses: the decline of social housing

that there should be no council housing in inner London boroughs, that only the rich 'deserve' to live there, and that the poor should travel in early in the morning from far away to service the rich, clean the streets, work as security guards and staff the shops.

Often it is through housing, and the taxation related to it, that the poorest are punished. From April 2013, cuts to council tax benefit were introduced of about £500 million, or 10 per cent of the total bill. The result was that some 156,563 vulnerable people were summoned to court in the following six months for failing to pay their new, raised level of council tax. Many simply did not understand what was happening to them. Only a minority of councils have so far reported how many of their residents they have taken to court. It is estimated that, in all of the 326 English councils, up to half a million people may already have been summoned by early autumn 2013, but the precise figures are not yet available. The official government response to this news was simply to claim that the survey it was based on was 'shoddy'.[70]

As poverty rises with inequality, public mental health also deteriorates. A commentator in the *Economist* put it succinctly: to afford to live in central London today, you have to be either on a six-figure salary or on benefits. The middle class, along with the poor, are being cleansed from the centre.[71] The half-million court summonses – a disproportionate number of them in the capital – resulting from caps to housing benefit mean that fewer of those on benefits can afford to live there. As housing becomes harder to secure and hold on to, the number of cases of depression climbs. It is estimated that 25,000 more mothers will suffer from mental illness by 2015 than in 2010, when an additional 100,000 families will be forced to live on less than 60 per cent of median income; but median income is falling more than expected, so that estimate might be reduced despite none of those families being any better off.[72]

Simultaneously, if current trends continue to 2015, some 40,000 more UK families will suffer overcrowding and more will become more economically vulnerable,[73] despite the existence of sufficient housing were it better distributed. We do not have enough housing to leave much of it empty or underused in the centre of the capital, and it is almost always owner-occupied housing that is in that unused state, rising in value as an investment month by month. The 2011 census revealed that there were more rooms per person than ever before in British history. Britain is a rich country, but it is set to share out what it has ever more unfairly, ensuring that the 1 per cent get even richer.[74] The top 10 per cent of people in Britain have average net wealth of around £1 million, while the poorest tenth have just £13,000 on average, most of which is the value of a few household goods and a second-hand car (see Figure 4.5).[75]

When the economic situation of all families is considered, the possibility of rising solidarity among the 99 per cent is evident. It is clear that the poorest tenth still suffer the most harm from benefit cuts; but proportionately the rest of the 99 per cent are very similarly affected by spending cuts, by the rise in VAT and National Insurance changes – and, at the

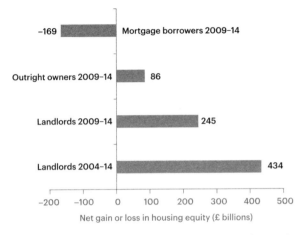

Source: Based on research carried out by Savills and reported by Kate Allen in the *Financial Times*, 2014 – K. Allen, 'Home buyers left behind in Britain's two-speed housing market', 18 January.

Figure 4.5 Gains and losses in the UK housing market, 2004/2009 to 2014

top end, loss of child benefit. The top 1 per cent are the least affected by the loss of child benefit (many do not bother to claim it), and in 2012 received a tax reduction from 50 per cent to 45 per cent on incomes over £150,000.[76] Figure 4.5 illustrates who has gained and lost most from housing since 2009 and 2004.

Reducing the Wealth Gap

> Bostridge expresses his views not as a war cry but with gentle passion. 'There's huge anxiety in middle-class London', he continues. 'I don't see how my children are going to be able to afford to live here. Four or five generations of my family have lived in London. I love London. Gosh …' Smiling sheepishly, Bostridge realises he has sounded off more than he might have wished. We order coffee and change the subject.
>
> Ian Bostridge, quoted in the *Financial Times*, November 2013[77]

We too often order coffee and change the subject. The subject is excruciatingly embarrassing because it is about not having enough money, and concerns some of the best-off among the 99 per cent as well as the poorest. It is shaming for rich and poor alike. In the past, anger about that shame fuelled the drive for greater equality, led by people from all walks of life who were shocked by what the very richest were then getting away with.

In 1908 Edward George Villiers Stanley, 17th Earl of Derby, enjoyed an income that was 1,000 times the national average. The main source of his income was rent on homes. By the time the 17th Earl died, in 1948, most of that income and wealth had been taxed away.[78] The growing equality between 1918 and 1978 meant that many of those homes are now owned by the people who would, in the past, have been his tenants. Since the 1970s, however, wealth inequalities have grown again. This partly explains why more people are now renting. A majority of young adults simply cannot afford to save the deposit needed to start to buy their home, and their families are not wealthy enough to lend or give them even small amounts of money.

Some of the world's leading economists place rising inheritance as the third-most-important factor driving up income inequality, after lower taxes on the rich and the recent lowering of the collective bargaining power of unions.[79] The Earl of Derby did not give up his riches happily. He was forced to by the collaboration of many in the elite fearful that revolution, or at the very least frequent riots, might be sparked by the impoverishment of the masses. Today, the elite again fears a growing social and political unrest resulting from escalating wealth and income inequality. In 2012 the head of the Institute of International Finance, representing the world's banks, told the BBC: 'if this inequality increases in income distribution or wealth distribution we may have a social time bomb ticking and no one wants to have that.'[80] His definition of 'no one' was perhaps narrow, as it is hard to see what the

Verso/Leo Hollis
One Nation under CCTV: the end of trust according
to Banksy

bottom half of society has to lose now they have so few assets
and so much debt.

Fear among the superrich elite is palpable. They buy cars
that weigh several tonnes because of the need to be both
bullet- and bomb-proof.[81] Fear of kidnap is growing rapidly
among the very rich in the United States, because the richest
obviously have the means to pay good ransoms. In the US,
between 2007 and 2010, the share of wealth of the poorest 40
per cent of citizens fell from just 0.2 per cent of all US household assets to a total of −0.9 per cent, or −1.6 per cent if their
home ownership was added.[82] Calling that debt 'ownership' is
a particularly sick joke.

While four out of ten Americans are facing absolute immiseration, debt and destitution, one in every 4,000 has never
been richer; nevertheless, despite this gulf, some of the very
rich appear to share the same dreams and aspirations as the
poor. They just realise their dreams differently. Top executives
in the US fly their families to places like Disneyland at their
company's expense. One reason they give is that this apparently gives them more time to work. Another excuse for such
expense-fraud is that they have to fly their families using their
company jet for security reasons: the family is at risk of hijack.
Of course, the more they pay themselves, and the less they pay
others, the greater that risk becomes.[83]

Not all the very rich share similar dreams to the rest – too much money can eventually warp one's aspirations. In late 2013 a report circulated of a 'luxury shantytown where rich can pretend to be poor'. As Professor Mathew Flinders of the University of Sheffield described it, this was the zenith of bad taste. A fake South African township had been built with the explicit intention of allowing the rich 'to experience the grinding life of the poor'.[84] He went on to explain that the delights apparently included an unlicensed bar, a 'long-drop' toilet, and shabby shacks complete with rusty corrugated-iron walls and roofs. One night in a fake shanty-town shack costs the same as an average month's wage in South Africa. But why do rich American tourists fly all the way to Africa to experience extreme poverty? They could just as easily find it at home.

On average, the few homes that the poorest 40 per cent of Americans own are worth less than nothing, due to their mortgage debt. In the UK, wealth inequality is, as yet, nowhere near this level, and fear of kidnap is much less; but as UK wealth inequality rapidly increases, we need to look to the US to see where we are heading. By 2012 almost 50 per cent of the UK population were no longer satisfied with their personal financial situation, and less than a fifth expressed high satisfaction (Figure 4.6).

What would make the rich safer and more secure is being less wealthy. Inheritance tax was low a century ago. It was introduced by a parliament made up of the rich to protect their riches, and the riches of their nation. Inheritance taxes had been brought in mainly to help repay government war debts. Most wars are started by people in the 1 per cent. The First World War began as an argument within an aristocracy and European royal family that simply could not imagine its consequences. In 1894 Death Duties had a maximum rate of 8 per cent. In 1914 they became Estate Duty – with a maximum rate of 20 per cent, rising to 40 per cent in 1939 and to 80 per cent in 1949. It was only in 1945 that the first government not consisting mostly of rich men gained power in the UK. Death

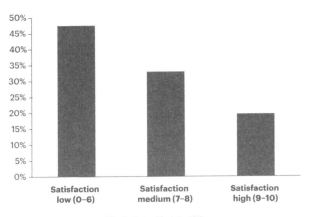

Source: Opinions Survey, Office for National Statistics, 2012

Figure 4.6 Adults in Britain satisfaction with their financial situation 2012

Duties became Capital Transfer Tax, with a maximum rate of 75 per cent in 1975, falling to 60 per cent in 1984. It was renamed Inheritance Tax after 1985, and reduced again to achieve a top rate of 40 per cent in 1988, where it still stands. Many rich families avoid paying even this by establishing trust funds to 'shelter' their wealth from redistribution.

The 1970s – the era of maximum redistribution – are now often pilloried. However, the 1970s were the best decade in which to be normal, not a bad decade in which to be poor, but a terrible decade in which to be rich. Inflation ate away at wealth. No wonder there is now an attempt to rewrite history and describe those times as terrible, when for most they were so good.[85] The rewriting of history has worked, and the media today presents a persistently gloomy assessment of the 1970s, as if the long, hot summer of 1976 never occurred. Wealth taxes were reduced after the 1970s because the rich gained increasing control over the levers of power and over political parties, and increased their influence by paying lobbyists to represent their interests, while often pretending to be representing the interests of 'business' or 'industry'. In the US and the UK the rich spent an ever greater share of their money to protect the rest of it. As a result, their assets ballooned in value while most people's share of wealth began a gradual decline.

In the 1970s the average politician represented the interests of the median voter. Researchers have shown that political representation has moved from representing the median voter to representing mainly the views of the 1 per cent. Centre-right parties perform this task, while other parties promote policies that serve the interests of those not that far below the elite. The researchers conclude: 'in spite of these correlations, we are not able to explain the circumstances that brought developed societies to the low democratic standards that they are suffering.'[86] Others are less circumspect. As the comedian Russell Brand put it in May 2013, when it comes to the UK Houses of Parliament, 'The whole joint is a deeply encoded temple of hegemonic power.'[87] In other words, the UK parliament's main function today is not to represent the people, but to preserve the power of a few. But neither Brand nor rigorous social scientists can explain how it got to be that way, and why the 1 per cent did not gain a similar degree of control over the political process in other affluent nations. By gaining so much control by the early 1980s and then changing financial regulation in their favour, the 1 per cent sowed the seeds of future instability, massive precariousness, and eventually the financial crash of 2008.

During the 1980s, income tax was reduced substantially in the US, and the UK followed suit. The increases in wealth and income inequality that followed can be closely linked to what caused the crash of 2008. In Ireland, where the crash was devastating, the richest 1 per cent had seen their share of national income double between 1995 and 2000. No wonder the Irish in general began to behave so recklessly. By 2010, researchers in Ireland had linked the recent rise in inequality there to the 2008 financial crisis.[88] In 2013 a wealth tax on the 1 per cent was being proposed, to be levied on all those living in Ireland with assets in excess of €1 million. By 2014 that measure had not been implemented but the Irish tax authorities were receiving 1,500 returns every day that spring for people registering to pay the new Local Property Tax,[89] at the same time the tax rate on interest received from savings was raised from 33 per cent to 41 per cent on 1 January. Capital Gains Tax had been increased to 33 per cent in 2012, and a domicile levy of €200,000 was introduced on anyone with property worth more than €5 million.[90]

The original suggestion in Ireland was that the 1 per cent be taxed annually at a rate equal to 0.6 per cent of their wealth. Currently most tax in rich countries is levied on income or expenditure. Less than 1 per cent is levied directly on wealth across the OECD, although tax on the interest accrued from wealth is a minor current wealth tax.[91] During 2013 a Europe-wide wealth tax was proposed.[92] In 2014 the German government suggested that (debtor) countries such as Ireland should impose it more firmly.[93] In 1990 half of all OECD countries had a net wealth tax, but that had declined by 2000 to one-third. Since then the number has fallen further, with Spain, Sweden, Finland, Iceland and Luxembourg all abandoning their wealth taxes after 2006. But Spain, Ireland and Iceland are reintroducing wealth taxes to cope with their financial emergencies.[94] The most effective wealth taxes are on fixed assets. In Iceland the disposable income of the 1 per cent collapsed from 20 per cent of all income to 10 per cent in just one year, as a result of measures taken to deal with the financial crisis; in Spain the 1 per cent take less than 10 per cent of annual income, and their share has fallen in the latest four years recorded.[95] It is possible to tax the wealth of the richest successfully.

In the UK the fixed assets of the rich are mostly in housing, especially in the form of rented property. In 2013 the *Financial Times* explained how the practice of subsidising the rich to allow them to become landlords had got completely out of control: 'It has driven up prices for the very smaller [*sic*], cheaper homes first-timers are after. Still more damaging is its effect in tilting the rental sector towards amateur landlords and short-term lettings that leave those who need larger properties and longer-term stability with nowhere to go. The practice thus damages the British housing market three times over.'[96]

The rich who buy to rent can get a tax rebate on the interest paid on any mortgage on those properties, and offset the costs of maintaining the property against tax. They also benefit from tax relief on insurance and other expenses. An owner-occupier has none of these advantages. In other words, those buying property as an investment are subsidised by government, making costs more affordable to them than to poorer buyers just wanting a home of their own.

It is not easy to study the very richest – the multi-millionaires; but in 2012 Skandia, an international wealth-management business, managed to survey 1,503 of their clients with net disposable assets (excluding their main property of residence) of at least £1 million. Of these, 436 lived in the UK, 94 per cent of whom were British. Despite their wealth, 21 per cent said they were not wealthier than their parents, and 31 per cent said they had become millionaires before the age of thirty. A third had not been to university. Of those who had started their own businesses, the majority had done so before they were twenty-five – mostly with help from their parents.[97] The rich rarely become so through their own efforts – and it is partly because it is not their work that has made them rich that many so carefully orchestrate the defence of their wealth – those who stay rich usually work hard in at least one way: to defend their riches.

At the suggestion of an annual mansion tax – say, on properties worth over £2 million – uproar results. The rich suggest that they simply do not have the money, or that they might have to pay someone to damage their home to reduce it in value, or, almost amusingly, that they will no longer be able to open their home to public view. One letter to the *Telegraph* began: 'SIR – I live in a family house that is open to the public, but, like many people in that position, I am asset-rich but cash-poor.'⁹⁸ Perhaps they should take in lodgers? When you hear stories like this you need to consider what will occur if the UK and other countries in Europe do not increase the taxation of wealth. If countries allow wealth inequality to remain high, or even to increase, they will eventually become as unequal as the US.

When graphics exposing the superrich began to spread across the internet at the end of the last decade, they often had to rely on data from just before the 2008 crash. One prepared in 2011 shows that a few years earlier the top 1 per cent had more than a third of all wealth in the US, and the bottom 90 per cent barely a quarter. Figure 4.7 reproduces the same data. The authors of the original graphic noted that the bottom 60 per cent of Americans had 65 per cent of their net worth tied up in their homes. The top 1 per cent, in contrast, had just 10 per cent of their wealth locked up in the bricks and mortar of their property. Consequently: 'The housing crisis has no doubt further swelled the share of total net worth held by the superrich.'⁹⁹ Taxing the rich through their property holdings alone may not be enough.

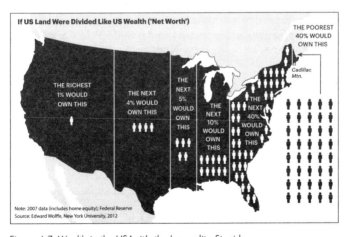

Figure 4.7 Wealth in the USA: it's the Inequality, Stupid

By 2012 it had become apparent that these graphics, pub-
licised widely in the US during 2011, were badly out of date.
Using data for 2010, Edward Nathan Wolff of the University
of New York showed that the bottom 40 per cent of US households were now usually in debt, with their debts averaging
$14,800 non-home wealth per household; in contrast the
middle 20 per cent had wealth averaging only $12,200 per
household (a quarter less than in 1983); the next 20 per cent
had $100,700 per household; and the top 20 per cent $1.7
million each on average (almost double the figure for 1983 in
real terms). If Figure 4.7 were redrawn using these numbers,
the bottom half of Americans would all be drowning in the
Atlantic when it comes to depicting their negligible wealth
holdings no matter how they were measured.[100]

Division at the Top

> Britain in the twenty-first century is a deeply divided nation.
> Whilst a handful of people at the top have never had it so good,
> millions of families are struggling to make ends meet. Growing
> numbers of Britons are turning to charity-run foodbanks, yet
> at the same time the highest earners in the UK have had the
> biggest tax cuts of any country in the world. And whilst low-
> paid workers are seeing their wages stagnate, the super-rich are
> seeing their pay and bonuses spiral up.
>
> Oxfam, 2014[101]

In 2012 it was revealed that the top tenth of people in Britain
by wealth were almost 500 times richer than the bottom tenth.
But those riches were not shared equally within the top tenth –
the top 1 per cent had the lion's share.[102] That share of wealth
now appears to be growing as the rest of the best-off 10 per
cent see cuts to their average take-home income, meaning that
the richest 1 per cent above that group are rapidly moving
away from the rest of the 'top tenth'. The last time these inequalities reached such a peak in the UK was over a (long)

lifetime ago. When inequality is at its highest, it can feel as if there is nothing that can be done to bring it down – but sooner or later it is always reduced.

Today it can appear that there is a new aristocracy, especially in the US. Rather than profiting from the land around their stately homes, or the coal under that land, or the steel mills they had monopoly control over – like the old UK aristocracy or the US robber-barons ('industrialists') – the new aristocracy characteristically has other 'investments', or a share in some form of copyright that they bought or inherited – for example, shares in the drug patents of pharmaceutical firms: 'Many keep their fortunes by simply avoiding paying taxes, using loopholes created by legislators who are re-elected with that same money they help to evade. In reality, most wealth in the world is the product of inequality and it stays in the same hands thanks to the systems that reinforce that inequality.'[103] Never before, however, has so much attention been focused on the tax-evading and other illegal behaviour of those at the top. Increasingly, suggestions are being made as to how the rich might be better controlled.[104]

Wealth taxes in rich countries have been changing in recent years. The target of taxation has moved away from inheritance, away from taxing the dead. Inheritance tax is too easy to avoid when the rich transfer a large amount of their wealth

Pudelek

Luxembourg, tax haven and home to Amazon.com

while they are alive. Thus, taxation of the beneficiaries of gifts in general, and other forms of capital gains has risen, and attention has begun to focus on the potential for land taxes.[105] The taxation of other forms of property, such as pharmaceutical patents, also needs urgent attention. Any form of wealth-hoarding that harms the well-being of others is now seen as a very legitimate source of public concern.

There are many good signs that the times are changing, but also some indicators that a fightback has already begun. In 2013 one 'wealth management firm' reported that it had 'established an internal university to train our advisors on recent tax, legal, financial, and regulatory innovations'[106] – implicitly signalling an intention to avoid taxation. Big landowners, including the richest of farmers, own the most expensive land. This group is specially protected by the Coalition government. Just as the UK government went to the European Court to try to protect the incomes of bankers from EU legislation capping banking bonuses, it has also opposed limiting the amount of subsidy any farm can receive from Europe to €300,000 a year.[107] Cameron's government does not want the richest farmers to have their annual incomes capped; it wants to ensure they receive enough money from Europe as income to remain part of the 1 per cent. Of course, the richest farmers and landowners say they need this subsidy just to scrape by.

The distribution of ownership of commercial real estate, of land, and of all property that is not its owner's main home is almost totally skewed towards the very rich. We are often told that 'pension funds' control much of our wealth; but most people do not have private pensions, and the vast majority of the money held in such funds will benefit just a very few rich pensioners in the future. The richest fifth of all households hold the smallest share of their wealth in the form of their main residence – just 50 per cent for the richest fifth of Europeans – whereas almost 30 per cent of their wealth is held as other real estate, leaving 20 per cent in other forms such as stocks, shares and gold.[108] As noted above, in the US the richest hold an even lower share of their vast wealth in the form of their main residence.

The current 'quantitative easing' policies of central banks have had the effect of making the rich richer. The *Financial Times*, quoting the chief executive of the finance and insurance firm Legal and General, has described the policy as 'designed by the rich for the rich'. Even the *Financial Times* has now insisted that enough is enough.[109] Quantitative easing has been described as printing money to prevent prices falling when wages fall and the economy slumps. However, if it were that simple then the money should at least have been evenly distributed among the population. A progressive government would have given more to those who had least – especially since all of the money would then have been spent, rather

www.squashcampaign.org

Priced out of London: wealth, prices, rent, housing and Occupy, 2013

than hoarded, and might have then boosted demand (see the illustration on the previous page).

What quantitative easing has actually entailed is the buying back of government bonds or other assets using government money created out of thin air. Financial institutions and individuals normally buy government bonds and wait to get their money back, plus interest, after a fixed period, but the bonds can be sold on. As a result of all the extra buying, the value of the bonds rises, but the returns do not rise, so they cease to be a good investment. The result is that bond-holders sell the bonds back to the government, and end up with more cash in hand. The hope was that this money will stimulate the economy by making loans to businesses more easily available. This is not what happened.

The rich started investing more in private shares, prime housing, art, wine and cars. The values of the most expensive of these items increased over the ten years to 2013 by over five times in real terms (at 17.5 per cent a year above inflation). This compares to a roughly three-fold increase in the price of gold. Quantitative easing has, in the short term, allowed the very rich to get much richer simply by owning assets that rise in value as the not-quite-so-rich stop buying bonds. More of the 1 per cent have then spent their money on luxury collectables.[110] Imaginary money has created imaginary extra value in luxury goods.

The Bank of England itself has noted that Britain's richest 5 per cent own almost half of all the assets that have increased most in value due to quantitative easing.[111] Beneath them, the not-quite-so-rich traditional savers have seen the real value of their savings decline. These factors have combined to push the 99 per cent closer together in the UK. This appears to also be true globally, but it is very hard to prove because household surveys are very bad at measuring the wealth and consumption of the very wealthy. As Kevin Watkins, the newly appointed director of the UK's Overseas Development Institute, recently explained: 'The top 5 per cent in the global wealth distribution have enjoyed a windfall: collectively, they have captured 44 per cent of the increase in world income since the late 1990s.'[112] And among this top twentieth, it is the richest of all who have most recently – within most of the world's children's lifetimes – taken the most.

The current era of opulence among the very affluent is unprecedented. Even in the 1920s and 1930s the superrich faced constraints. They might have had the first-class cabins on the Titanic, but they sailed on the same ship as everyone else. Today chartered planes can fly from private airports, and the rich can avoid the queues, the traffic and the noise. Transatlantic flights must use big planes and big airports – and that means queuing, even for the rich. But soon it is planned that, the richer you are, the faster you will be able to move through key airports such as London's Heathrow. There will be shorter queues for the 1 per cent. The UK Border Agency said in 2012 that it soon wished 'to offer fast-track passport lanes to speed up wait for passengers of "high value" to the airlines or British economy'.[113] Soon there will be no waiting before you board your plane to cross the oceans, turning left into the first-class cabin. Soon the very rich will know even less about the lives of the rest. But the rest are learning more and more about them, and the harm that comes from their current extremely expensive existence.

5
Health

As the divide between the top percentile and everyone else widens, inequality is an issue that will not go away. And as the body of evidence accumulates, a clearer picture is emerging of inequality and its relation to health, self-worth, the ability to participate in society and to take control of one's life. Knowledge, as they say, is power – especially in the hands of 99 per cent of the population.

Editorial, *New Scientist*, 2012[1]

All sections of society live longer in countries that are more egalitarian. On average the life-expectancy gap is more than four years between the least and most equitable of the richest nations: people in Japan usually live more than four years longer than people in the US. The opposite was the case when the US was more equal and Japan much more unequal, but average Japanese life expectancy increased by about 13.7 years during the first decade after the Second World War, despite the country's post-war poverty. This was partly due to medical progress, but also to legislation that reduced inequality.[2] The strongest correlation can be found between wealth inequality and life expectancy.[3]

The damaging effects of economic inequality are greater still when variations in mental health are considered. The improvement to mental health in the UK that could be expected from even a modest lowering of inequalities has been estimated to be worth £24 billion annually to the economy in reduced NHS costs.[4] In 2013 it was reported that one in ten of all Americans were taking antidepressant drugs in any given year, and some 13.6 per cent of white Americans were being prescribed them.[5] That was almost one in seven of all adults – an unprecedentedly high proportion of a society requiring constant medication just to cope with living.

One-tenth was the highest proportion recorded in any rich nation bar Iceland, and 13.6 per cent is unprecedented for any social group. The proportion in Iceland reached 10.6 per cent in 2011, no doubt due to the effects of national bankruptcy.[6] Before the US figure was released and depression in Iceland peaked, only Scotland had achieved a record of one in ten of the population being prescribed antidepressants. In Iceland, Scotland and the US, the better-off might escape many of the effects of inequality on physical health, but have no immunity to poor mental health; however, we now suspect that the better-off also tend to bear more of a responsibility for promoting the thinking that is most often used to defend widespread inequalities, and that in turn makes them so much more likely to be sick, especially psychologically, than the better-off in more equitable countries.

Just as the *New Scientist* was revealing a consensus that inequality was bad for health, the British prime minister announced that he no longer wanted the UK government to assess the effect its policies have on social equality:

> Let me be very clear. I care about making sure that government policy never marginalises or discriminates … I care about making sure we treat people equally. But let's have the courage to say it – caring about these things does not have to mean churning out reams of bureaucratic nonsense. We have smart people in Whitehall who consider equalities issues while they're making the policy. We don't need all this extra tick-box stuff. So I can tell you today, we are calling time on Equality Impact

Assessments. You no longer have to do them if these issues have been properly considered.[7]

Cameron made this announcement at a time when many Whitehall officials were working on changes to the Health and Social Care Act which were bound to impact on health inequalities. It is difficult to see how they could 'properly consider' these issues once the standard assessments used to gauge how policies affect various social groups had been scrapped, all in the name of clearing away 'bureaucratic nonsense'.

The 2012 Health and Social Care Act only got through parliament with the aid of members of the House of Lords who had declared financial interests in profit-making healthcare companies.[8] The bill was driven through by the financial interests of the 1 per cent. But it was a shoddy piece of legislation and criticised from all quarters. As one well-informed commentator remarked: 'It would seem that the recently enacted Health and Social Services Bill has some very serious "real world" flaws, in that it is not possible to do in the real world that which the bill purports to achieve.'[9] Nevertheless, the 1 per cent pushed it through. It also pushed through a series of cuts – not least to social care visits – that were closely followed by an increase in the mortality rate among the elderly. When the social system begins to break down, things that were once taken for granted – such as frail elderly people being visited by care workers – suddenly become the exception rather than the rule (see Figure 5.1).

The 1 per cent sees the NHS as a river of money coming from the government which can be partially diverted into private healthcare – an historically lucrative source of income for them. Meanwhile, private healthcare companies do not fund the education of their NHS-trained staff; they pick and choose the lucrative aspects of healthcare, and when necessary pass the buck back to the NHS. In the United States, where there is no equivalent to the NHS, the 1 per cent most ill people each require some \$116,000 a year to be

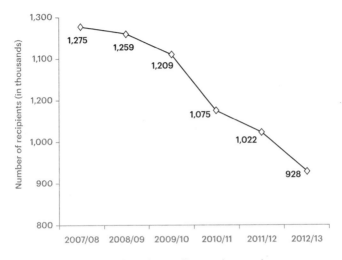

Source: Figure 1 of http://careandsupportalliance.wordpress.com/

Figure 5.1 Change in reported number of social care recipients, England (in thousands)

spent on their healthcare – a figure representing only their insurance premiums and other direct costs, not the cost of providing care, which would be even greater. In the US, if you do not have insurance then you do not receive that care.[10] In fact, only the 1 per cent can afford to be seriously ill in the US.

The 2012 Act allows up to 50 per cent of beds in an English hospital to become private beds (Wales and Scotland now have different rules). The use of hospital beds is more efficient in the NHS, just as the use of bedrooms is more efficient in social housing. As a result, the Act ensures that in the future there will be a hospital bed crisis. The 1 per cent thus damages health directly through its incompetence, as well as indirectly by promoting health-damaging environments.[11]

Health in the UK is at its worst, overall, in Glasgow, where GPs in very deprived areas report that benefit cuts mean

Chris Upson at Geography.co.uk
The Red Road flats in Glasgow

increasing numbers of their patients cannot afford to heat their homes, with direct impacts on overall health and life expectancy.[12] In the UK, the 1 per cent live at least ten years longer than average.

Men who die in Kensington and Chelsea are, on average, fourteen years older than men who die in Glasgow; for women, the gap is twelve years. If the richest are compared to the poorest, the average gaps are far wider.[13] When the very richest in society die prematurely, their cases can make headlines worldwide. When the poor die, there is no news at all. The strongest predictor of poor health and early death is poverty.[14]

The Child Poverty Action Group has calculated that, for the youngest in society, the Coalition government cuts mean that a baby born to a low-income family after April 2012 will be around £1,500 worse off a year than a sibling born in April 2010. Their parents have lost a £190 Health in Pregnancy grant, a £500 maternity grant, a £500 Child Trust Fund, and £545 of the baby element of child tax credit, offset by only £255 in its child element.[15]

By the summer of 2013 it had become clear that in England and Wales an extra 23,400 people died in 2012 and early 2013 compared to earlier years. That amounts to a 5 per cent rise in mortality. Within a month of the rise in mortality becoming known, Public Health England produced a report suggesting it might have been due to flu. But the president of the Faculty of Public Health, Professor John Ashton, commented that this was unlikely to be the case.[16] There was no more evidence of flu being the cause than there had been for the 12,000 deaths from smog in London in 1952/53, when the Conservative government of the time had used the same excuse. Spending cuts were surely to blame.[17]

Growing economic inequality as the richest take more and more for themselves is bad for everyone's health, possibly even for some of the very best-off. The reasons may be myriad, but the outcomes are clear. And this, above all else, is why the money taken by the 1 per cent needs to be reduced, to improve our health and perhaps even save some lives. To see what happens if we do not do this, we need only look to the US.

In the US the average height of Americans peaked in 1975. Falling nutritional standards due to lower incomes for the poor and especially for black women are thought to be to blame. According to a University of Connecticut professor, Peter Turchin, this stagnation in general human health and a worsening for the very poorest is directly attributable to the inefficiencies caused by the elite capture of ever more income and wealth in the US since 1975. Turchin also suggests that levels of inequality have reached such extremes that the general social system in the US is breaking down, including the financial system.[18] As long ago as 1991, the poorest fifth of black people in the US had a median net worth of just $1, as compared to $10,257 for the poorest fifth of whites.[19] In 1995 it was understood that:

> Racial and socioeconomic inequality in health is arguably the single most important public health issue in the United States. The evidence reviewed indicates that [socioeconomic status] inequalities in health are widening, and the health status of at

least some racial groups has worsened over time. The ranking of the United States relative to other industrialized countries in terms of health has been declining over time, while America continues to spend more on medical care per capita than any other country in the world. The evidence reviewed suggests that a serious and sustained investment in reducing societal inequalities can enhance the quantity and quality of life of all Americans and create the necessary liberty for the pursuit of health and happiness.[20]

Twenty years later, the situation in the US has become much worse – and the UK is accelerating towards the US model.

Let Them Eat Marketing

Demand for positional luxury goods by the rich crowds out the basic needs of the poor.

Christine Greenhalgh, *Cambridge Journal of Economics*, 2005[21]

The diets of British children and adults within the poorest tenth of households changed dramatically in the years following the financial crash. Because of this the Institute of Fiscal Studies found that by 2013 the poor were spending less overall on food, reducing their calorie intake, but had increased their consumption of saturated fat and sugar, while eating much less fresh fruit and vegetables than they had in 2008. Fresh fruit purchases by the poorest tenth fell by a fifth since 2008, fresh vegetable purchases by a seventh.[22] Similarly, unprocessed meat purchases fell by a fifth, but the consumption of meat pies, burgers and meat-based ready meals increased by a third, and purchases of chips increased by a fifth.[23]

Before 2007 an improving dietary trend had been in place, demonstrating that it is not poor attitudes but poor incomes that harm health. There is a pernicious and persistent myth that it would be a waste of money, or even harmful, to give poor parents more money, as they would only spend it frivolously. This is an uncharitable myth based on anecdote, not on scientific evidence.[24] The evidence we have is that, if the incomes of poor families increase, they spend more on their children and buy better food.

In the UK from 1998 to 2003, when child poverty was falling and the incomes of poor families were increasing, it was found that 'low-income families with children have increased their spending on children's footwear and clothing, books, and fruit and vegetables, relative to other families with children, but have decreased their spending on alcohol and tobacco'.[25] The research that uncovered this did find that there were areas where low-income families were not catching up – most obviously in their relative inability to afford computers – but their diets had definitely improved with their increased income.

Tragically, the current UK government suggests that what the poor need is not more money, but more marketing. Poorer people's lifestyles and behaviours are to be better managed – socially engineered – by targeting specific advertising at those deemed to be misbehaving the most.[26]

Unsurprisingly, there has been a great deal of criticism about this marketing of 'good behaviour' deliberately

NHS Choices/Live Well

Figure 5.2 A balanced diet: marketing rather than nutrition

diverting attention from the known causes of health inequality – income and wealth inequalities. In this blame-the-poor approach, the apparent aim is to get those at the bottom of the 99 per cent to accept their lot, to live a subsistence lifestyle on their meagre means, to quit smoking and try their best to get by.[27] It has been known for a century that most of the poor are highly responsible within the confines of their economic circumstances, contrary to the prevailing opinions of those who are much better off.[28]

Today, of the 158,000 people living in the Royal Borough of Kensington and Chelsea, some 213 per 100,000 die each year before their seventy-fifth birthday. Twice as many die young in similarly populated Blackpool – 432 per 100,000. Kensington and Chelsea is usually one of the top ten healthiest areas of the country – although not for deaths attributed to liver disease. When these figures were released, Labour's then shadow public health minister, Diane Abbott MP, said that the Coalition's savage cuts to local services would only 'hit poorer areas harder and make health inequalities even worse'.[29] And high income and wealth inequalities are not associated just with wide variations in health within a country, but also with lower overall quality of health and life expectancy of the population as a whole (see Figure 5.3).

The mechanisms that cause overall population health to be worse in more economically unequal countries are many and varied. There are many ways in which living in a very unequal society can harm your view of yourself and others. Social experiments have been conducted to show that, if you put two strangers together for five minutes, as soon as one has determined that he is the richer or more powerful, he is much more likely to stop paying attention to his companion.

You know what it is like when someone stops paying you attention: it is hurtful and annoying. Psychologists can measure disregard using hidden cameras. Someone is uninterested in you when they do not nod or laugh appropriately, or when they express disregard through their facial expression,

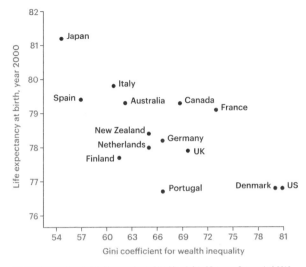

Source: Nadine Nowatzki, 'Wealth Inequality and Health: a Political Economy Perspective', 2012

Figure 5.3 Life expectancy at birth and wealth inequality, fourteen OECD countries

when they look over your shoulder because something more interesting has caught their eye, or when they take over the conversation just a little too often. This occurs more when there is more inequality. Eventually, most people simply stop talking to those in much lower or higher social class groups, because both see it as a waste of time.

Human beings evolved to distinguish fake smiles from genuine concern or appreciation. It has been hypothesised that for the vast majority of human history we needed a mechanism to ensure effective cooperation without exploitation.[30] The genuine smile, where the skin by your eyes wrinkles like crow's-feet, is the reliable signal for communicating cooperative intent and kindness. It is very hard to fake. Charles Darwin was among the first to note the implications of our emotions for cooperation and survival.[31]

We have all had it done to us and we have probably all

done it to others, but the higher up in rank we are, the more likely we are to be guilty of the snub – ignoring people who sweep the waste around our feet, or guard the entrances of the buildings we enter. The snub is not paying another person the same attention you would like to receive yourself. In a very unequal society, it becomes hard not to ignore others when so many people around you appear to be doing 'trivial' mundane tasks. In more equal societies, fewer people are employed to do such things, and everyone has more in common.

In extremely inequitable societies, it can be excruciating even to maintain a conversation across the social divide. Social psychologists from Berkeley and Amsterdam have studied pairs of strangers placed together in artificial situations where one subject told the other of a difficult personal experience, such as a divorce or the death of a close relative. The researchers then studied the reaction. What they found was that the larger the social gap between the two individuals, the less compassion was shown by the more powerful towards the hardships of the weaker person. In contrast, the poorer in each pair of strangers tended to be much more understanding. The researchers concluded that poorer people are better attuned to interpersonal relations, both with members of their own social strata and with more powerful people. They were better, at least, than the rich – because they have to be.[32] So if you do find conversation with others who are unlike you hard work, you are probably the better-off person within the group.[33]

The easiest place in the rich world to observe people being given the cold shoulder is the United States. Evidence has been amassed which shows that university students in the US do not recognise homeless people as human when shown images of them. This was found when MRI scans were taken of university students' active brains while the students were looking at images of homeless people: 'Notably, the homeless people's photographs failed to stimulate areas of the brain that usually activate whenever people think about other people, or themselves. Toward the homeless (and drug addicts), these areas simply failed to light up, as if people had stumbled on a pile of trash.'[34]

If university students can come to see homeless people as nothing more than refuse, it is not hard to imagine how a small group of more elite students might come to see those working on a university campus, cleaning the buildings or sweeping away leaves. Travel to a very unequal country, such as India, and you will be able to observe the rich almost completely ignoring the poor. In the UK, if someone has had far less spent on their education than was spent on yours, it may not be hard to think of that person as intrinsically less valuable. After all, if they were not of less value, then all the money spent on you might have been wasted.

Great inequality can have bizarre outcomes. One is the phenomenon of 'social death' – of no longer being seen as being human. This occurs to inmates in the prisons of the most unequal countries, to refugees, to people with severe mental illness and to the homeless.[35] It is in the US that the concept of social death has been observed most clearly and defined most exactly:

> Social death is the effect of a social practice in which a person or group of people is excluded, dominated and/or humiliated, to the point of becoming dead to the rest of society. They may speak, but their voice is not heard and their words do not matter. They may protest, but their action remains unsupported and ultimately ineffective. They may analyse the central dynamics of power and privilege in twenty-first-century America, but their analysis gets lost in the news cycle and buried by official rhetoric.[36]

The rich often suggest that, as long as the poor have enough to get by, the wealth of the 1 per cent has no negative impact, and may even be a source of employment for the poor. But meticulous research has shown that huge inequalities in income and wealth result in the poor having very similar feelings of shame across a range of environments. This has been found to be true

License under Creative Commons

The inevitable result of austerity: increased homelessness and desperation

in settings ranging from Uganda to India, within urban China, in Pakistan, South Korea and the United Kingdom, as well as in both (far more equitable) small-town and urban Norway. The resulting sense of shame has very bad effects on mental health.

The shame that comes from living in relative poverty was found to cause the people affected to withdraw further from society, and in extreme cases to have thoughts of suicide – all as a result of 'the attitudes and behaviour of those not in poverty, framed by public discourse and influenced by the objectives and implementations of anti-poverty policy'.[37] In other words, saying that the rich do good and create wealth, and that the poor need help because of their deficiencies, makes the effects of poverty worse.

In 1979 the sociologist Peter Townsend concluded that shame was the core issue of poverty – a position that was echoed by economist Amartya Sen in 1983.[38] The converse of the shame of the poor is the belief of the rich that they deserve their good luck. Such a conviction, however, requires a remarkable lack of empathy. As psychologist Daniel Goleman notes, 'Reducing the economic gap may be impossible without also addressing the gap in empathy.'[39] If we look carefully, it is not hard to see attacks on empathy all around us.

In the UK the groups most blamed for our current woes are not the 1 per cent, but immigrants. Increasingly the poorest of newly arrived immigrants fall into the 'human trash' category. Since 2010 in the UK, voters have been promised that there will be a reduction in net migration. Multiculturalism has been vilified and migrants' rights reduced – including the right to receive benefits and healthcare. The European Union predicts that net migration will soon fall, in what appears to be an attempt to reduce fear (see Figure 5.4). Perhaps this is done because anti-migrant talk is now so popular.

The UK government has even funded advertising vans urging illegal migrants to 'go home'. As Mathew Goodwin, Britain's foremost expert on far-right parties, explains: 'More and more voters are moving from the mainstream to the margins, guided by a toxic and – to be frank – nasty group of opinion-makers in our society who appear to relish sowing the seeds of xenophobia, protest and division.'[40] Even at the level of the European Union, citizens are placated by the technocrats' promise that there will be a sharp decline in immigration after 2020, rather than seeing net immigration as a boon compared to net emigration.[41]

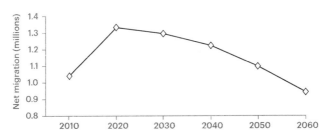

Source: EU Directorate General for Economic and Financial Affairs and Eurostat, 2012

Figure 5.4 Officially projected annual net migration into the EU-27, 2010–60

Everywhere politicians and policy-makers, from David Cameron through to the European Commission, promise that there will be fewer immigrants in future – as if immigrants were the source of problems in housing, employment, education or health in countries where the rich increasingly monopolise living space, salaries, school and health spending. Immigrants are a useful diversion from the actual causes of scarcity. When immigrants come to Europe they tend to join societies that are in debt, and they reduce that debt by taking a share in it. They are mostly young and fit, and ready to give more than they ever took in childhood. In contrast, others are finding ways of taking more and more – and most of them were born here. By and large they had rich parents, but they are nevertheless trying to find ways to surpass their parents' wealth.

Services Become Businesses

> Growing inequality is one of the biggest social, economic and political challenges of our time. But it is not inevitable.
> A special report from the *Economist*, 2012 [42]

You don't want your doctor to be paid more the sicker you get. Where that happens, in the United States, female life expectancy has stagnated or declined in almost half of all US counties since 1985 (areas smaller than states). In many counties, women in the US are now dying at younger ages than their mothers. When this was first reported, the journalist filing the report wrote, 'The worst part is no one knows why.'[43] The symptoms of rising inequality are manifold, making their cause hard to detect at times.

In 2013 when it became clear that some 8,350 more elderly people had died in the UK in 2012 than in 2011, the prime suspect was austerity – a rise in deaths due to flu was found to account for only 5.8 per cent of the increase.[44] The President of the Faculty of Public Health's (John Ashton's) fears, documented earlier in this chapter, were vindicated. Many care homes had been affected by financial crises.[45] Subsequent research suggested that around 483,000 people in England were not receiving social care visits in 2012–13 who would have received them in 2005–06[46] (see Figure 5.1, on page 133). The life expectancy of people aged over sixty-five in England and Wales fell during 2012.[47]

By spring 2014, it had been revealed that, thanks to the cuts, a further 168,000 older people in the UK were no longer receiving care, at a time when the number of elderly people was rising. The BBC described this as 'catastrophic'.[48] The director of the charity Age UK said this was now putting older people at 'significant risk'.[49] What she did not add was that the apparent savings made by the reduced number of visits to the elderly were tiny in comparison to the amount being used by a small number of bankers. On the very same day that Age UK released its statistics, it became clear that some 481 Barclays bankers in 2013 had been paid £1 million or more – some fifty-three more than a year earlier – and that 'eight individuals got more than £5m, and another fifty-four earned between £2.5m and £5m. Again, those tallies were higher than in 2012. Overall, the bonus pool was increased from £2.2bn to £2.4bn.'[50]

As the bankers take more and more, the old and poor begin to die younger.[51] Death causes fear, especially for those who are used to controlling almost everything else in their lives. At the extreme, there are billionaires who fund research on lifespan extension. Some are planning to be cryogenically frozen at the point of death, and thawed when technology allows them to be revived.[52] A few are willing to invest their fortunes in the tragic project of trying to keep their own miserable frames breathing forever.[53] Often these people would not countenance being taxed one iota more for the immediate benefit it could give to the life expectancy of countless others.

Even in more equitable countries that experienced an increase in income inequality, and where that increase has been much less pronounced than in the UK, there has been a subsequent rise in health inequalities. In Finland about half the increase in health inequality outcomes is directly attributable to a surge in the relative poverty of the poorest since 1987.[54] In Finland, however, everyone lives longer, on average, than in the UK. The rich live longer than the rich in the UK, and the poor live longer than the poor in the UK – and all this despite Finland's cold, snow and very long, dark winters. Greater equality can overcome a great deal. In contrast, in the UK, the life expectancy of women over sixty-five fell for the first time in many years in 2012 (see Figure 5.5) – not long after the implementation of those swingeing cuts to the living standards, care visits, and hope of the elderly, and especially women.

The US is light years behind a country like Finland when it comes to sharing resources more fairly – but even a small move in that direction can appear to be a great achievement. Where such progress is made, people can become briefly elated, but the campaigning is hard and the reversals often dispiriting. For outsiders, it can be shocking to discover that

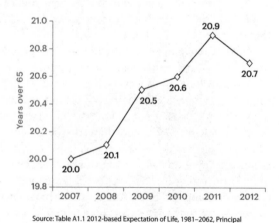

Source: Table A1.1 2012-based Expectation of Life, 1981–2062, Principal Projection, United Kingdom, December 2013

Figure 5.5 Life Expectancy of Women aged sixty-five in the UK

a sixty-one-year-old in the US needs to pay $10,000 dollars a year just to receive what they see as basic healthcare – and that measures by the current Obama administration to improve this are said by some to be making the situation worse.[55] But the spirit embodied in Obama's 'yes we can' campaign rhetoric gave widespread hope to those desperate for change.

In Puerta del Sol, Madrid's central square, on 7 June 2011 – before the Occupy movement took off elsewhere – a young woman who joined the *indignados* tried to explain what it felt like to make her voice heard: 'It's impossible to switch off … I dream about it at night. It was hard work learning how to conduct the assemblies, especially the big one … We learn

Zaruteman
'Listen to the anger of the people', Indignados, Madrid 2011

something new every day.'[56] Protesting in Spain – like enacting progressive legislation in the US, like researching the changing influences on life expectancy in Finland – can be a cause of elation; but much of it is also a bitter grind, with only the occasional moment of celebration. One such moment came recently, when the locksmiths of the Spanish city of Pamplona announced that they would no longer change the locks on the doors of people who had been evicted, making eviction impossible.[57]

Between the extremes of the protestors in the central squares of Europe demanding their rights, and the isolation of one sixty-one-year-old not sleeping in the US through fear of failing to pay for her personal healthcare, there are millions of small battles being fought to maintain our dignity, financial security and mental health. Student fees in the UK are an instructive case in point. From 2015 onwards, the first students to have been charged £9,000 a year for their studies will have to start paying back their loans. Those loans could well increase future inequality and harm health in more direct ways, as they exacerbate anxiety.

The outstanding debt on UK student loans goes up every year in line with the retail price index (RPI), and then is increased by up to 3 per cent more, on a sliding scale, for incomes between £21,000 and £41,000. If inflation rises, the debt will increase dramatically. Once the loans are privatised, they will become just another 'hedge' that the rich can use. By lending students money the students protect the future wealth of the rich against inflation. The static threshold of £21,000 is effectively lowered when inflation goes up. The amount you have to pay off through the tax system each year then increases with earnings over £21,000, irrespective of how little that increase might be worth in real terms. If the current growing student loan book was seen as the potential health risk that it is, it would be understood very differently.

The UK government produced a repayment calculator utilising an RPI of 3.6 per cent, and working with starting graduate salaries from £15,795 to £70,000. It allows for a maximum loan, including maintenance and tuition, of £50,025 for a three-year course.[58] If you enter a starting salary of £15,795, then it takes thirty years to pay off a loan of £21,000, at a cost of £56,000; but if you borrowed £50,000, you still only had to pay back £56,000. With a starting salary of £26,000, though, your £50,000 loan would eventually cost £166,150.

The repayment calculator might come in handy in future should students take legal action against a government that turned millions of young people's university educations into a fail-safe investment opportunity for a few thousand of the 1 per cent. The rich now have an even bigger financial interest in suppressing tax increases to fund tertiary education: after the full student loan book is privatised, investors will lose money if students need to borrow less.

Another way of looking at this problem is in terms of how a student's tax will be calculated, using current rates. The first £9,440 of income is untaxed; the next £11,660 is taxed at 20

STUDENT LOAN DEBT

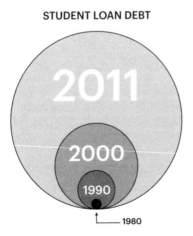

Source: Economic Research, Federal Reserve Bank of St. Louis, 2013

Figure 5.6 The US student loan debt bubble

per cent; the next £23,440 is taxed at 29 per cent, instead of 20 per cent – and anything above £44,440 is taxed at 49 per cent (instead of 40 per cent), until the loan is paid off, irrespective of its initial size. While much richer people and the government that introduced this scheme say that the imposition of a marginal 50 per cent tax rate on their income would be totally unacceptable, they are happily imposing it on the children of parents who cannot afford university tuition fees. Inequalities in income and wealth will rise in future as a result of the student loan system – and when such inequalities rise, inequalities in health follow suit.

As R. H. Tawney noted, 'During the past two and a half years every artifice has been employed to create the impression that public expenditure on education is recklessly extravagant.'[59] That sounds as if it was written about the year 2004, but in fact it dates from 1934. The effect of that same rhetoric eighty years later – in 2011 – was policies that caused some 32,000 fewer students to stay on at school after age sixteen than in 2010.[60] This was the first recorded fall, in both absolute and relative terms, for many years. Numbers rose the year after, as 'insecure, low-paid work without prospects, including mostly so-called "traineeships" … explain[ed] why so many eighteen-year-olds [were] still prepared to pay so much for so little in exorbitantly priced higher education'.[61]

Between 2007 and 2011, the number of suicides among men in higher education in the UK rose by more than a third, while the number among young women almost doubled – although the female rate remained less than half the male rate.[62] Health and education are linked in many ways. A combination of rising financial and academic pressures on students coupled with recent cutbacks to university support services might be partly to blame, as well as the rapid dwindling of job prospects.

It is clearly no coincidence that the two countries with the highest student fees in the rich world are also the two with the highest number of extremely rich households. At the last full census of the world's rich,[63] in 2011, there were found to be almost 3,000 families in the US with at least $100 million in private wealth. The UK has only a fifth of the population of the US, but has more very rich families per head. Some 1,125 families in the UK hold $100 million or more in assets – far more than in any other country in Europe, despite other countries such as Germany being both more prosperous and more populous.

Taxes for the Rich, Not Debt for the Young

> Unequal political power is the endgame of widening inequality – its most noxious and nefarious consequence. Big money has all but engulfed Washington and many state capitals – drowning out the voices of average Americans, filling the campaign chests of candidates who will do their bidding … [The reason] conservative Republicans would rather talk about poverty than about inequality is because they can then characterise the poor as 'them' – people who are different from most of us, who have brought their problems on themselves, who lack self-discipline or adequate motivation. Accordingly, in their view, any attempt to alleviate poverty requires that 'they' change their ways.
>
> Robert B. Reich, former US Labour Secretary, 2014[64]

The alternative to putting the young into debt is to tax the rich. In late 2013 the International Monetary Fund (IMF) cast doubt on the UK government's claim that taxing the rich at only 45 per cent on their very high incomes raised more tax than would a higher tax rate, for the dubious reason that the rich apparently then hide less of their money. The IMF concluded that a better top rate of tax would be 60 per cent, and that this would raise an extra £4 billion a year just from the 1 per cent.[65] The rich have become richer by cutting the tax rates that apply to them (see Figure 5.7), and directly and indirectly increasing taxation on others – including the new student loan regime.[66] Only the very rich appear to benefit from such policies.

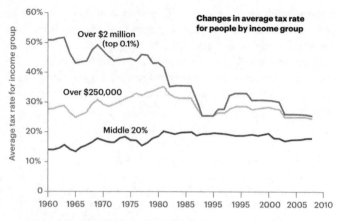

Source: Paul Krugman, 'The Long Run History of Taxes', 12 July 2012

Figure 5.7 The rich got richer by cutting their taxes and raising taxes on others (US)

So much needs to change if our societies are to become fairer and our overall health and welfare improve. The withdrawal of public funding for the education of the young must be recognised as an unfair tax levied on behalf of the old and the rich. Welfare to Work needs to be scrapped, and resources diverted to create good jobs, not cajole people into bad ones.[67] The dangers of not following such a course are that the UK will begin to run ever faster in a global race towards the bottom, to a place where there is no solidarity and precious little empathy. When it was revealed in 2011 that over 700 of those elderly care homes might close due to higher levels of rent being demanded by landlords, and that the residents would be evicted, it was first reported by the BBC as an item of business news, rather than health news.[68]

There is a danger that the UK government will soon copy the actions of more conservative groups, even from places as poor as India. Such factions highlight the financial success of a few initially very poor entrepreneurs, and then suggest that all of the poor can pull themselves up by their own bootstraps if only they pull hard enough. The implication is that 'there is little need for the state to wade in with things like effective training, cheap credit, and a decent public infrastructure'.[69] But we can now see what happens, after more than thirty years of promoting economies based on the 'survival of the nastiest' economics – inequality rises, and the 1 per cent takes more from a shrinking pot.

In 2013, the OECD noted that, across all of Europe, 'excluding the mitigating effects of the welfare state, via taxes and transfers on income, inequality has increased by more over the past three years to the end of 2010 than in the previous twelve'.[70] In other words, the crash has widened the gap between the 1 per cent and the 99 per cent across most of Europe. The crisis created by the rich has been turned to their own advantage. However, in contrast to the 1970s and 1980s, when the rich took the rest of the top 10 per cent with them and the income and wealth of that entire group rose, in the UK today – much as in India a few years ago – it is only the very richest who are really doing well.

Now only the 1 per cent can achieve enough wealth to escape what the majority fear. As wage inequality has risen in the UK since 1967, the number of workers in the private sector with private pension schemes has fallen from 8 million to under 3 million today – the lowest level of private sector pensions held since the 1950s. Some 20 per cent of all employees now believe they will never be able to afford to retire.[71] And how will university students retire in their early seventies if they have not been able to contribute to pension schemes in their thirties and forties because they have been paying off their student loans?

The best-off 1 per cent of Americans now have $1.3 million or more each in their retirement accounts, as well as that part of the rest of their wealth which they don't give to their children (see Figure 5.8). Many in the 1 per cent are so wealthy they do not need a pension. Even the worst-off of the top 10 per cent of Americans have an average pension account worth

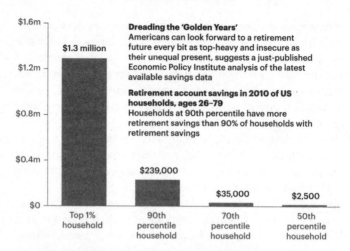

Source: Monique Morrissey and Natalie Sabadish, Economic Policy Institute. 'How the 401(k) revolution created a few big winners and many losers'. September 2013

Figure 5.8 Be afraid of your futures: pensions pending in the US

$239,000 – about a hundred times the average retirement savings of the middle American. But that account will not give them a very high annual pension; in old age, they will have more in common with the rest of the 99 per cent than with the 1 per cent. The poorest half of all pensioners will have to rely almost entirely on whatever they can glean from the state, their families, and charity.[72]

Money Works Better Spread Around

> And money is like muck, not good except it be spread. This is done chiefly by suppressing or at least keeping a strait hand upon the devouring trades of usury.
>
> Francis Bacon, former attorney general
> and lord chancellor of England, 1625[73]

Francis Bacon's line on money being like muck is often quoted, but few know the next line, condemning usury and debt.

Reducing inequality requires that lines be drawn between right and wrong. We know that, for healthcare, 'it is immoral to profit from another's illness'.[74] The alternative is bleak, not just for those at the bottom of society, but all the way up to just below the 1 per cent. When money is spread around as poorly as today, the stink of corruption becomes very hard to disguise, and the harm caused to those at the bottom, who are robbed of almost every last penny, becomes palpable.

Writing about the growth in food banks and the middle class's rising fear of poverty, UK commentator Richard Seymour explains that, as we have shifted from welfare towards the punishment of people for being poor, 'those fortunate enough to stay just the right side of this divide will have added motivation to be compliant; docile toward social superiors, viciously competitive towards everyone else'.[75] But it doesn't have to be this way.[76] We could drastically reduce the retirement age to sixty, or at least move it back to sixty-five. The government says we cannot afford this, but that is clearly incorrect. The state pension is roughly the same as Jobseekers' Allowance. Every older worker who wishes to retire but cannot without a state pension could create a job for someone unemployed. There may not be a fixed amount of work available, a 'lump of labour', but there is a finite pay chest.

Compared to young people, older retired people are much more likely to take up voluntary work in the community – and thus increase social capital. There is also less of a stigma attached to being retired than to being unemployed, resulting in less depression and other mental illness. Making the elderly work until they die is not good for their health. Keeping the young out of decent work is not good for their health. People should be able to choose to work and to retire when they want to. Being forced to work is a recipe for bad work, and at the extreme is slavery.

We need to realise that we only achieved full employment when we had a far more equitable distribution of wages and salaries and people had choices over what work they did. That condition of equity may have emerged out of war, but it was maintained for decades by government policy. However, as businesses become increasingly automated, the downward trend in employment will continue.

Left to its own devices, the private market will employ ever fewer people on good wages, who will then be expected to work ever harder to secure ever greater profits. This will hold true not only within organisations but between them. Where one person is taken on, for instance, to work in a supermarket, more than one loses work elsewhere – such as in local grocers and independent petrol stations.[77]

Government efforts to create and maintain high-quality jobs is not just good for public health – it is justified by the fact that every well-employed individual creates positive benefits for society, such as tax revenue and the maintenance of dignity. In contrast, as the 1 per cent takes an ever higher share of income, unwanted costs are created, such as high levels of unemployment, or a proliferation of part-time and low-paid work. All of these factors have negative effects on our overall health and happiness.

A government that wanted to improve public health would promote the employment of more conductors on buses and trains – not least in order to encourage people to use them instead of cars. It would promote more face-to-face interactions at post offices, rather than more impersonal, labour-saving and apparently efficient work through demoralising call centres. We would see more teachers, smaller class sizes in schools, and fewer executives paid millions of pounds a year. All this in the past created the dual benefits of increased and sustainable employment and increased social capital.

In the words of John Kay, writing in the *Financial Times*, 'policy to give the low-paid more money rather than benefits is worthy of debate and only a rabid ideologue could fail to appreciate that pay is not purely a question of productivity; it is also a question of bargaining.'[78] Left in the control of the 1 per cent, the not-so-free market can destroy jobs and livelihoods faster than it creates them. Life needs to be less precarious if stress is to be reduced and health improved. The government must ensure that firms embrace employment sustainability, along with environmental sustainability. There should be an end to the practice, used even by government, of forcing workers to reapply for their own jobs at a reduced rate of pay.

People in power often suggest that, as the demand for labour falls, full employment can be maintained by reducing real wages – for example, by ensuring that any wage increases are less than the rate of inflation. But the wage level at which this full employment is achieved does not necessarily allow human dignity, or even survival. Also, as real wages fall, those who are still employed spend less. Good jobs become scarcer. Simultaneously hate crime and other forms of violence increase. And everyone's health suffers.[79]

In Britain today, around 1 per cent of all young men under twenty-five are in prison – the highest rate of imprisonment in Europe. In the US, well over 1 per cent of all men are in prison – the highest rate in the world. These rich countries are also those that deny prisoners the vote.[80] Crime influences health and well-being in many ways. In Britain between 1974 and 2005, as income inequality increased, so too did the scale of property crime. But the falling real price of consumer goods such as televisions, video players and DVD players contributed to a reduction in the number of those crimes which were domestic burglaries during this period.[81] Since the crash of 2008, the value of these goods relative to people's disposable income has risen, and so it is no surprise to hear that domestic burglaries are on the increase – especially in parts of the UK that are still in the depths of recession.[82]

Poverty campaigners understand that if you ignore the concentration of wealth, you cannot be serious about dealing with its absence.[83] Researchers from the Center for American Progress found that around half of all parents in the US believe their children will be poorer than they are. They dis- covered that poorer children tended to do far better if they were growing up in regions with fewer very rich people, but more average incomes, concluding: 'Giving tax breaks and other benefits to the wealthy will only perpetuate the current era of diminished mobility; to reignite opportunity, policy- makers must grow and strengthen a vibrant middle class.'[84] The middle can only grow and be vibrant if both fewer people are rich and fewer people are poor.

How do the extremely rich react to hearing the message that greater equality is essential to increasing overall well- being, and that they are part of the problem? They compare their plight – as venture capitalist Tom Perkins did in January 2014 – to that of the Jews victimised by the Nazis on Kristallnacht.[85] By March 2014, billionaire Ken Langone was repeating the analogous claim that those who were hounding the rich were acting just as Hitler had acted in 1933, causing the London *Evening Standard* to quote Alexander Pope: 'We may see the small value God has for riches by the people he gives them to.'[86]

Conclusion: Towards a Fairer Society

> Revolutions break out on ships, and utopias are lived on islands.
>
> Judith Schalansky, 2012 [1]

José Gonzalo Rodríguez Gacha, a Mexican drug lord, was reputed to be so rich that he had his four initials embossed in gold leaf on the toilet paper he used. But, despite all the advantages of money, his life came to a horrible conclusion. He killed himself in 1989 by detonating a grenade by the side of his face, just after watching his son being shot dead by police. We have a fascination with stories of great wealth, but clearly it is not always better to be rich. [2]

To counter our older concepts about rich men – and their despair at camels failing to fit through the eye of the needle – there exists a new, often subconscious, message that existence is only fully realised with the aid of great wealth. It is a message disseminated through the smiling faces on magazine covers and on primetime television. Contrast these with the miserable faces of the poor, or merely 'normal', that the media presents every day. Many well-known television dramas in both the UK and US have at their heart the implicit message 'the rich only have your best interests at heart'. Think of *Downton Abbey*. [3]

Our grandparents' generation created the National Health Service while ours came up with the National Lottery. That is a sad indictment of our times, but it does at least allow a natural experiment to be carried out to answer the question of what happens to people if they are simply given a large amount of money. The answer, most often, is that they become rapidly and sometimes rabidly more right-wing. In particular, lottery winners who live in poorer, more left-leaning areas appear most likely to shift towards the right in their political beliefs after having 'come into' some money. The relationship has been shown to be 'of a "dose-response" kind: the larger the win, the more people tilt to the right'.[4] Can it be so different for the very rich?

Some 1 per cent of the UK's top 1 per cent are lottery winners. In October 2012 Camelot, the organisation that runs the UK National Lottery, published research claiming that, since 1994, the 3,000 lottery winners who had won over £1 million each – who had claimed a total of £8.5 billion between them – had contributed £750 million to GDP, because each millionaire winner generated roughly six jobs – servants, cleaners, gardeners and, in 5 per cent of cases, personal beauticians.[5] At no point did this study mention the money taken out of the economy to buy lottery tickets – nearly £7 billion in the year 2012/13 alone. Furthermore, the list of jobs created is hardly edifying.

The Camelot-sponsored report made no mention of how often winning large sums of money ruins people's lives, despite the often heard story of the family torn apart by its windfall. In November 2013 that story was of Adrian and Gillian Bayford, divorcing a year after winning £148 million in the Euro lottery – a win that, at the time, they said would bring their family closer together. They had celebrated 'with a pizza with their daughter, eight, and son, six, before heading off on holiday to a Scottish caravan park'.[6] Now their children see them separately. The *Sun* reported a neighbour commenting on Adrian and Gillian: 'It's such a shame because they are a lovely family with two young kids. And everyone around here was so happy for them when they won. They worked hard all of their lives and then came into this wonderful bit of good fortune. That's why it's so sad it's ended like this.'[7] But, of course, such stories are as old as the hills.

In 1961, Viv Nicholson and her then husband won a small fortune on the football pools, and vowed to 'spend, spend, spend'. Since then, Viv has gone through both widowhood and her third, fourth and fifth marriages. In 2007, at the age of 71, having finally managed to conquer her alcoholism, she was living on a pension of £87 a week, had an overdraft, and was searching for work.[8] Even more extreme stories are now routinely told in the US, where it sometimes seems as if people will do anything for the chance of a fortune and routinely have their lives ruined through the ill effects of gaining riches.[9] For millennia, we have known that greed harms and having too much can be damaging; but we seem able to forget faster than we can remember.

In November 2013 Boris Johnson, Conservative mayor of London, made a speech in which he explained why he believed that greed was good:

> Like it or not, the free market economy is the only show in town ... No one can ignore the harshness of that competition, or the inequalities that it inevitably accentuates [but] the top 1 per cent contributes almost 30 per cent of income tax; and indeed the top 0.1 per cent – just 29,000 people – contributes fully 14 per cent of all taxation.[10]

The implication is that those who grab the most for themselves also somehow give the most back, even if unwillingly, through taxation.

The rich do not, in fact, pay tax very willingly, and certainly take far more than they pay in tax. It is also very hard to argue that they have really earned what they pay tax on through hard work, rather than guile. Income tax is only 26 per cent of total government revenue – national insurance contributions raise 18 per cent, and VAT raises 17 per cent.[11] The rich pay such a large proportion of income tax because their incomes are now so extraordinarily large, because they have worked so hard to raise their take and swallow up so much of what is available. Owing to VAT and other regressive levies, the 20 per cent least well-off of all households pay 36.6 per cent of their income in tax, while the wealthiest 20 per cent pay 35.5 per cent.[12] Boris Johnson's figure of 30 per cent of all income tax revenue equates to under 8 per cent of all government revenues, so there is no way that the top 0.1 per cent can be contributing 14 per cent of all taxation. Boris was wrong. When it comes to numerical rather than verbal dexterity, he is not a 'top cornflake'.

Boris went on to say that he wanted more social mobility: 'to get back to my cornflake packet, I worry that there are too many cornflakes who aren't being given a good enough chance to rustle and hustle their way to the top'. His analogy is more apt than he realised. As with people, there is not that much difference between one cornflake and another. To go on to suggest that only the ones at the top are really worth very much would be absurd. You can try to dismiss Boris Johnson as a buffoon, but he has many supporters and a realistic hope of becoming the next Conservative leader. His words were carefully chosen to appeal to the beliefs of his core supporters, although we cannot know whether he believes them himself or is being consciously deceptive. He may just crave power, and choose his words and shape his demeanour as a way of winning votes.

The day after Johnson's speech, the European Banking Authority issued figures showing that 2,714 bankers in the UK in 2012 had each earned more than €1 million (£833,000) – 11 per cent more people than in 2011, by far the highest number of any country in Europe, and ten times the number in Germany, which came second on the list. Average total pay – including salaries, pensions and bonuses – for London's top-earning bankers surged by 35 per cent to €1.95 million (£1.6 million) in 2012.[13] In Sweden, only eleven 'investment' bankers earned more than €1 million that year; in Spain, thirty-seven; in France, 117; in Germany, just one hundred – and in the United Kingdom, 2,188.[14] Of the 526 non-investment bankers in Europe earning this amount, all were in the UK. The UK is not normal.

Similar trends were found among UK FTSE 100 chief executives, whose total annual remuneration increased fivefold between 2000 and 2012 to hit an average of £4.2 million. The pay of the next-best-off 150 UK CEOs also rose quickly, but not quite as quickly, to average £1.1 million by 2012. Reporting these statistics, and in contrast to Boris, Conservative MP Jesse Norman explained that 'no reputable study has found a significant correlation between senior executive pay and long-term corporate performance'.[15] The UK has a very expensive problem that the rest of Europe has managed largely to avoid: an overpaid and underachieving 1 per cent. They are expensive not just in direct financial terms, but in terms of the damage they go on to cause. Pay the most and you are likely to get the greediest, who in turn are unlikely to curb the greed of those around them (lest their own greed be exposed). These exceptionally highly paid bankers are the people who caused the financial crisis in the UK. The subsequent Libor scandal dwarfed all previous financial scams in the history of markets, and now there is a possibility that the Forex scandal could be just as serious. And the UK's banks are still by far the most indebted in Europe.[16] So much for paying the most to get the best.

In the UK, unlike anywhere else in Europe, bankers are protected by law through the Corporation of the City of London, which is governed by a plethora of unelected bodies including the Worshipful Company of International Bankers.[17] The only place in the world where similar if even more bizarrely named bodies can be found is the US, where organisations such as Kappa Beta Phi operate. This is a semi-secret fraternity that was founded at the start of the Great Depression, around 1929, and which includes among its members 'both incredibly successful financiers (New York City's Mayor Michael Bloomberg, former Goldman Sachs chairman John Whitehead, hedge-fund billionaire Paul Tudor Jones) and incredibly unsuc-cessful ones (Lehman Brothers CEO Dick Fuld, Bear Stearns CEO Jimmy Cayne, former New Jersey governor and MF Global flameout Jon Corzine)'.[18] In early 2014 the fraternity was exposed in the British newspapers, one of which reported that 'the upper ranks of finance are composed of people who have completely divorced themselves from reality'.[19] The jour-nalist did not make the obvious connection to financiers in London. He was writing in the *Daily Mail*.

Why does the UK appear determined to continue to be such an exception? It is not just that the UK is home to almost all of Europe's most greedy bankers and highest-paid chief executives. The UK, and especially southern England, is also the European exception when it comes to private education. As we saw in Chapter 2, simply by segregating rich children from poor children, private education encourages a sense of personal superiority.[20]

The sense of superiority engendered by private education is closely related to that fostered in a segregated society – not least because the most expensive schools could not continue to function as they do without a small number of very highly paid individuals to pay the huge fees. Exclusive private educa-tion, of which the UK has by far the most in Europe, often instils the belief that others – educated by state or lesser private schools – are inferior to your classmates, and that self-interest and the exploitation of those others is good business. It is hard to see how it could avoid fostering a ridiculous level of conceit. Why else would it be worthwhile for the parents spending so much on their children if they did not believe that their chil-dren were, or should be, worth far more than other children?

Private education is basically a financial investment expected to generate a financial return. The existence of such a large private sector compared to the rest of Europe makes other unusual divisions within UK schooling appear normal. A number of Christian sects and Jewish state-funded schools have existed for years. The new UK free schools policy allows any religion or educational ethos to establish state-funded schools. All private schools could apply to become free schools with government backing, unless of course they want far more spent on their children than on others'. Variety is not bad, except where the purpose is to push others down and your little group up. We should not condone many times more being spent on the education of a select few. By the same token, when there is less to go round, why do the poor have to suffer the greatest cuts (see Figure 6.1)?

The UK is an oddity compared to the rest of Europe. The Coalition government now plans tougher benefit cuts for the poor, having already reduced the top rate of tax to 45 per cent for the very richest. It plans to reward the top 1 per cent, giving a few of the rest of the top fifth slight increases in their take-home pay in the years up to 2016 while everyone else is impoverished. This conclusion is based on the Office for Budget Responsibility's own assessments of government policy.[21] In the UK the elite is unashamed of its selfishness. Elsewhere in Europe, where austerity has been better shared

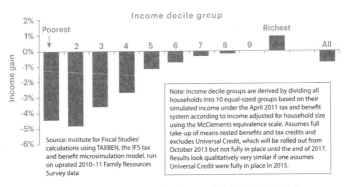

Figure 6.1 Planned UK tax and benefit changes 2012 to 2015/2017

out, the result has been that overall suffering has been far less.[22]

In the long term it is children who will suffer most from spending cuts, rather than working adults or pensioners. The effects of the tax, benefit and other spending measures now under way are far greater for households with children, which make up only a third of all households in England, but which will suffer around two-thirds of the cuts. On average, couples with no children will lose 4 per cent, couples with children 9 per cent, and lone parents 14 per cent of their net income. The spending cuts alone are equivalent to 2 per cent of net income for couples with children in the top income decile, but 9 per cent of net income in the bottom decile; for lone parents, these figures are 2 per cent and 11 per cent, respectively.[23] Because of this, the children's commissioner for England remarked in June 2013: 'We consider that the overall impact of the tax-benefit reforms is likely to be in breach of Article 2 of the UNCRC – non-discrimination.'[24] A tiny number of government measures will help a few children through early years and increase some school spending, but the vast majority of measures will harm many more, especially the children of the poorest and second-poorest tenths, and lone parents' children will suffer far more than those with two parents (see Figure 6.2).

There is a group that is even worse hit than those with children in the UK: the youngest of adults. Already,

since the recession, it is no surprise to see that the household incomes of adults in their 20s have been falling faster than those of any other age group since 2007–08. This is despite the fact that about 40 per cent of the group live with their parents, and that this has tended to cushion the impacts on their household incomes.[25]

In real terms, the median income of households containing those young adults fell by 12 per cent over the following four

Couples with children

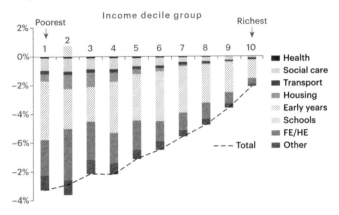

Lone parent families

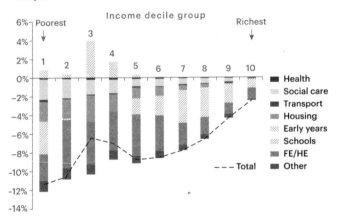

Source: Social Mobility and Child Poverty Commission, 2013

Figure 6.2 Relative effects of spending reduction of £29 billion by 2016 on families in England

years, after no growth in the previous six years.[26] But when it comes to suffering through poor health, it is those over sixty-five, and especially poorer elderly women, who have seen their life expectancy falling despite pensions being maintained. As documented above, cuts to home visits have coincided closely with the deteriorating health of the very elderly. Increased suffering can be identified in almost every group – excluding the 1 per cent.

When a society becomes as unequal as the UK now is, avarice rises. As inequalities increase, people already at the top become ever more motivated solely by greed. The source of inequality is a failure to control the greedy. Often they feel that they need more money despite all their wealth. They are made to feel that way because status and respect are increasingly measured in purely financial terms. Just over thirty years ago, Neil Kinnock, then Labour Party leader, remarked: 'If Margaret Thatcher wins on Thursday, I warn you not to be ordinary. I warn you not to be young. I warn you not to fall ill. I warn you not to get old.' What he did not add, which would have been most prescient, was: 'I warn you not to reach adulthood alongside Thatcher's grandchildren. I warn you not to be young then, not to want to study then, not to want a rewarding job then, or to grow old then.' Years after Thatcher's policies have made the rich so much richer and stripped so much power from the poor, Kinnock's words are no longer a warning but a description. Had he known, he could have explained that in more equal societies there is much less need to be mercenary. When inequality rises, more people become less concerned about how their behaviour impacts on others.

Following the financial crash in the rich world, only six out of thirty OECD countries saw a reduction in market (pre-tax and benefit) income inequalities. Of all OECD countries, it was in Spain that disposable income inequality rose fastest in the first three years after the financial crash.[27] Ireland saw the highest increase in market income inequality, but state action resulted in the increase in disposable income inequality being modest (see Figure 6.3). The greedy used the crash to become richer, to buy assets cheaply, and to make new profits out of others' impoverishment. But it doesn't have to be this way. State action resulted in disposable income inequality falling in another dozen countries, most dramatically in Iceland,

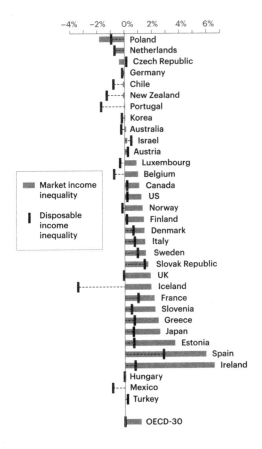

Source: European Centre for Disease and prevention Control, 'Health, Inequalities and the Financial Crisis', 2013

Figure 6.3 Change in income inequalities in rich countries between 2007 and 2010

reversing the changes in market income inequality. Around the rich world the same shock is being handled very differently from one country to another. The crash tended to increase inequality, but there were large differences in how well various countries succeeded in tempering that increase.

What is to be done? One option is simply to let things carry on as they are, wait until the average price of property in London doubles to £1 million a house, step back, and even-tually watch the greatest bubble in history burst, along with what is left of the credibility of London's banks and finance sector, which did nothing to stop the new bubble growing – and then hope that a chastened and poorer country becomes more equal again. But that is a giant gamble that might result in a poorer and even more unequal future.

What will it take for those towards the top of the 99 per cent who are losing out, as well as those who are falling out of the 1 per cent, to realise that even many people with healthy lifestyles and relatively well-paid jobs are heading for a fall? Currently they just blame it on bad luck when someone like themselves goes under, but eventually they will realise that it is due to an unsustainable system – especially when they look at the dramatically varying economic fortunes of their children and wider family.

In the world's most affluent and unequal of countries, those at the top often say that people are poor because there are too many of them, either too many being born or too many immigrating. This is a common refrain of the elite. David Attenborough recently put it more subtly: 'We are such a densely populated country ... The world is only so big. You simply can't go on increasing forever, so something's going to stop it. Either we can stop it or the natural world will stop it for us.'[28] David is wealthy enough to be a member of the 1 per cent, and he was quoted on the BBC website having said this on the *Today* programme. When he says 'we can stop it', he may not have a very wide conception of 'we'. I think we can stop inequality rising, and I know population growth is rapidly slowing; but part of stopping the crises to come will involve confronting the views of many people in David's economic position.

Research published in *Behavioural Ecology* finds that elites like the 1 per cent can emerge when a lack of free-flowing information gives a few a growing advantage. The effect of such rising elitism on the group as a whole is doubly harmful. It is not only that less good gets done as the gaps between us are widened, but that ignorance is fostered. Those with power simply know very little about the lives of the majority. They can come to see 'the masses' as a seething sea of out-of-control bodies; but, looking up from below, the powerful appear to have very poor vision.

Technically speaking, rising elitism has harmed us all in the past because 'the loss of efficiency of stratification is due to the lengthened information channels, whereas the additional loss of efficiency in the elite network is due to the information bottleneck emerging between the elite clique and the rest of the group'.[29] The result is a rising culture of entitlement that is damaging to all. Increasingly, the rich feel that they are entitled to as much as they can possibly get away with – that they are entitled to say outrageous things and that no one else is entitled to anything much.

In the US and UK, the culture of entitlement among the richest has arisen that is not found to be as strong in other rich nations. Elitist views and behaviour are now seeping into the mainstream, so that even the poor are heard to call for lower taxes. That is how deep the confusion goes. A 2011 study of eighteen OECD countries found that the optimal top tax rate for the marginal earnings of the very rich might be over 80 per cent. With that, a country could increase productivity (which could be green productivity), while 'no one but the mega rich would lose out'.[30] The authors of the study show top tax rates to have fallen since the 1970s, and the income share of the richest 1 per cent to have grown in almost perfect correlation (see Figure 6.4).

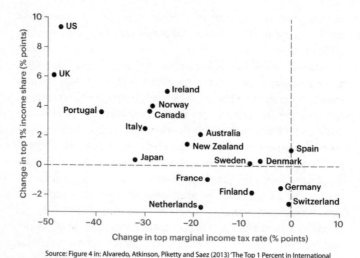

Source: Figure 4 in: Alvaredo, Atkinson, Piketty and Saez (2013) 'The Top 1 Percent in International and Historical Perspective', *Journal of Economic Perspectives*, 27: 3 (Summer 2013), pp. 3–20

Figure 6.4 The effect of top tax rates on pre-tax incomes of the top 1 per cent since 1960

Countries that have not reduced top income tax rates since the 1960s have also prevented their elites from taking too much. It is clear that higher taxation can reduce greed at the top more effectively than any other mechanism. Put simply, if taking more for yourself gains you very little (because of what the government takes), it pays to let that money go to people paying much lower tax rates. High taxes at high incomes help the greedy to be less greedy. The alternative is to see the 1 per cent become richer and richer, pollute more, and lecture the rest of us on our behaviour, while they plot ever more elaborate ways of behaving badly. This might include taking personal trips into space – which makes flying private jets to Necker Island look like environmental awareness. But a new mood is developing. The *Wall Street Journal* asks: 'Why do Leonardo DiCaprio and Richard Branson lecture us about carbon consumption while plotting trips to space?'[31]

There are many positive signs that people are coming to realise that the rich must be helped to take less. But we face a major problem that often hinders progress: self-congratulation. In order to achieve long-term improvement, it is necessary to retain a sense of anger. Stop to celebrate one small victory (the locksmiths in Spain, the peoples' parliament in Iceland, the land tax in Ireland, new forms of protest in the US) and, before you know it, the greedy have snatched back that little part of the wealth you had liberated, and found another tax loophole. The left, greens and anarchists can appear a dour bunch, because of their fear of being complacent and compliant. All of us need to believe more strongly that better outcomes can be achieved – just as feminists, anti-racists and democrats have done in the past.

A Slow Revolution

> [The 1 per cent] have been able to divide everyone else by geography and by identity. They have produced an unequal market system, and have privatised public resources, pushing the costs on the rest of society ... People need to be citizens again, not consumers. They need to have more choices and they need to demand more.
> Elvin Wyley, speaking at Occupy Vancouver, 2011 [32]

What we need is a slow revolution. The 1 per cent cannot control itself. It is easy to blame its members, but blaming them may exonerate others who, while not having been so greedy themselves, could have acted and could still act to curtail the greed of others. To gain entry into the 1 per cent often requires a certain lack of self-restraint. It is up to the rest of us to control these people – for their own good as well as ours. We can document their greed, the size of their yachts, the frequency with which they fly and the pollution caused by all the expensive vehicles they use to move around as fast as they can; but documentation is not enough. [33] This stupidity needs to be halted. In the past it has not been revolution, in most cases, but war that has quickly relieved the 1 per cent of much of its assets. Today a non-violent war of attrition on concentrated wealth is needed, and it is beginning.

In the US in 2013, the president finally acted. Top tax rates for the richest 1 per cent were increased from 35 per cent to 39.6 per cent of income received over a high threshold, and capital gains tax was increased from 15 to 20 per cent in that same year.[34] There are now many calls to increase these rates even more, raising capital gains taxes up to a maximum rate of 50 per cent for the very richest Americans. Many of these calls are coming from much nearer the mainstream than has been the case for decades. Celebrate ever so slightly, have a beer, smile a bit more – but above all else do something to help build the momentum.

Why did the US president act in 2013? One answer is that in the US it became clear by the summer of 2012 just how enormous the fallout from the financial crash was:

> median wealth plummeted over the years 2007 to 2010, and by 2010 was at its lowest level since 1969. The inequality of net worth, after almost two decades of little movement, was up sharply during the late 2000s. Relative indebtedness continued to expand [from 2007 to 2010], particularly for the middle class, though the proximate causes were declining net worth and income rather than an increase in absolute indebtedness. In fact, the average [new] debt of the middle class (in real terms) plunged by 25 percent.[35]

In other words, the middle were becoming poorer through no fault of their own – and falling into ever greater debt to the richest despite not having asked to borrow more.

The calls to curtail the excesses of the 1 per cent in the US are not made now in obscure outlets, but – at the extreme – in *Forbes*, the favoured journal of the rich.[36] Even *Forbes* writers who have been hedge-fund managers, and have headed the Fortunes and Options Division of Lloyds TSB bank, can see what is coming and say: 'We can't afford another Dust Bowl.'[37] It is not hard now to collect hundreds of calls for change coming from all directions, but will they be enough? A slow revolution is hard to sustain, and it has many enemies.

How are the very richest in the US reacting to the threat to their wealth? Some are playing the markets and try to move their money abroad;[38] others are writing directly to their employees recommending that they do not vote Democrat. Until 2010 it was illegal for companies to act in this way, but corporate executives lobbied to change the law so that they could spend part of their profits on trying to entice their employees to vote to keep company profits high and their employer's wage and tax bills low. A slow revolution requires repeatedly exposing such bullying attempts to persuade people to act against their own interests.

Major US companies now send their employees letters recommending that they vote Republican. Before the last US presidential election, 'some letters warn[ed] that if President Obama [was] re-elected, the company could be harmed, potentially jeopardizing jobs'.[39] Simply expressing slightly progressive views in the office will mark you out as a threat not only to your bosses, but also to your peers. One lawyer who commented on the story noted, 'By hinting at the possible loss of employees' jobs, [it] appeared to cross the line into improper coercion.'

In the US Obama may be no saint, but he 'enrages the 1 per cent'[40] because he explains to the wider population that it has been their business strategies which have enriched the elite and impoverished the middle of American society. He is also finally starting to act because his policy advisors can now show him so easily how far countries like the US and the UK are out of step. Information about the 1 per cent has entered the public domain, touching off a ferocious response, and a level of vitriol not seen for decades. Between 1981 and 2002 the attitudes of the majority of Americans had no significant impact on public policy.[41] Now that is changing.

The UK is different. In the UK the prime minister was a member of the 1 per cent by dint of his wealth long before he entered parliament. He presides over a cabinet containing more members of the 1 per cent than has been the case for decades, and has appointed a series of close advisors not just from the 1 per cent, but often from his own school; and, hardly surprisingly – and unlike Mr Obama – he does not explain to his electorate how the business strategies of his friends have impoverished the middle of British society. As even Cameron's secretary of state for education, Michael Gove, complains: 'Mr Cameron, who went to Eton, numbers four Old Etonians among his inner circle: Oliver Letwin, minister for government policy; Jo Johnson, head of his policy unit; Ed Llewellyn, chief of staff; and Rupert Harrison, George Osborne's chief economic adviser.'[42] Is it any wonder inequalities in the UK continue to rise?

In the UK the leader of the opposition, Ed Miliband, although to the left of Obama, takes conspicuous care not to enrage the 1 per cent. Instead, he speaks very tentatively: 'The early signs, Miliband claims, are that the greatest beneficiaries of a recovering economy will also be a privileged few. Rewards in the banking sector in London grew nearly five times faster than the wages of the average worker last year. He argues this is not an accident, but a function of how the coalition views growth can be achieved.'[43] Such carefully worded statements are more than a generation away from Denis Healey's promise of February 1974 to 'squeeze property speculators until the pips squeak' – and Healey was to the right of Labour at the time.[44]

When you hear of slow progress in the UK and US, it may surprise you to learn that income inequality may not be rising everywhere. Globally, according to the World Bank, inequality has been falling since 2000. In Brazil income inequality peaked in the 1980s. In the US it is currently at a peak, but in Sweden it appears to have been falling again just as it has fallen worldwide (see Figure 6.5).[45] Such claims for falling

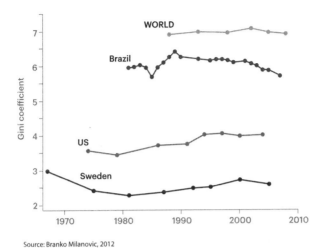

Source: Branko Milanovic, 2012

Figure 6.5 Global and selected countries' income inequality Gini coefficients 1966–2006

worldwide inequality are, of course, disputed; and measures of inequality that are more sensitive to the 1 per cent taking an ever greater share may not be as forgiving of extreme greed as the Gini coefficient; but inequalities within the middle of the distribution can nonetheless fall.

Shortly after the release of the 2012 World Bank report suggesting that global income inequality was falling, another organisation published its major findings, stating: 'Poverty has not declined to the extent claimed and inequity has risen.'[46] It may be that, between the mildly rich and the relatively poor, some equalisation is occurring. Whatever the precise global trend is, it remains the case that inequality has risen more in the US and the UK than elsewhere, and that, because other places have had more success in preventing this trend, it is not inevitable that it should continue. Increasingly, inhabitants of the US and the UK are learning from the example of other countries, coming to conclude, as Uffe Elbaek and Neal Lawson recently did: 'For the first time in a long time, radical egalitarian democrats face a future in which there is hope, real hope.'[47]

Less than one hundred years ago we had very little idea just how unequal our society was. Hugh Dalton, a boy from Eton, was awarded a PhD in 1920 from the University of London, and wrote an academic paper on income inequality in the UK.[48] He concluded his study with a declaration that 'the chief practical necessity is the improvement of existing statistical information, especially as regards smaller incomes'. He described measures of variance and distribution that were only just being discovered. In 1945 he became chancellor of the exchequer, where he helped the UK to become more equal, and helped the 1 per cent to contribute more and to become less of a drain on the nation, continuing a tradition that had begun in 1918 and would run through to 1978.

Orthodox economics suggests that, in the long run, prices and incomes will come back into alignment. It also provides a bizarre justification as to why some nations are rich and others are not.[49] Marxists say that price and value are a product of underlying social relations, not free-floating market forces. Keynesians say that in the long run we are all dead, and thus need to do something about the short run. All should know that the rich are currently being let off the hook, all those from the bottom of the 1 per cent up to those in control of the largest corporations. In 2012 Barclays 'secured a non-prosecution agreement and agreed to pay a penalty of more than $450 million, a comparatively paltry sum for a bank that had more than £32 billion ($50 billion) in revenue in 2011'.[50] But in 2013 Barclays was forced to begin to reveal more of its activities in order to avoid paying part of a $4.3 billion EU antitrust penalty.[51] The 1 per cent is finding it progressively harder to hide its money and its corruption.

Many people argue that concerted political action, including much more effective banking regulation, is needed to address the problem of increasing inequality. A global tax on capital was seriously proposed in 2014 by Thomas Piketty, one of the world's leading economists, and a best-selling author in the US and UK that year.[52] But successful social movements in the past, rather like the victors in wars, wrote their own history, and may have overstated the importance of overt politics. Campaigners want to say why they mattered; academics want to try to influence policy, and so look for evidence of their personal impact. But much change consists of gradual, almost imperceptible, transformation – a slow revolution of the wheel, a change in the mood, a subtle shift in what becomes morally acceptable, one that is almost never due to any great leaders or great speeches. Gradual transformations in societal motivations are not easily monitored. It is often not obvious how they occurred, and usually difficult to quantify their extent.

Today, another such transformation may be under way – a slow revolution in attitudes to greed. The highest-ever level of concern about rising inequality in Britain was recorded by Ipsos MORI in their winter polling of 2013.[53] Trends can form without the necessity of a lobby group or an organisation trying to profit from them. 'Societal motivation' and 'changing fashion' are almost synonyms. By December 2013, further polling evidence revealed that most UK voters believed any recovery was likely to favour the wealthy few rather than 'families like them', and that a majority favoured taxing the rich more rather than further cuts, especially to protect key services like health and education.[54] By that year we were no longer surprised that the majority thought this way – only that the rich still did not get it.

As pointed out earlier in this book, but well worth considering again in conclusion, in 2009 the ailing commentator and journalist Clive James predicted: 'Getting rich quick – and having much more money than you ever need – will look as pointless as taking bodybuilding too seriously.'[55] He helped begin the slow revolution. He explained how this kind of change has happened before, using the example from long ago of when the codpiece went out of fashion. That item of clothing, designed to create the illusion of a large penis, went from being normal in one era to the object of ridicule in the next.[56] James mocked the greediest of bankers: they were not just bad, they were embarrassments.

But it may not be us, or any activism at all, or any great change in mood or huge social transformation that changes things, and it may be that a slow revolution is not enough. But the rise in the income and wealth of the 1 per cent will come to an end, because it always does.

Just before he died, another veteran commentator, Alexander Cockburn, wrote: 'Is it possible to reform the banking system? There are the usual nostrums – tighter regulations, savage penalties for misbehaviour, a ban from financial markets for life. But I have to say I'm dubious. I think the system will collapse, but not through our agency.'[57] Alexander was certainly correct that, if the greed of the 1 per cent is not controlled, then the system will collapse. But just as the Elizabethan age did not end with men wearing larger and larger codpieces until they could no longer stand, so our current world may not come to an abrupt halt when – one day – a company realises that the severance pay it has promised a departing chief executive equals all of its turnover, and it has to close, triggering a cascade of more closures until all the pay-outs are worthless.[58]

These two points of view, both offered by people towards the end of their lives, are widely varying in prescription. One says that salvation is already upon us – it is just that we have not yet noticed that getting rich quick has lost its lustre. The other says that the end is nigh because of greed, and all will not end peacefully. Both agree that in the UK and US we cannot continue to allow the 1 per cent to take ever more, and drive inequality up ever higher (see Figure 6.6). Both predictions agree that it will end. The only question is how.

The Price of Inequality

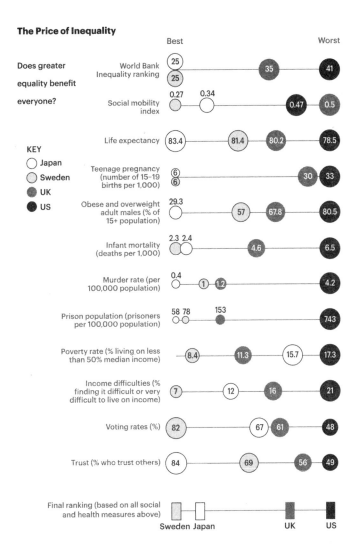

Source: Equality Trust, 2012

Figure 6.6 The price of inequality, four countries, 2012

Afterword

In 2009, Clive James made a prediction for the coming year. 'Getting rich quick for its own sake', he wrote, 'will look as stupid as bodybuilding does at that point when the neck gets thicker than the head.'[1] Already, the modern obsession with excess wealth 'was gone like the codpiece'. In various of his musings, James had noted that the codpiece did not suddenly go out of fashion. It took time. A small group of men were still strutting around with clothing designed to imply each was endowed with an enormous 'manhood' long after most of the Tudor aristocracy had become embarrassed by such stupidity. In the same manner, greed tends to reach an apex and then decline. Worldwide greed rose with renewed vigour during our lifetimes, especially in the most unequal countries of the rich world, including the UK.

A couple of days after the 2015 UK general election James received a special award from the British Academy of Film and Television Arts; a year earlier he had been awarded their president's medal. The smooth-tongued prophet of our times has been showered with awards, but it is unlikely he will live to see his prediction come true: the end of fashionable greed. It is still uncertain whether the tide will turn after the 2015 election, or whether future generations will face an even more rapacious society. None of us know what is about to unfold.

The Conservatives won by a narrow majority in May 2015. The result shocked a London-based commentariat. This was hardly surprising as the capital swung to Labour and London remains where life's winners congregate, a place from which losers must be expelled. It was life's losers who did not turn out to vote for the main alternative on offer, a watered-down version of Conservative austerity being sold to them by Ed Miliband. We were then told the Labour Party did not appeal enough to those who were aspirational and wanted more, including people who wanted more irrespective of who would end up with less. But perhaps fear and fantasy greatly played their part, too. An eighth of the English electorate voted for the UK Independence Party (UKIP).

In Scotland greed really did go the way of the codpiece. All but three of the constituencies fell to the Scottish National Party. No longer a nationalist party, the SNP had become a national party. It now represented as wide a cross-section of society as it is possible to imagine. The former Royal Bank of Scotland oil economist Alex Salmond became an MP alongside young students and aged socialists. So fifty-six SNP MPs set off to London to take their seats and spread their message. Not since 1918, when Sinn Féin took seventy-three seats in Ireland, has a third party performed so well in the United Kingdom. Change is underway, but many of the English elite remain so blindly arrogant they cannot see what's coming. To them the Scots are no better than restless children.

As the impact of the May 2015 election became felt throughout England, new voices were heard and grew louder. They said the Labour Party had stumbled not by choosing the wrong leader or electoral strategy, but because it had forgotten how to cooperate and be kind. Labour did not ally itself with the Greens or the SNP, and there was little unity among its own members in the Shadow Cabinet. Instead, Labour saw the election as a two-horse race where being the sole winner was all important.

One now-hardened commentator, Zoe Williams, explained: 'The problem is so much deeper than who the leader is; and so much more exhilarating.'[2] Labour had not been offering change, just a diluted version of what had gone before. What for some was exhilarating in the days and weeks after 7 May was the opening up of new possibilities and radical alternatives. There were few signs of optimism among the population at large, but for some there were at least glimmerings of hope. Other commentators, such as Bill Gidding, pointed out that in England the votes for radical alternatives rose, and there was no swing from Labour to Conservatives between 2010 and 2015.[3]

The May election crystallised the thinking of many who in one way or another oppose the power of the 1 per cent. Rebecca Winson, a writer and an activist for GMB Young London, wrote on the day after the election: 'Labour, Green, Tusc [Trade Union and Socialist Coalition] and even Lib Dem progressives must work together to oppose what's going to happen. We're all on the same side now.'[4] She ended her piece by saying:

> If you can, be kind to those you argue with, because compassion changes more minds than anger, even though it's harder to muster. Be kind to the poor, the disabled, the immigrants, the workers and to anyone who's a bit different. The government won't be, you see.

Concern about the implications of rising inequality is growing among the well-to-do, who occasionally deign to look down from the hill from over their high garden walls and worry that neither hill nor walls are high enough. Today, the London Riots of 2011 are often referred to when you speak to the rich about inequality. Clearly, for many of the elite, poverty and inequality would only be of minor concern were it not for the fear of insurrection. As the poor are pushed out of London, the elite feel safer, but all the time more people are living on the breadline, especially in London where rents are skyrocketing. Forecasts published the week after the election suggested that London house prices could double to average £1 million a property by 2030, and surveys were released showing that the richest fifth in Britain held on average 105 times the wealth of the poorest fifth.[5]

It is not just in the UK and in the capital that a fear of the impoverished is growing. This is now an international concern. The Canadian Liberal Party leader, Justin Trudeau, issued a dire warning to Canadians as to what may lie ahead if the gap between rich and poor doesn't narrow:

> In short, fairness for the middle class and those working hard to join it is good for all of us. It's good for Canada, and, I might say, if we don't deliver fairness, Canadians will eventually entertain more radical options. All of the time I've spent with Canadians tells me that the status quo is not sustainable. Change is coming, my friends. What we need is leadership and a plan to shape that change responsibly, for the benefit of all.[6]

'My friends', Justin said, underscoring the fact he was addressing people like himself, a well-heeled gathering at the Canadian Club. He was inviting his audience to talk about people like 'them', those who might be driven to undefined radical options out of desperation. But is this kind of talk too late? Isn't it high time the men and women outside the gates of the wealthy pursued those more radical options?

The day before the election, it was revealed that the Coalition government's Department of Work and Pensions (DWP) had conducted forty-nine reviews of benefit-related deaths. Many of those deaths had been recorded as suicides, but some could have been deaths from starvation. We have no way of knowing, as the DWP refused to release the information, leading to an investigation from the government's own information watchdog.[7]

Those forty-nine are a tiny sample of all the deaths thought to be connected to benefit cuts made since the coalition government took power in 2010. Between 2010 and 2013 many thousands of working-age people died in the days and weeks after they had their benefits withdrawn.[8] In 2013/14 the ledger of deaths grew longer.[9] The records do not even include the elderly who died earlier than they otherwise would.[10] A twenty-four-minute silent movie lists some of the younger victims. I stopped watching it nine minutes in. At that point you learn of Christelle, thirty-two, who was pregnant and died clutching her five-month-old son, Kayjah. I could not watch it anymore. She jumped from a third-floor balcony after her benefits had been stopped. We do not know if Christelle and Kayjah's are two of the forty-nine cases that have been reviewed in secret.

The coalition government was not kind, and the new government will be even less so now the Conservatives are working alone. Not everyone was callous in the Coalition, but most of those with any sympathetic feeling left of their own accord if they weren't pushed. In late summer 2013, by chance I met Lib Dem MP Sarah Teather, then the education minister. She was walking alone and in tears. A few days later I heard she had been sacked from the cabinet as part of a broad government reshuffle. Nick Clegg said he was 'disappointed' by Ms Teather's subsequent decision to stand down as an MP in 2015. Sir Menzies Campbell, the Liberal Democrats' former leader, said, 'Coalition is not for the fainthearted.'[11]

In November 2012 Sarah Teather had voted against the coalition for the first time, having called the Benefit Cap 'immoral and divisive'. Between April 2013 and February 2015 as many as 59,000 households had their housing benefit capped, 45 per cent of these lived in London, where rents are so much higher.[12] Almost all those households will have included children. At any one time, over twenty thousand households were being capped, but when you get evicted for rent arrears you come off the list. Her government were not kind, but Sarah was – so she had to go because she couldn't take part in the heartlessness any longer.

In 2012, 1,046,398 sanctions were applied to people claiming jobseeker's allowance. The minuscule weekly income of the very poorest people in Britain was being docked, almost always for a petty misdemeanour. These offences included not attending a meeting in a jobseeker office because the claimant was attending an interview for an actual job elsewhere. A further 32,128 people scraping by on the employment and support allowance, because they were not working due to illness or disability, had their benefits cut for some similar infringement. On top of this a further 44,000 lone parents receiving income support, because they had little or no other income, were sanctioned for indeterminate stretches of time during that year and lost income they needed to prevent them and their children from going hungry. Lives are being destroyed, people shamed, and moral crimes verging on atrocities being committed. Many thousands of elderly women have died prematurely, many times the number Harold Shipman killed and each of them suffering a more painful fate than his lethal injections.

We have no record of how many children were harmed by the 1.1 million financial sanctions applied in just one year to Britain's poorest families. Every single one of these families was already living on less than the Minimum Income Standard for the UK. We know that because benefit levels in Britain remain pegged far below the level deemed minimal to provide an acceptable standard of living by the British public, and those benefits drop further every year.[13] What we do know about the scale of mass sanctions is a result of the tireless research carried out by David Webster of the University of Glasgow, who stated:

Decisions on guilt are made in secret by officials who have no independent responsibility to act lawfully. Yet the 'transgressions' (DWP's own word), which are punished by this system, are almost exclusively very minor matters, such as missing a single interview with a Jobcentre or Work Programme contractor, or not making quite as many token job applications as the Jobcentre adviser demands.[14]

Webster noted that, in the same year that 1.1 million sanctions were applied, Great Britain's magistrates' and sheriff courts of Great Britain imposed a total of only 849,000 fines. Not only that, but the scale of penalties handed out by courts is less punitive than the sanctions visited on benefits claimants. The failure to make the correct number of token job applications in a week leads to a harsher punishment than shoplifting does. What better incentive could there be to encourage shoplifting, especially now that even taking out-of-date food from supermarket waste-bins counts as theft?[15] No wonder Sarah Teather was in tears by the end of the summer of 2013. She knew what was happening and could no longer stomach it, could no longer condone the sadism, unlike so many of her Liberal and almost all of her Conservative colleagues.

Some people are rarely kind. What made them cruel or keeps them that way is often a mystery, but they are a minority. Being kind is not an attribute usually associated with acquiring riches or getting ahead in right-wing politics. And it is easy to make cuts if you don't sympathise. It is easier if you think of others as less deserving than you, or otherwise different, or not worthy of respect for any of a wide variety of ill-conceived reasons.

It's easy to make cuts if you don't sympathise and it is easier not to sympathise if you are protected from the cuts and they don't immediately affect you. The income of the 1 per cent has been protected while incomes and benefits for the poorest have been slashed and sanctioned. At the same time there have been huge cuts to local authority budgets (with more to come) and subsequently massive cuts in services for the most vulnerable – to social care, youth services, mental health services –

developments which leave the 1 per cent, and indeed many others, largely unaffected. Wealthier members of society can afford to go private when it comes to health care or education.

If we look at the demographics of the people most affected by the cuts, what we see is very telling. Since 2010 some 79 per cent of all cuts have hit the income of women. In part, this is because most parents raising a child alone are women, but austerity has also taken a heavy toll on public services used by women, and a disproportionate number of women who were working in public services have lost their jobs or been made to go part-time.

In 2012 an estimated 3.5 million children were living in poverty.[16] In 2013 the Fawcett Society estimated that a total of £14.9 billion had been cut from benefits, tax credits, pay and pensions, with 74 per cent of this being taken from women's incomes. By 2014 they found that the inequality gap between women and men was actually rising.[17] Data from 2014 shows that two-thirds of all the welfare cuts in Scotland came from families with children. Lone parents have lost £1,800 a year, £400 more than families with two parents and more resources. But the cuts have been even deeper for the disabled, who have, on average, £2,000 less to live on.[18]

Because the UK government hid and delayed the publication of the statistics, academic researchers in England have been forced to use data passed to the European Statistical Office. That data shows that George Osborne misled parliament in March 2015 when he said people were better off than they had been in 2010. Data collected across the whole of the UK actually revealed that living standards had fallen for all but the very richest. Increasing numbers of people have reported falling behind with their rent or struggling just to pay fuel bills. Almost half the population cannot now afford to repair or replace their fridge or cooker immediately should one or the other break down. 'Only the very richest (those who could make ends meet very easily) saw no perceived fall in their living standards.'[19]

In the UK, the lives of the 1 per cent have followed a very different trajectory to those of the rest of the population. Those who get by 'very easily' have not seen a drop in their incomes. But that does not mean they feel any better off. Inequality within the 1 per cent is growing rapidly. At the very top of the 1 per cent, the richest 1,000 families have seen their wealth double since 2005, with each family worth an average of £547 million by 2015. Yet even that is a fairly meaningless average because there is more inequality within the 1,000 richest families in the UK than there is in the rest of the 1 per cent.[20]

At the top of British society it is easy to feel envious. For example, a young man on an annual income of £160,000, without children, who just scrapes into the 1 per cent category, knows that, in his probably modest but very central London apartment, he is a world away from those living in the largest mansions to be found, as the crow flies, a few minutes away. He is unlikely ever to comfortably keep up with those he sees as his peers. It is a world in which you can never have enough money or enough of the things it can buy.

Living in a society that tolerates gross wealth and income inequalities makes it hard to empathise with a wide range of other people. The very rich may ignore you in the same way you sometimes don't notice the person sweeping the street as you walk by. Or the very rich try not to notice you – just as you might have learnt to try not to notice the people sleeping rough in the entrance to the Tube or bus station. You are as far down, and your life as frightening to the very rich, as the destitute are to you.

It becomes almost impossible to get through the day at the top of British society if you look down. The vertigo is too hard to bear. What difference can it make to someone so far beneath you if they have to live on a few less pounds a day? Surely they just need to budget better. When you cannot empathise with another group, it is very hard to think kindly towards them. It is when you feel "we're all in it together" or at least "there but for the grace of God, go I" that kindness comes naturally.

The UK is on a trajectory to become the most unequal of the richest twenty-five nations in the world.[21] Those in power in the most unequal of rich countries today, especially the UK, cannot imagine that kindness works. They see kindness as weakness. Had they been kinder, less aggressive, when they were younger and making their way in the world, they would probably not have got to where they are today.

Kindness is a trait to be shunned and derided by those currently in power. Violence, action, force and what they call 'civility' is what is needed.[22] Kindness does not help the poor, they say, and instead they offer the 'tough love' of sanctions. And if the poor die early, well they were weak and this is survival of the fittest at play. When the elite now in charge hear of a young mother, denied benefits, jumping from a balcony holding her child, some do not shudder. They think this is 'collateral damage' in their 'war on poverty'. Such thinking began with the deaths we inflicted on civilians living abroad in wars for resources in the Middle East. Casualties become seen as inevitable.

The rich are like you and me, the same flesh and bone, the same fundamental mortality; it is just that the rich do not think like us. That is why you are shocked by what they do when they hold power. 'How can they do this?' you ask. 'Can't they see?' The answers are first, 'Easily', and second, 'No.' They are working for what they believe to be a greater good – and you are unfortunate flotsam and jetsam that happen to be in their way. Just as the roofless and the beggars and the poor are 'unfortunate', so too are you. It is just unfortunate you are not rich enough to pay your university's fees and have to take out a loan; unfortunate you don't have a trust fund or at least an inheritance to look forward to. They are simply lucky to be 'privileged', or so they are taught to think. With gross inequality comes segregation and a consequent lack of knowledge about how the other person lives.

There was a time when hardly anyone was roofless in the UK, when you never met a beggar and those with least

were not that different from those in the middle – they had
enough to feel included in society. I was young then. As I age
it becomes harder to remember when I first saw teenagers
sleeping rough, or was first asked for 'the price of a cup of
tea', or first realized that because I could make some choices
whereas others couldn't, that they were no longer free. But I
grew up in a country without many youngsters bedding down
in sleeping bags, without people jumping from third-floor
balconies clutching their children because their dole had been
cut, without people choosing to die to avoid having to beg and
feeling that they have no other choice.

Luckily, you don't have to rely on the memories of the old
to know that a more equal world is possible, a world where
the 1 per cent take a far smaller share of the cake. The 1 per
cent by definition will always be those taking the largest slice,
but it needn't be such a great fat slice if it leaves only slithers
for the rest. Question those who say that it can only be this
way. Try to question them kindly rather than with incredulity.
A society based on merit would be remarkably equitable compared with what we face today. No one is worth 3,000 times
someone else. But someone who only just qualifies to be in the
1 per cent according to income and who saves carefully will,
even after several years, still be worth 3,000 times less than an
average member of the *Sunday Times* 'rich list'. The 3,000-fold
inequalities within the 1 per cent are just as indefensible as
those between them and the other 99 per cent.

A slow revolution means you are in it for the long haul.
But it will be worth it when finally we begin to create a more
equal country for all. It will be worth it because we will know
that although no one can predict the future, the next generation and those that follow them will not have to grow up in a
world of ignorant untruths, among them the notion that only
a few people are truly able and the rest are commodities and
worth very little on the job market. Do we pay them a living
wage or a minimum wage, we muse? These are differences in
sums of money tiny to many of us.

It will be worth it if we turn the tide because, even if we do not care that much, in our old age, people who have the time and peace of mind will care for us, not least because we cared for them when they were younger. It will be worth it because we will know that it could have been much worse had we stood by and done nothing unselfish. No one who is sane dies thinking that if they had just tried a little harder they could have made another million. But they do die lamenting a world they are leaving becoming more cruel, greedy and callous. And they do worry about the generations to come.

Gross inequality creates a lack of respect for anyone who is not like us. There is contempt among the rich for the poor, and that will seed the same among the poor for the rich. Cruelty and hate flourish. This pervasive lack of respect is not new and has grown between groups many times before, over religion, race, nationality, social class, sex and sexuality. These older divisions remain and can easily tear us apart. However, nowadays it is financial inequality, both globally and in the UK, that is the greatest source of division.

What is needed is understanding and generosity, hope and perseverance, but above all kindness. Kindness is patient, it does not envy, it does not boast, it is not proud, it is not self-seeking.[23] Every kind action is worthwhile. The greedy waste the lives of others but they also waste their own lives through their greed. They are not worthy of envy.

May 2015

Acknowledgements

Many people helped to inspire and fill this book with their comments and ideas. Some are referenced in the endnotes, but particular thanks are due to Derek Heptinstall, a retired journalist who I have never met (other than on email) and who very kindly read through an early draft, and to Steve Nicholson, a citizen of Oxford and retired from many jobs, who kindly read through a much later draft. Simon Reid-Henry of Queen Mary, University of London, also commented early on, and helped me avoid some pitfalls. Tina Fawcett of the Environmental Change Unit at the University of Oxford helped greatly with references on the consumption patterns of the rich, and Patrick Ainley of the University of Greenwich helped with advice about their culture. Dimitris Ballas of the University of Sheffield and Ben Hennig of Oxford University commented on the structure and evidence. Avner Offer and Stuart Basten at Oxford gave me good advice at a crucial stage, and Stuart in particular encouraged me to visit the pub to prevent me from trying to write it all at once. Bronwen Dorling and David Dorling helped iron out some errors, and made very useful suggestions, as did Leo Hollis, my editor at Verso, who restructured the text, moved what I had put at the end to the start – to save you the suspense – and did much 'cutting of the crap' with his red pen. I am very grateful for that – but you should be more grateful still! Leo altered both the structure of the book, and the precise detail of the social structure of its object of study. Charles Peyton diligently copy-edited the text and Mark Martin at Verso went through with many further suggestions to tighten it up and further clarify. Andy Pressman advised on the graphics and Ailsa Allen at the University of Oxford very kindly drew and redrew them all.

During 2013 and 2014 I was fortunate to be invited to present some of the ideas that later developed into this book as part of a series of talks, and I am grateful for the comments I received from both strangers and colleagues at those events, which included the New Economics Foundation; the Sheila McKechnie Foundation; the Institute of Child Health; University College London; the Centre for Census and Survey Research; the Institute for Social Change in Manchester; the Radical Statistics Group; the Manchester and Leeds Salons; the Bristol Festival of Ideas; the York Festival of Ideas; the Royal Statistical Society; the Department of Sociology of the Lisbon University Institute; the Centre for Crime and Justice Studies; the Royal Irish Academy; the Centre for Social Relations at the University of Coventry; the London Radical Book Fair; Friends of *Le Monde Diplomatique*; the Centre for Labour and Social Studies; Birkbeck University's June 2013 symposium, 'Surplus, Wealth, Waste, Excess'. I am also grateful for comments arising from talks on inequality given at Kings College London; the Houses of Parliament; One Sheffield Many Cultures; the Edinburgh Book Festival; the Hay Festival; the TUC Congress; the Annual Conference of the Howard Reform League; the Royal Geographical Society; the London Battle of Ideas; the ESRC Festival of Science; Oxford University's Department of Education; the Equality Trust Annual Supporters and Local Groups meeting, during the Barts and the London School of Medicine and Dentistry Global Health week; the Regional Studies Association 'Global Urbanisation: Challenges and Prospects' conference, at Newman University (Birmingham); Nuffield College, Oxford; the World Economic Group Meeting on the World Economic and Social Survey (United Nations); the Institute of Applied Social Studies, University of Birmingham; the Oxford Civic Society; the Centre for Social Relations, University of Coventry; the National Institute for Economic and Social research (London); and during the International Symposium on Homelessness, Health and Inclusion, held in London in March 2014. Travelling and talking, rather than lecturing, is a good way to learn.

Ant Harwood, my agent, helped me think more carefully about doing a short book on inequality and the 1 per cent just as I was arriving at the University of Oxford, which gave me the opportunity to observe some things about the 1 per cent a little more closely. I am very grateful to him and to my new colleagues at Oxford for their patience and forbearance. I am especially grateful for a very kind and friendly welcome at St Peter's College and to find so many people there interested in privilege and injustice. In particular I would like to thank the alumni of the School of Geography and the Environment, who came to my 2014 inaugural lecture on 'Geography, Inequality and Oxford', and the many who so helpfully commented and corresponded with me afterwards – especially about their personal experiences of having been an undergraduate, often many years ago. Finally, I should thank my family for the time they have given me to write this book when I should have been spending more of it with them. It might be time to slow down a little, having got my views on that most contentious of issues – 'inequality and the 1 per cent' – off my chest and on the record.

Thanks to Nic Brimblecombe, Florence Rose Burton, David Dorling, Vicky Duckworth, Leo Hollis, Mark Martin and Khadija Rouf for commenting on and editing the afterword.

Danny Dorling, Marston, Oxford, 2015

Notes

1. Can We Afford the Superrich?

1. B. Wilkins, 'Nobel Prize Winner Shiller: Inequality Biggest Problem Facing US', *Digital Journal*, 15 October 2013, at digitaljournal.com.
2. G. Sargent, 'There's Been Class Warfare for the Last 20 Years, and My Class Has Won', *Washington Post*, 30 September 2011.
3. R. Morin, 'Rising Share of Americans See Conflict Between Rich and Poor', Pew Research and Social Trends, 11 January 2012, at pewsocialtrends.org.
4. J. Cribb, A. Hood, R. Joyce and D. Phillips, 'Living Standards, Poverty and Inequality in the UK: 2013', Institute for Fiscal Studies Report R81 (2013), pp. 30, 45, at ifs.org.uk (receiving £160,000 a year before tax is roughly the same as about £115,000 a year from all income sources after having paid income taxes, or £9,600 a month take-home income).
5. A. Park, C. Bryson, E. Clery, J. Curtice and M. Phillips, eds, 'British Social Attitudes: The 30th Report', London: National Centre for Social Research, 2013, at bsa-30.natcen.ac.uk.
6. '[M]ost people perceive the distribution of wealth in the UK to be far more equal than it actually is.' Inequality Briefing, 'Inequality: How Wealth is Distributed in the UK – animated video', *Guardian*, Comment is Free, 8 October 2013, at theguardian.com. In the US the equivalent is Think Progress,

'Wealth Inequality Video Highlighting Difference Between Perception And Reality Goes Viral', *Huffington Post*, 3 April 2013, at huffingtonpost.com.

7. I. Ortiz, S. Burke, M. Berrada and H. Cortés, 'World Protests 2006–2013', Working Paper, New York: Initiative for Policy Dialogue and Friedrich-Ebert-Stiftung, September 2013, at policydialogue.org.

8. D. Dorling, 'Fairness and the Changing Fortunes of People in Britain', *Journal of the Royal Statistical Society* A, 176: 1 (2013), at dannydorling.org.

9. Cribb et al., 'Living Standards', p. 40. See also, in the same source, Figure 3.3, which states: 'Percentiles 1–4 and 99 are excluded because of large statistical uncertainty.'

10. The difference between the tenth-percentile and ninetieth-percentile individual was only 0.7 per cent. See IFS, 'Green Budget: Summary', London: Institute for Fiscal Studies, 2014, pp. 4–5, at ifs.org.uk.

11. Which?, 'State Pension Explained', 2014, at which.co.uk.

12. Others suggest the Palma ratio of the income share of the top 10 per cent divided by that of the bottom 40 per cent, which tends to vary around 1. While better than the Gini measure, it is still not as simple as the 1 per cent measure, and may well not correlate as well with social problems. On the Palma ratio, see A. Cobham, 'Palma vs Gini: Measuring Post-2015 Inequality', Centre for Global Development Blog, 5 March 2014, at cgdev.org.

13. D. Runciman, '*The Democracy Project: A History, a Crisis, a Movement*, by David Graeber – review', *Guardian*, 31 March 2013.

14. When the very well-paid, now publicly owned, financial institutions such as Royal Bank of Scotland are excluded. See ONS, 'Labour Market Statistics', 16 October 2013, at ons.gov.uk.

15. We know it is roughly fifteen times as much, because that figure is given by the World Top Incomes Database – the most respected source in the world. This average income of the 1 per cent is calculated by multiplying the mean average income in the UK by the proportion of national income received by the 1 per cent in the UK, reported by the World Top Incomes Database to be 15 times average incomes in 2007. Thus, as £24,596 times 15 is £368,940, that is mean 1 per cent income. See topincomes. g-mond.parisschoolofeconomics.eu.

16. E. Fahmy, D. Dorling, J. Rigby, B. Wheeler, D. Ballas, D. Gordon and R. Lupton, 'Poverty, Wealth and Place in Britain, 1968–2005', *Radical Statistics* 97 (2008), pp. 11–30, at dannydorling.org.

17. In April 2013, according to the MIS, a single working-age adult needed a budget of £200 per week; a pensioner couple needed £240; a couple with two children need £470; and a lone parent with one child needed £285. See jrf.org.uk.

18. ONS, 'The Effects of Taxes and Benefits on Household Income, 2011/12', London: Office for National Statistics, 10 July 2013, at ons.gov.uk.

19. Open University, 'Teaching Salary – What You Can Expect to Earn', Open University website, November 2013, at qualificationstobeateacher.co.uk.

20. Technical Steering Committee, 'GP Earnings and Expenses 2011/12', Health and Social Care Information Centre, 25 September 2013, at hscic.gov.uk.

21. J. Kaffash, 'Revealed: One in Five GPs on CCG Boards has Financial Interest in a Current Provider', *Pulse*, 4 January 2014, at pulsetoday.co.uk.

22. Because those few top-earning GPs do fewer surgeries, there is about a one-in-fifty chance that you will meet one if you are ill (personal communication, David Dorling, January 2014).

23. A rate of 1:1.64. See E. Currid-Halkett, 'The 21st Century Silver Spoon', *New York Times*, 9 November 2013, at opinionator.blogs.nytimes.com.

24. It is probable that the existence of the extremely unequal societies, such as the UK and USA, puts a brake on the most equal becoming more equitable. A general trend to more equality would not be limited to the most unequal of countries, but might require a widespread cultural change in fundamental beliefs.

25. The dataset can be found at topincomes.g-mond.parisschoolofeconomics.eu.

26. N. Pearce, 'Thomas Piketty: A Modern French Revolutionary', *New Statesman*, 3 April 2014.

27. D. Hirsh, 'A Minimum Income Standard for the UK in 2013', Joseph Rowntree Foundation, 2013, at jrf.org.uk.

28. In the UK, '[p]oorer children have worse cognitive, social-behavioural and health outcomes in part because they are poor, and not just because poverty is correlated with other household and parental characteristics, such as levels of education or

attitudes to parenting'. K. Cooper and K. Stewart, 'Does Money Affect Children's Outcomes?', Joseph Rowntree Foundation Report, 22 October 2013, at jrf.org.uk.

29. A. Walker, D. Gordon and R. Levitas, *The Peter Townsend Reader* (Bristol: Policy Press, 2010).

30. A. Sedghi and J. Burn-Murdoch, 'UK Wage Gap Widens. Get Data for the Past 25 Years', *Guardian*, 9 November 2012.

31. In the UK, 'rising bonuses paid to bankers alone accounted for around two-thirds of the increase in the national wage bill ('earnings pie') taken by the top one percent of workers since 1999.' B. Bell and J. Van Reenen, 'Bankers and Their Bonuses', Centre for Economic Performance Occasional Paper 35 (2013), London School of Economics, at cep.lse.ac.uk.

32. P. Crush, 'HSBC Circumvents EU Bankers' Bonus Cap', Chartered Institute of Professional Development, 25 February 2014, at cipd.co.uk.

33. As revealed by Canadian data, a proxy for the US/UK. S. Breau, 'The Occupy Movement and the Top 1 Per Cent in Canada', *Antipode*, 27 August 2013, at onlinelibrary.wiley.com.

34. Official website of the British Monarchy, at royal.gov.uk.

35. G. Smith, 'The "Value for Money Monarchy" Myth', Republic Campaign, 2013, at republic.org.uk.

36. Imagine the boost to tourism from having over a thousand royal families! There would be some 10,000 royal places to visit and jobs for hundreds of thousands of servants. Over the summer months, Buckingham Palace alone employs an extra 350 staff on zero-hours contracts to cope with the summer visitors, staff the palace shop, and monitor the state-rooms that tourists traipse through. See S. Neville, M. Taylor and P. Inman, 'Buckingham Palace Uses Zero-Hours Contracts for Summer Staff', *Guardian*, 30 July 2013.

37. J. Bingham and P. Dominiczak, 'Cutting Benefits Part of a "Moral Mission", Cameron Tells New Cardinal', *Telegraph*, 18 February 2014.

38. See Z. Bauman, *Does the Richness of the Few Benefit Us All?* (Cambridge: Polity, 2013), p. 10, for a very well-articulated opposing view that current trends do now appear to be a little like just such a machine.

39. Dorling, 'Fairness and the Changing Fortunes of People in Britain'.

40. For a short history of UK tax, see 'Income Tax' at politics.co.uk.

41. There are many sources. One that is easily edited but currently good is 'History of Taxation in the United Kingdom', at en.wikipedia.org.

42. W. Streeck, 'The Crises of Democratic Capitalism', *New Left Review* II/71 (September–October 2011).

43. D. Box, 'Bond Markets, Not Politicians, Control Our Future', *Ecologist*, 29 April 2010, at theecologist.org.

44. P. Roscoe, *I Spend Therefore I Am* (London: Penguin, 2014), p. 154.

45. Dorling, 'Fairness and the Changing Fortunes of People in Britain'.

46. F. Alvaredo, A. B. Atkinson, T. Piketty and E. Saez, 'The Top 1 Percent in International and Historical Perspective', *Journal of Economic Perspectives* 27: 3 (2013), pp. 3–20, at pubs. aeaweb.org. For the data, see topincomes.g-mond.parisschoolof economics.eu.

47. R. Ramesh, 'Coalition's Austerity Policies Are Hitting the Poor Hardest, Says Think-Tank', *Guardian*, 4 June 2013.

48. I. Denisova, 'Income Distribution and Poverty in Russia', OECD Social, Employment and Migration Working Papers, No. 132 (2012), OECD Publishing, at dx.doi.org.

49. B. Klimke, 'Oligarchs in London: super-rich Russians let the ruble roll' *Berliner Zeitung*, 25 March 2014.

50. BBC, 'Russian Tycoon Usmanov Tops *Sunday Times* Rich List', BBC News, 20 April 2013, at bbc.co.uk.

51. A. Reuben, 'Sunday Times Rich List: The Changing Face of Wealth', BBC News, 18 April 2013, at bbc.co.uk.

52. ONS, 'UK Worth £6.8 Trillion', news release, 16 August 2012, at ons.gov.uk.

53. ONS, 'The National Balance Sheet, 2013 Estimates', 15 August 2013, at ons.gov.uk.

54. A similar map of the US appeared here at revista-amauta.org. For the UK, the figures are from D. Dorling, 'Underclass, Overclass, Ruling Class, Supernova Class', in A. Walker, A. Sinfield and C. Walker, eds, *Fighting Poverty, Inequality and Injustice* (Bristol: Policy Press, 2011).

55. K. Garthwaite, 'The Language of Shirkers and Scroungers? Talking about Illness, Disability and Coalition Welfare Reform', *Disability and Society* 26: 3 (2011), at tandfonline.com.

56. One Society, 'How National Minimum Wage is Falling Behind Top Pay, and the Damage This Does to Living Standards and the Economy', Briefing, 1 October 2012, at onesociety.helencross. co.uk.

57. David Cameron's November 2006 Scarman lecture, quoted in: J. Strelitz and R. Lister, eds, 'Why Money Matters: Family Income, Poverty and Children's Lives', Save The Children, 2008, p. 2, at savethechildren.org.uk.

58. H. Yousuf, 'Obama Admits 95 Per Cent of Income Gains Gone to Top 1 Per Cent', CNN money, 15 September 2013, at money. cnn.com.

59. N. Davies, *Dark Heart: The Shocking Truth about Hidden Britain* (London: Vintage, 1998), p. 144.

60. M. Taylor, 'Margaret Thatcher's Estate Still a Family Secret', *Guardian*, 9 April 2013. Her neighbours on the square included Roman Abramovich and Nigella Lawson. The Finns have a saying: 'money is a little bit like snow. It tends to gather in heaps.'

2. Childhood

1. D. Reay, 'What Would a Socially Just Education System Look Like?', Centre for Labour and Social Studies, 2012, p. 12.

2. See OECD, 'Skills Outlook', Copenhagen OECD, 2013, Table A2.7, p. 265, at skills.oecd.org.

3. SFS, 'UK Private School Class Sizes "Smaller Than State Schools and OECD Average"' School Fees Trust, 14 September 2011, at sfs-group.co.uk.

4. M. Friedman, 'Public Schools: Make Them Private', *Washington Post*, 19 February 1995.

5. L. Macmillan and A. Vignoles, 'Mapping the Occupational Destinations of New Graduates', research report for the Social Mobility and Child Poverty Commission, October 2013, at gov. uk.

6. J. Henry, 'Comprehensive School Pupils Do Better at University, Two New Studies Confirm', *Observer*, 15 June 2013.

7. S. Berg, 'Five Schools "Send More to Oxbridge than 2,000 Others"', BBC News, 8 July 2011, at bbc.co.uk.

8. Sutton Trust, 'Degrees of Success: University Chances by Individual School', 2011.

9. R. Muir, 'England Should Follow Scotland on Access to University', *Independent*, 12 June 2013.

10. J. Grove, 'Poor Aren't Making Inroads into Elite Universities', *Times Higher Education*, 13 February 2014.

11. S. Collini, 'This Literacy Report Is Not a Story of England's National Decline', *Guardian*, 8 October 2013.

12. S. Vine, 'Sarah Vine: Why I Want My Daughter to Go to a State School', *Guardian*, 7 March 2014.

13. S. Collini, 'Sold Out', *London Review of Books*, 24 October 2013.

14. A. McGettigan, 'Who Let the Dogs Out? The Privatization of Higher Education', *Radical Philosophy* 174 (July/August 2012), p.24.

15. G. Paton, 'Number of Pupils in Private Schools Drops amid Rising Fees', *Telegraph*, 25 April 2013.

16. Joy Schaverien, quoted in S. Partridge, 'Boarding School Syndrome: Disguised Attachment-Deficit and Dissociation Reinforced by Institutional Neglect and Abuse', *Journal of Attachment: New Directions in Psychotherapy and Relational Psychoanalysis* 7: 2 (2013), pp. 202–13.

17. J. Harris, 'Grammar Schools Do Not Aid Social Mobility. Stop This Deluded Thinking', *Guardian*, 11 November 2013.

18. R. Garner, 'Academies "Increase Divisions Between the Rich and Poor": Study Finds Segregation Made Worse by a Wider Choice of Schooling', *Independent*, 4 September 2013.

19. E. Dugan, 'Only One in 10 Britons Has Best Friend of Different Race Survey Reveals Extent of Social Segregation in UK – along Both Ethnic and Class Boundaries', *Independent*, 7 August 2013.

20. 'Society in the UK continues to reproduce itself in terms of life chances. Social mobility may happen in small pockets … but failure is deeply embedded in other communities.' M. Collins, M. Collins and G. Butt, 'Social Mobility or Social Reproduction? A Case Study of the Attainment Patterns of Students According to Their Social Background and Ethnicity', *Educational Review*, at tandfonline.com.

21. Reay, 'What Would a Socially Just Education System Look Like?', p. 10.

22. T. Slater, 'The Myth of "Broken Britain": Welfare Reform and the Production of Ignorance', *Antipode*, 18 December 2012.

23. Quote originally seen on this poster http://owsposters.tumblr. com/page/4.

24. E. Allen, 'Is Your Tooth Fairy Fair? Children Get £5 Under Their Pillow in London ... But Only 5p in Hull', *Daily Mail*, 9 November 2011.

25. Halifax, 'Parents Loosen Purse Strings as Pocket Money Increases', press release, 24 August 2013, at lloydsbanking-group.com.

26. Only 2 per cent of children fit into this category in the most exclusive of state schools. Free school meals taken up at any time in the last six years is the measure used to allocate the pupil premium, so is becoming a widely available statistic. On the 2005 figure, see Sutton Trust, 'Rates of Eligibility for Free School Meals at the Top State Schools', 2005.

27. Halifax, '8–15 Year Olds Receiving Most Money since 2007', report, 15 August 2013, at lloydsbankinggroup.com.

28. Staff Reporter, 'Girls Left Out of Pocket Money while Boys Earn More for Chores', *Independent*, 6 August 2013.

29. D. Cummings, 'Some Thoughts on Education and Political Priorities', self-published thesis of Dominic Cummings, at s3.documentcloud.org. Footnote 193 draws in turn on J. Wai, 'Investigating America's Elite: Cognitive Ability, Education, and Sex Differences', *Intelligence* 41: 4 (July–August 2013), pp. 203–11, at sciencedirect.com.

30. The three-times figure (in fact nearer 3.6) is 25 per cent divided by 7 per cent from Reay, 'What Would a Socially Just Education System Look Like?'.

31. Press Association, 'Drop in Number of Pupils Staying in School After 16', *Guardian*, 28 June 2012.

32. H. Williamson, 'NEET Acronym Is Far from a Neat Description', *Times Educational Supplement*, 5 March 2010.

33. P. Scott, 'Universities Are Becoming Finishing Schools for Gilded Youth', *Guardian*, 2 July 2012.

34. S. Higgins, M. Katsipataki, D. Kokotsaki, R. Coleman, L. E. Major and R. Coe, 'The Sutton Trust–Education Endowment Foundation Teaching and Learning Toolkit', Education Endowment Foundation, 2014, at educationendowmentfoundation. org.uk.

35. G. Paton, 'Universities "Forced to Lower Entry Grades to Fill Places"', *Telegraph*, 28 April 2013.

36. Z. Williams, 'What's the Point of Social Mobility? It Still Leaves Some in the Gutter', *Guardian*, 23 May 2012.

37. A. Milburn, 'Fair Access to Professional Careers: A Progress Report by the Independent Reviewer on Social Mobility and Child Poverty', Cabinet Office, UK, 2012, at cabinetoffice.gov.uk.

38. As above, 'top twenty' as defined by the employers who target the graduates of this group the most. And most of these firms do not even recruit from all of the 'top twenty' universities, which are Aston, Bath, Birmingham, Bristol, Cambridge, Cardiff, Durham, Edinburgh, Exeter, Leeds, Liverpool, London, Loughborough, Manchester, Newcastle, Nottingham, Oxford, Sheffield, Southampton and Warwick.

39. High Fliers Research, 'The Graduate Market in 2012: Annual Review of Graduate Vacancies and Starting Salaries at Britain's Leading Employers', High Fliers Research Limited, 2012, p. 8, at highfliers.co.uk.

40. N. Pearce, 'What Should Social Democrats Believe?' *Juncture*, 19 September 2013, at ippr.org.

41. G. Whitham, 'Child Poverty in 2012: It Shouldn't Happen Here', Save the Children, 2012, p. 2.

42. B. Benjamin and B. Pourcain, 'Childhood Intelligence Is Heritable, Highly Polygenic and Associated with FNBP1L', *Molecular Psychiatry* 19 (February 2014 (note that the paper is very badly titled, given the whole genome association study being reported which is then not highly heritable because the association is so polygenic – personal communication George Davey Smith, one of the many authors).

43. Pearce, 'What Should Social Democrats Believe?'. If you are wondering what an abstract metric of material equality is, it could be the 1 per cent! It is material (about money), it is a metric (a measure), it is abstract – you can't see the 1 per cent all sitting together in Wembley Stadium. They would never all agree to attend the same event. The 1 per cent are a group you have to imagine. That does not mean they do not exist, or alter the fact that the effect of having such a separated sector of society is not only palpable but distorts how we all think.

44. One would appear to be Mr Gove: 'England's Secretary of State for Education Michael Gove to Address 6th Annual National Summit on Education Reform', Tallahassee, Florida, Marquee Education Event, atexcelined.org.

45. Mr Gove was speaking at The 'Foundation for Excellence in Education', the background of which can be found at excelined. org. That Foundation is supported by some of America's richest families (Gates, Walton, Bloomberg). A list of donors can also be found at excelined.org.

46. Often they confound gene-given and god-given potential. Press Association, 'Church Could Take Control of Secular Schools under New Deal, Report Says', *Huffington Post*, 4 July 2013, at huffingtonpost.co.uk.

47. Although it is speculated that he attended Durham School, a private all-boys school that only started taking girls from 1985. See 'List of Old Dunelmians', at en.wikipedia.org.

48. J. Merrick, 'Michael Gove Held Talks with "IQ Genes" Professor', *Independent*, 13 October 2013, at independent.co.uk.

49. Benyamin et al., 'Childhood Intelligence is Heritable'.

50. C. M. A. Haworth, K. Asbury, P. S. Dales and R. Plomin 'Added Value Measures in Education Show Genetic as Well as Environmental Influence', *PLoS One* 6: 2 (2011). As of October 2013, this paper had only been cited by two other studies, both of which had Plomin as their last listed author.

51. G. Paton, 'GCSE Results "Influenced by Children's Genes, Not Teaching"', *Telegraph*, 25 July 2013.

52. M. Wakefield, 'Revealed: How Exam Results Owe More to Genes than Teaching, *Spectator*, 27 July 2013.

53. The Faculty of Education at the University of Cambridge hosts a large website providing material for anyone interested – learningwithoutlimits.educ.cam.ac.uk – from which the quote is taken.

54. A. Asthana, T. Helm and T. McVeigh, 'Black Pupils "Are Routinely Marked Down by Teachers"', *Guardian*, 4 April 2010.

55. C. Witchalls, 'James R. Flynn: Are We Really Getting Smarter Every Year?', *Independent*, 27 September 2012.

56. S. Loughan, P. Kuppens, et al., 'Economic Inequality Is Linked to Biased Self-Perception', *Psychological Science* 22: 10 (2011), at psychologicalscience.org.

57. B. Johnson, 'The Annual Margaret Thatcher Lecture', London, 27 November 2013, at cps.org.uk. An astute reply to Boris would be that 2 per cent of the population have IQs of under seventy, and many of them have known medical problems which would warrant their being given special consideration. There

is no such justification for giving people with IQs above 130 special consideration – they should cope just fine, although some might find social interactions difficult.

58. S. Jones, 'There's Much More to IQ than Biology and DNA', *Telegraph*, 14 October 2013. In response to criticism from Steve Jones, Cummings suggested that Jones might not have read his essay properly. D. Cummings, 'What I Actually Said about Genes, IQ and Heritability', *Telegraph*, 15 October 2013.

59. J. Bakija, A. Cole and B. Y. Heim, 'Jobs and Income Growth of Top Earners and the Causes of Changing Income Inequality: Evidence from US Tax Return Data', 2012, revised analysis available on author's webpage at web.williams.edu.

60. The Boston Consulting Group analysis was reported in turn in R. Neate, 'China and India Swell Ranks of Millionaires in Global Rich List', *Guardian*, 31 May 2012.

61. BBC, 'Small Drop in Teenagers Scoring Five Good GCSEs', BBC News, 18 October 2012, at bbc.co.uk.

62. S. O'Hagan, 'A Working-Class Hero Is Something to Be … But Not in Britain's Posh Culture', *Guardian*, 26 January 2014.

63. Office of the Children's Commissioner, 'A Child Rights Impact Assessment of Budget Decisions – Children and Young People's Version', 27 June 2013, at childrenscommissioner.gov.uk.

64. D. Leigh Scott, 'How the American University was Killed, in Five Easy Steps', *OpEdNews.com*, 19 August 2012, at opednews. com.

3. Work

1. J. Stiglitz, 'Inequality Is a Choice', *New York Times*, 13 October 2013, at opinionator.blogs.nytimes.com.

2. Including a growing number of Nobel Laureates such as Joseph Stiglitz and Robert Shiller (see Chapter 1, above). Ever since Sweden's own banking crisis, more laureates have been awarded to more sceptical economists.

3. K. A. Weeden and D. N. Grusky, 'Inequality and Market Failure', *American Behavioural Scientist*, 2013 (pre-print).

4. B. Bell and J. V. Van Reenen, 'Extreme Wage Inequality: Pay at the Very Top', Centre for Economic Performance, Occasional Paper 34 (2013), at cep.lse.ac.uk.

5. I. Brinkley, K. Jones and N. Lee, 'The Gender Jobs Split: How Young Men and Women Experience the Labour Market', *Tounchstone Extras*, TUC, 2013, at tuc.org.uk.

6. A. Bennett, 'Young Women In Low Paid Jobs Triples In 20 Years, Warns TUC', *Huffington Post*, 1 November 2013, at huffington-post.co.uk.

7. H. Chowdrey and L. Sibieta, 'Trends in Education and Schools Spending', IFS Briefing Note BN121, Institute for Fiscal Studies, 2011, at ifs.org.uk.

8. E. Saez, 'The Evolution of Top Incomes in the United States (Updated with 2012 Preliminary Estimates)', University of California, Berkeley, press release, 3 September 2013, at elsa.berkeley.edu.

9. Note that the BBC put the proportion at 19.3 per cent, and said: 'The top 1 per cent of American households had income above $394,000 (£250,000) last year. The top 10 per cent had income exceeding $114,000'. BBC News, 'US Income Inequality at Record High', 10 September 2013, at bbc.co.uk.

10. J. Kay, 'Higher Pay Boosts Economics and Politics', *Financial Times*, 2 October 2012.

11. D. Boffey, 'Super-rich on rise as number of £1m-plus earners doubles', *Observer*, 2 June 2013.

12. D. Horsey, 'Obscenely high CEO salaries are stark marker of U.S. wealth gap', *Los Angeles Times*, 16 April 2014.

13. World Bank, 'Ending poverty requires more than growth, says WBG', World Bank Group (WBG) press release, 11 April 2014, at worldbank.org.

14. Z. Goldfarb and M. Boorstein, 'Pope Francis Denounces "Trickle-Down" Economic Theories in Critique of Inequality', *Washington Post*, 26 November 2013.

15. M. Haddad, 'The Perfect Storm: Economic Stagnation, the Rising Cost of Living, Public Spending Cuts, and the Impact on UK Poverty', Oxfam, 2012, at policy-practice.oxfam.org.uk.

16. B. Milanovic, *The Haves and the Have Nots: A Brief and Idiosyncratic History of Global Inequality*, (New York: Basic Books, 2012).

17. M. Kumhof and R. Rancière, 'Inequality, Leverage and Crises', IMF Working Paper, November 2010, at imf.org.

18. M. Kumhof and R. Rancière, 'Leveraging Inequality', *Finance and Development*, 47: 4, (December 2010) pp. 28–31, at imf.org.

19. S. Lansley, *The Cost of Inequality: Why Economic Equality is Essential for Recovery* (London: Gibson Square, 2012).

20. At least they said that in an earlier draft. The final draft was a little more toned down. Haddad, 'Perfect Storm'.

21. M. Gill, 'Our Instinct for Equality', *New Statesman*, 27 February 2012, p. 15.

22. And it is not just us. A paper was published in *Nature* in 2003 concerning experiments with monkeys being fed with cucumbers, or preferably grapes, in which the monkeys rejected being rewarded unequally, opting for no reward rather than an unfair one. S. F. Brosnan and F. B. M. de Waal, 'Monkeys Reject Unequal Pay', *Nature* 425 (2003).

23. See the description of top bosses and the high frequency of unfortunate childhood experiences suffered by many of them in R. Peston, *Who Runs Britain? And Who's to Blame for the Economic Mess We're In?* (London: Hodder & Stoughton, 2008).

24. J. Henrich, R. Boyd, S. Bowles et al., 'In Search of Homo Economicus: Behavioral Experiments in 15 Small-Scale Societies', *American Economic Review* 91: 2 (May 2001), at umass.edu.

25. E. Proto and A. Rustichini, 'A Reassessment of the Relationship Between GDP and Life Satisfaction', Working Paper 94, Centre for Competitive Advantage in the Global Economy, Department of Economics, University of Warwick, 2012. They argue that the first to suggest the mechanism behind this was J. S. Duesenberry, *Income, Saving, and the Theory of Consumer Behaviour* (Cambridge, MA: Harvard University Press, 1949). The classic reference is R. A. Easterlin, 'Does Economic Growth Improve the Human Lot? Some Empirical Evidence', in R. David and M. Reder, eds, *Nations and Households in Economic Growth: Essays in Honour of Moses Abramovitz* (New York: Academic Press, 1974).

26. K. Van den Bos, P. A. M. Van Lange, E. A. Lind, L. A. Venhoeven, D. A. Beudeker, F. M. Cramwinckel, L. Smulders and J. Van der Laan, 'On the Benign Qualities of Behavioural Disinhibition: Because of the Pro-Social Nature of People, Behavioural Disinhibition Can Weaken Pleasure with Getting More than You Deserve', *Journal of Personality and Social Psychology* 101 (2011), at paulvanlange.com.

27. P. A. M. Van Lange, R. Bekkers, A. Chirumbolo and L. Leone, 'Are Conservatives Less Likely to Be Pro-Social than Liberals? From Games to Ideology, Political Preferences and Voting', *European Journal of Personality* 26 (2012), at paulvanlange. com.

28. L. C. Groopman and A. M. Cooper, 'Narcissistic Personality Disorder', American Medical Network, 2006, at health.am.

29. K. Rowlingson and S. McKay, 'What do the Public Think about the Wealth Gap?', University of Birmingham Wealth Commission Report, 2013, at birmingham.ac.uk.

30. J. Treanor, 'Barclays to Reveal as Many as 600 Staff Earn More than £1m a Year', *Guardian*, 26 February 2013.

31. P. O. Hosking, 'Britain Tops League of Millionaire Bankers', *The Times*, 16 July 2013 – behind a paywall, so read the *Guardian* instead: J. Treanor, 'More than 2,400 UK bankers paid €1m-plus, EU regulator says, *Guardian*, 15 July 2013.

32. 'Bankers Use Cocaine and Got Us Into this Terrible Mess', headline reported in *The Week*, 16 April 2013, covering the story behind the *Sunday Times* pay-wall.

33. Staff reporter, 'Fraudster Bernie Madoff "Had So Much Cocaine in His Office It Was Dubbed the North Pole"', *Daily Mail*, 21 October 2009.

34. Robbie Williams may have heard the joke via Richard Pryor: J. Kossoff, 'Why Cocaine Isn't Kosher', *The Telegraph Blog*, 11 August 2008. Incidentally the UK doesn't just have the highest rate of cocaine use per head. It also has the highest number of plastic surgery operations of any country in Europe: BBC, 'UK tops Euro plastic surgery league', 11 March 2002, at http://news.bbc.co.uk/. This will not be unrelated.

35. S. Anthony, 'Cocaine: Why We Are All Talking About It', *Observer*, 1 December 2013.

36. As revealed on 21 November 2012 at 7.18 a.m. on the BBC Radio 4 *Today* programme business news, hosted by Simon Jack, and reported a day earlier in P. Walker, 'City-Wide "Addiction"', *Guardian*, 20 November 2012.

37. J. Arlidge, 'The Debt Collector', *Sunday Times Magazine*, 7 October 2012.

38. M. Stein, 'A Culture of Mania: A Psychoanalytic View of the Incubation of the 2008 Credit Crisis', *Organization* 18 (2011), at sagepub.com.

39. J. Salmon, 'Barclays Fat Cat Rich Ricci Retires at 49 Just Weeks after Pocketing £18m Shares Windfall (… and He's Getting a Year's Salary as His Pay-Off)', *Daily Mail*, 19 April 2013.

40. G. Hiscott, 'Bob Diamond: Shamed Former Barclays Banker Claims He "Never Did Anything for Money"', *Mirror*, 2 May 2013.

41. A. Osborne, 'Ex-HBOS Chief Sir James Crosby Gives Up Knighthood and Part of Pension', *Telegraph*, 9 April 2013.

42. BBC, 'Former RBS Boss Fred Goodwin Stripped of Knighthood', BBC News, 31 January 2012, at bbc.co.uk.

43. J. Treanor, 'RBS Chairman Reveals Employee Lobbying over Banker Bonuses', *Guardian*, 11 November 2013.

44. S. Fleming, 'Bank of England Is Urged to Clamp Down on Bank Bonuses', *Financial Times*, 2 March 2014.

45. Ipsos MORI, 'Politicians Trusted Less than Estate Agents, Bankers and Journalists', 15 February 2013, at ipsos-mori.com.

46. H. Dixon, 'Judges Lose Their Sky TV at Taxpayer Funded Lodgings', *Telegraph*, 14 October 2013.

47. A. Foster, 'Jeremy Paxman Takes 20 Per Cent Pay Cut to Stay at Newsnight – But Still Gets £3M over Four Years', *Evening Standard*, 8 February 2011.

48. A. Smith, *An Inquiry into the Nature and Causes of the Wealth of Nations, Book I*, Chapter II: 'Of the Principle which Gives Occasion to the Division of Labour', Section 1.2.4 (London: Methuen, 5th edn, 1904 [1776]), at econlib.org.

49. BBC, 'David Cameron Suggests Cutting Benefits for Under-25s', BBC News, 2 October 2013, at bbc.co.uk.

50. C. Hope, 'Exclusive: Cabinet Is Worth £70 Million', *Telegraph*, 27 May 2012.

51. R. Fergusson, 'Punishing the Young Unemployed', Centre for Crime and Justice Studies Report, 15 October 2013, at crime-andjustice.org.uk.

52. OECD, 'Crisis Squeezes Income and Puts Pressure on Inequality and Poverty', New Results from the OECD Income Distribution Database, OECD, 2013, at oecd.org (see Fig. 8, p. 7).

53. J. Berman, 'Nick Hanauer's TED Talk on Income Inequality Deemed Too "Political" for Site', *Huffington Post*, 17 May 2012, at huffingtonpost.com.

54. Equality Trust, 'Wealth Increase of Britain's 100 Richest Would Pay For 1.75 Million Living Wage Jobs', Press Release, 19

February 2014, at equalitytrust.org.uk.

55. On what more is needed, see P. Ainley and M. Allen, *Lost Generation? New Strategies for Youth and Education* (London: Continuum, 2010).

56. N. Morris, 'Overqualified and Underemployed: Britain Faces "Youth Talent Crisis" as New Figures Reveal More than a Million Young People Working Menial Jobs', *Independent*, 19 March 2014.

57. Unemployment was the third-largest risk out of thirty-one evaluated, and climate change was second. WEF, 'Worsening Wealth Gap Seen as Biggest Risk Facing the World in 2014', press release, 16 January 2014, at weforum.

58. J. Lugo-Ocando, *Poor News: Global Journalism and the Reporting of World Poverty* (London: Pluto, 2014).

59. N. Ahmed, 'Nasa-Funded Study: Industrial Civilisation Headed for "Irreversible Collapse"?', Earth Insight blog, *Guardian*, 14 March 2014.

60. See Figure 1 in I. Preston, V. White, J. Thumim and T. Bridgeman, 'Distribution of Carbon Emissions in the UK: Implications for Domestic Energy Policy', JRF, 2013, at jrf.org.uk.

61. G. Ananthapadmanabhan, K. Srinivas and V. Gopal, 'Hiding Behind the Poor: A Report by Greenpeace on Climate Injustice', Bangalore: Greenpeace India Society, 2007, at greenpeace.org.

62. W. Hutton, 'Blame Austerity, Not Old People, for the Plight of Britain's Young', *Guardian*, 23 June 2013.

63. J. Hall, 'Unemployment at Three-Year Low as Number of Britons in Work Reaches All-Time High of 30m', *Independent*, 13 November 2013.

64. M. O'Hara – personal communication from her research on austerity Britain, 2013, due to be published by Policy Press during 2014.

65. BBC, 'Q&A: What Will "Help to Work" Mean for Claimants?', BBC News, 30 September 2013, at bbc.co.uk.

66. J. Beattie, 'Forced Labour: Conservative Party to Force the Jobless to Work for Nothing or Lose Their Dole', *Mirror*, 30 September 2013.

67. Ibid.

68. 'Workhouse Rules' (letter), *Scotsman*, 1 October 2013.

69. P. Routledge, 'Michael Gove Is Patronising, Insulting, Nasty, Wrong and Arrogant', *Mirror*, 13 September 2013.

70. J. Lyons, 'Soaring Number of Starving Britons Who Rely on Food Banks Is National "Emergency", Experts Warn', *Mirror*, 4 December 2013.
71. BBC, 'Red Cross Launches Food Aid Campaign for Britain', BBC News, 11 October 2013, at bbc.co.uk.
72. Russia Today, 'EU Economic Crisis Causing Massive Rise in Poverty – Red Cross', *Russia Today*, 10 October 2013, at rt.com.
73. N. Morris, 'Hungrier than Ever: Britain's Use of Food Banks Triples', *Independent*, 16 October 2013.
74. C. Cooper and K. Dutta, 'Malnutrition Cases in English Hospitals Almost Double in Five Years', *Independent*, 17 November 2013.
75. C. Cooper, 'Food Poverty in UK Has Reached Level of "Public Health emergency", Warn Experts', *Independent*, 4 December 2013.
76. K. Willsher, 'Will France's Supertax Spark 'Patriotism' or a Brain Drain?', *Guardian*, 14 September 2012.
77. Source: A. Seely, 'Income Tax: The New 50p Rate', House of Commons Library, Standard Note SN249, 2013, at parliament. uk, p. 33.
78. C. Beatty and S. Fothergill, 'Hitting the Poorest Places Hardest: The Local and Regional Impact of Welfare Reform', Sheffield: Centre for Regional Economic and Social Research, Sheffield Hallam University, 2013.
79. I. Jack, 'It's Shameful the Way Britain Kowtows to the Super-Rich', *Guardian*, 9 March 2013.
80. K. Allen, 'British Workers Suffer Deepest Real Wages Cut since Records Began, Research Shows', *Guardian*, 12 June 2013.
81. J. Void, 'Salvation Army Fights Back – Calls Critics of Unpaid Work Offensive', *The Void Blog*, 17 December 2013, at johnnyvoid.wordpress.com. See also George Orwell's suggestion on how the Salvation Army should be viewed in the final paragraph of 'Down and Out in Paris and London', 1933.
82. S. Malik, 'Workfare Placements Must Be Made Public, Tribunal Rules', *Guardian*, 19 May 2013.
83. A. Beckett, 'What Is the "Global Race"?', *Guardian*, 22 September 2013.
84. F. Norris, 'Median Pay in US is Stagnant, but Low-Paid Workers Lose', *New York Times*, 26 April 2013.
85. D. Herzer and S. Vollmer, 'Rising Top Incomes Do Not Raise the Tide', *Journal of Policy Making* 35: 4 (2013), at ideas.repec.org.

86. R. H. Tawney, *Equality* (London: George Allen & Unwin 1952 [1931]), based on the Halley Stewart Lectures, for 1929. Quote on p. 11.

87. Z. Minton Beddoes, 'For Richer, for Poorer – Special Report: The World Economy', 13 October 2012.

88. R. Kutnor, 'The Task Rabbit Economy', *American Prospect*, 10 October 2013.

89. Trust for London, 'London's Poverty Profile, Key Facts, October', 2013, at londonspovertyprofile.org.uk.

90. The three countries in which the 1 per cent have experienced the most similar recent increases in income are the US, the UK and Canada. D. Dorling, 'How Only Some Rich Countries Recently Set Out to Become More Unequal', *Sociologia, Problemas e Práticas* 74 (2014), at revistas.rcaap.pt.

91. The full list of ratios is: Moscow 2.63; London 1.69; Paris 1.67; Johannesburg-Gauteng 1.50; Buenos Aires 1.47; Vienna 1.30; Stockholm 1.23; Tokyo 1.14; and Seoul 1.10. Calculated from Figure 4, p. 36, in G. Clark, 'Nations and the Wealth of Cities: A New Phase in Public Policy', Centre for London, 2014, at centreforlondon.org.

92. M. Gibson, 'Will Allegations of Drug Abuse Hurt Nigella Lawson's Career?' *Time Entertainment*, 14 December 2013 (which originally suggested her supporters were called 'Team Cupcake', but that was her staff).

93. These are the wage rates quoted on information boards at Blenheim Palace. Wages at the time of the first Duchess are given at blenheimpalace.com.

94. In a nod to understanding other people's money problems, the businessman explained that this was a 'huge luxury'. This butler used to work for the royal household – something the 'Dragon' was probably keen to make general knowledge. The vanity of this particular business mogul came to light when he 'appeared on the *Today* programme – 24 hours after he went on to promote the social mobility programme – to defend himself against charges of nepotism and hypocrisy'. See R. Neate, 'James Caan: "No Parent Is Not Going to Help Their Children', *Guardian*, 6 June 2013.

95. C. James, 'A Prediction That's a Safe Bet', *BBC News Magazine*, 2 January 2009, at bbc.co.uk.

4. Wealth

1. M. Sinclair, 'Why No Conservative Should Support a Mansion Tax', *Spectator*, 18 February 2013.

2. The figure of 98 per cent of people being empathetic was given by Roman Krznaric on the BBC Radio 4 *Today* programme on 28 October 2013, at 8.35 a.m. (bbc.co.uk). His forthcoming book is R. Krznaric, *Empathy: A Handbook for Revolution* (London: Rider Books, 2014).

3. Once you include those with a little empathy, there is a wider range of variance in levels of empathy, and of pro- and antisocial behaviour, as is often reflected through variations in political alliances. P. K. Hatemi, C. L Funk, S. E. Medland et al., 'Genetic and Environmental Transmission of Political Attitudes over Time', *Journal of Politics* 71 (2009).

4. Those countries are home to 53 per cent of HNWIs. Capgemini and RBC, 'World Wealth Report', Royal Bank of Canada Wealth Management Division, 2013, at worldwealthreport.com.

5. P. Bump, 'The World's Rich Got Richer in 2013 than You Will Ever Be', *The Wire*, 2 January 2014.

6. Staff reporter, 'Bill Gates Becomes World's Richest Person Again', *Irish Times*, 3 January 2014.

7. J. Kollewe, 'London Retains Crown as Favourite City of World's Ultra-Rich', *Guardian*, 5 March 2014.

8. R. Fuentes, 'Anatomy of a Killer Fact: The World's 85 Richest People Own as Much as the Poorest 3.5 Billion', Oxfam Blog, 31 January 2014, at oxfamblogs.org.

9. R. Wilkinson and K. Pickett, 'The Spirit Level Authors: Why Society Is More Unequal than Ever', *Observer*, 9 March 2014.

10. L. Elliott, 'Britain's Five Richest Families Worth More than Poorest 20 Per Cent: Oxfam Report Reveals Scale of Inequality in UK as Charity Appeals to Chancellor over Tax', *Guardian*, 17 March 2014.

11. K. Moreno, 'The 67 People As Wealthy As The World's Poorest 3.5 Billion', *Forbes Magazine*, 25 March 2014, at forbes.com.

12. D. Dorling, 'Fairness and the Changing Fortunes of People in Britain', *Journal of the Royal Statistical Society* A, 176: 1 (2013), at onlinelibrary.wiley.com.

13. Capgemini and RBC, 'World Wealth Report', p. 18, refers in turn to 'Outlook 2013', Art Market Update, Fine Art Fund Group, January 2013.

14. N. Shaxson, *Treasure Islands: Tax Havens and the Men Who Stole the World* (London: Bodley Head, 2011).

15. J. Hills, F. Bastagli, F. Cowell, H. Glennerster, E. Karagiannaki and A. McKnight, *Wealth in the UK: Distribution, Accumulation and Policy* (Oxford: Oxford University Press, 2013).

16. K. Roberts, *Class in Modern Britain* (Basingstoke: Palgrave Macmillan, 2011), pp. 169–92. Quoted in P. Ainley and M. Allen, 'Running up a Down Escalator in the Middle of a Class Structure Gone Pear-Shaped', *Sociological Research Online* 18: 1 (2013), at socresonline.org.uk.

17. John Scott's three-volume edited collection, *The Sociology of Elites*, published in 1990, is a good starting point for anyone interested in studying elitism in Britain. His *Stratification and Power: Structures of Class, Status and Domination*' (Cambridge: Polity Press, 1996) and *Corporate Business and Capitalist Classes* (Oxford: Oxford University Press, 1997) develop the same themes. Professor Scott (CBE) is the current Pro Vice-Chancellor for Research at the University of Plymouth. I collected together these references and gave them as part of a witness statement on behalf of Trenton Oldfield at his 9 December 2013 deportation hearing to make the case that the study of elites is part of the academic mainstream of the social sciences (unpublished, but in court papers).

18. I am grateful to Patrick Ainley for this suggestion (personal communication, March 2014). He continued to say that any oppressed group is likely to be the same, as Hugh McIlvenney wrote in *Docherty*: 'In ony country in the world, who are the only folk that ken whit it's like tae leeve in that country? The folk at the boattam. The rest can a' kid themselves oan. They can afford to hiv fancy ideas.' But another consideration is the changed nature of the state ... which increasingly just runs itself – or rather has been handed over to private monopoly capital to run so they were even complaining on radio the other day that MPs absent themselves from Parliament because there is less and less going on there nowadays.' Available at jim-murdoch.blogspot.co.uk. [note *Docherty* is written by William McIlvanney and was published by Canongate in 2013].

19. P. Collinson, 'Richest 10 Per Cent of UK Households Own 40 Per Cent of Wealth', *Guardian*, 3 December 2012.

20. Anonymous, 'What I'm Really Thinking: The Children's Entertainer', *Guardian*, 22 June 2013.

21. In India itself, luxury apartments are being designed for Mumbai that have a swimming pool built into each balcony. See P. Johnston, 'Ambitious Mumbai Development which Sees Balconies Replaced with Swimming Pools', Luxury Travel Blog, 16 April 2013, at aluxurytravelblog.com.

22. L. Hewitt and S. Graham, 'Getting Off the Ground: On the Politics of Urban Verticality', *Progress in Human Geography* 37: 1 (2010), p. 83.

23. R. Fry and P. Taylor, 'The Rise of Residential Segregation by Income', PEW Social and Demographic Trends, 1 August 2012, at pewsocialtrends.org.

24. It is easier to see why this might be if you look away from where you are used to: J. Mazzocchetti, 'Feelings of Injustice and Conspiracy Theory: Representations of Adolescents from an African Migrant Background (Morocco and Sub-Saharan Africa) in Disadvantaged Neighbourhoods of Brussels', *Brussels Studies*, No. 63, (26 November 2012), at brusselsstudies.be.

25. M. Farauenfelder, '12 Million Americans Believe Lizard People Run the US', Boing Boing Blog, 15 April 2013, at boingboing. net.

26. L. Mckenzie, 'The Realities of Everyday Life for the Working-Class in Neo-Liberal Britain (Part 2)', *New Left Project*, 31 August 2013, at newleftproject.org.

27. Alice, 'Eton's Scholarship Exam', *New Left Project*, 23 May 2013, at newleftproject.org.

28. Ibid., comment by David, made on 24 May 2013, 09:17.

29. See, for example: http://auction.westminster.org.uk/lots/a-one-week-internship-at-portas (accessible as of April 2014).

30. J. S. Henry, 'The Price of Offshore Revisited: New Estimates for 'Missing' Global Private Wealth, Income, Inequality, and Lost Taxes', Tax Justice Network, July 2012, pp. 8, 36, at taxjustice. net.

31. Oxfam, 'Working For The Few: Political Capture and Economic Inequality', Oxfam Briefing Paper 178, 20 January 2014, at oxfam.org.

32. Frank Knight Research, 'The Wealth Report 2012', London Citi

Private Bank, 2012, at thewealthreport.net, further details at: S. Ro, '10 Stats about How People with Over $100 Million Invest', *Business Insider*, 11 August 2012, at businessinsider.com.

33. C. Paikert, 'Courting the Next Generation of the Rich', *New York Times*, 16 October 2012.

34. S. Ro, 'Mo' Money Mo' Problems? At Wells Fargo, a $50 Million Account Will Get You a Psychologist', *Business Insider*, 2 April 2012, at businessinsider.com.

35. D. Barrett, 'One Surveillance Camera for Every 11 People in Britain, Says CCTV Survey', *Telegraph*, 10 July 2013.

36. M. Brown and N. Gil, 'Tax Exemption for Public Access to Treasured Artworks is "A Racket"', *Guardian*, 27 December 2013.

37. J. Fordham, 'Historic Houses Association Guidance for Applicants to the Heritage Lottery Fund's Our Heritage Programme', London, Historic Houses Association, February, 2013, at theheritagealliance.org.uk.

38. M. Kennedy, 'Stately Home Owners to Gain Access to Lottery Money', *Guardian*, 5 July 2012.

39. J. Vasagar, '"Buried" Report Praised Labour's School Building Programme', *Guardian*, 5 July 2012.

40. T. Middleton, 'Climate, Land and Homes', *Strike* magazine, 4 June 2013, at strikemag.org.

41. T. Wallace, 'London's House Prices Soar 12pc', *City AM*, 19 February 2014.

42. A. Molloy, 'Oxford is the Least Affordable City in the UK, where Houses Cost 11 Times Local Salaries', *Independent*, 10 March 2014.

43. K. Allen, personal communication on 'Cash Buyers Versus Mortgages, the Savills Analysis', 16 January 2014, published as K. Allen, 'Home Buyers Left Behind in Britain's Two-Speed Housing Market', *Financial Times*, 18 January 2014.

44. M. Griffith, 'Foreign Demand Comes with Risks' (letter), *Financial Times*, 5 March 2014.

45. B. Goldacre, 'Generation Game' (letter), *The Times*, 29 November 2013.

46. M. Duell, 'All Aboard My New Home! The Shipping Containers Being Rented Out for £75 a Week to Try to Solve London's Chronic Housing Crisis', *Daily Mail*, 9 October 2013.

47. N. Shaxson, J. Christensen and N. Mathiason, 'Inequality: You

Don't Know the Half of It', Tax Justice Network, 19 July 2012, at taxjustice.net.

48. L. Slater, 'Keeping Up with the Zahoors: Inside the Super-Rich World of Londongrad', *Times Magazine*, 23 November 2013, p. 41.

49. M. Seamark, 'Blairs Paid £1.35m in Cash for Home Number SEVEN: Splashed Out on a Four-Storey Georgian Townhouse for Son Nicky', *Daily Mail*, 2 February 2013.

50. NatCen, 'Mortgage Interest Rates Helping the Rich to Save More?', London, National Centre for Social Research, 2013, at natcen.ac.uk. Note: 'Not everyone saves money each month, but about 20 per cent of the lowest income group, 30 per cent of the 2nd quintile, 40 per cent of the 3rd quintile, 50 per cent of the 4th quintile and 60 per cent of the highest income group say they do. In 2011 the households in these groups were each earning on average £675, £1,114, £1,550, £2,203 and £4,226 per calendar month.'

51. S. Neville and K. Allen, 'UK Wealth Gap Grows as Homeowners Save More but Renters Suffer', *Financial Times*, 11 October 2013.

52. S. Hawkes, 'Biggest Drop in Savings for 40 years, Bank of England Figures Reveal', *Telegraph*, 2 December 2013.

53. Shelter are trying to have the law changed to make this type of eviction illegal. Shelter, 'Can't Complain: Why Poor Conditions Prevail in Private Rented Homes', London, Shelter, March 2014.

54. P. Collinson, 'Number of £1m UK Homes Up by Third in "Them and Us" Market', *Guardian*, 28 June 2013.

55. First-time buyers are also harmed. D. Johnson, 'Building Our Way Out of Crisis?', GLA report by Green Party Assembly Member, London, GLA, November 2012, at london.gov.uk. Note that it is not lack of supply but 'High Prices [that] are the biggest barrier holding back first time buyers in London'.

56. D. Johnston, 'Crumbs for Londoners', GLA Report by Green Party Assembly Member, London, GLA, November 2013, at london.gov.uk.

57. K. Allen, 'Wealth Survey Shows Stark North-South Divide', *Guardian*, 4 June 2013.

58. N. Lee, P. Sissons and K. Jones, 'Wage Inequality and Employment Polarisation in British Cities', York, Joseph Rowntree Foundation, 2013, pp. 3, 14, at jrf.org.uk.

59. W. White and P. Owen, 'Liberal Democrat Conference: The Spirit of Roy Jenkins Lives On', *Guardian*, 24 September 2012.

60. D. Dorling, *All that is Solid: The Great Housing Disaster* (London: Allen Lane, 2014).

61. GRO(S), 'Occupied and Vacant Dwellings in Each Local Authority (LA)', September 2012', Edinburgh, 2013, at gro-scotland.gov.uk.

62. D. G. Blanchflower and A. Oswald, 'Does High Home-Ownership Impair the Labour Market?' NBER Working Paper No. 19079, May 2013, at nber.org.

63. R. Ramesh, 'One in Four UK Children Will Be Living in Poverty by 2020, Says Thinktank', *Guardian*, 7 May 2013.

64. M. Hasan, 'Strivers vs Shirkers? Ten Things They Don't Tell You about the Welfare Budget', *Huffington Post*, 17 December 2012, at huffingtonpost.co.uk.

65. Figure 3.4 in Social Mobility and Child Poverty Commission, 'State of the Nation 2013, October 2013, London, Stationery Office, at gov.uk.

66. H. Reed, 'In the Eye of the Storm: Britain's Forgotten Children and Families – Methodological Summary', London, Action for Children – The Children's Society – NSPCC, 2012, p. 6.

67. G. Kelly, 'Stealth Cuts Are Making Universal Credit Toxic to the Working Poor', *Guardian*, 12 December 2013.

68. According to the research undertaken for the Children's Society and the National Society for the Prevention of Cruelty to Children. See Reed, 'In the Eye of the Storm'.

69. Nat Cen, 'Social Attitudes in an Age of Austerity', British Social Attitudes 2012, London, National Centre for Social Research, at bsa-29.natcen.ac.uk.

70. J. Werran, 'Lewis Disputes "Shoddy" Labour Figures on Council Tax Arrears', *Local Government Chronicle*, 11 October 2013, at localgov.co.uk.

71. DK, 'Mapping Gentrification: The Great Inversion', *Economist*, 9 September 2013.

72. T. MacInnes, H. Aldridge, S. Bushe, et al., 'Monitoring Poverty and Social Exclusion 2013', York, Jospeh Rowntree Foundation, 2013, at jrf.org.uk.

73. Reed, 'In the Eye of the Storm', reveals that, over the seven years leading to 2015, 'the number of children living in families with five or more vulnerabilities is set to rise by 54,000 to 365,000,

an increase of around 17 percent [and] the number of children living in extremely vulnerable families is set to almost double by 2015, to 96,000'.

74. Dorling, *All that is Solid*.
75. 'Here we have relied on the figures produced by the Office of National Statistics (ONS) in their report Wealth in Great Britain Wave 2, Wealth of the Wealthiest, 2008–10. The term wealth includes pensions, investments, housing, physical possessions and land. "£1,000,000" is rounded up from £967,000.' 'Inequality Briefing 1: Who Has What', 11 October 2013, at inequalitybriefing.org.
76. Reed, 'In the Eye of the Storm', p. 34.
77. Ian Bostridge, one of Britain's best-known tenors, won a scholarship to Westminster School, went on to gain a first in modern history at Oxford University, a master's degree in the history and philosophy of science at Cambridge University, and then a doctorate from Oxford. He is illustrative of the very top of the 99 per cent. A Londoner, he is possibly the last generation of his family to be able to afford to live in London. See A. Clark, 'Lunch with the FT: Ian Bostridge', *Financial Times*, 8 November 2013.
78. F. Alvaredo, A. B. Atkinson, T. Piketty and E. Saez, 'The Top 1 Percent in International and Historical Perspective', *Journal of Economic Perspectives*, 27: 3 (2013), p. 14, at pubs.aeaweb.org.
79. Ibid., p. 18.
80. BBC, 'Deutsche Bank Chief Ackermann Fears "Social Time Bomb', BBC News, 2 February 2012, at bbc.co.uk; Bloomberg TV Business Week, 'Bloomberg Most Wanted: Meet the King of Bulletproof Cars', 10 November 2013, at businessweek.com.
81. J. Ramsey, 'Production Bentley EXP 9 F Could Get Optional 3rd Row Au Pair Seating', Auto Blog, 24 August 2012, at autoblog. com: 'Armouring your vehicle is the latest craze among the uber-wealthy. Texas Armouring in San Antonio is the biggest private vehicle armouring company in the world, protecting celebs like T.I., Mel B and Steven Segal. They produce about 200 vehicles a year and project that number to double in the next five years due to a spike in demand in the US.'
82. E. N. Wolff, 'The Asset Price Meltdown and the Wealth of the Middle Class', Occasional Paper, New York University, 2012, p. 58, Table 2, at appam.confex.com.

83. Charles Elson, director of the US Center for the study of Corporate Governance, reacted to these revelations by saying, 'I find the security argument tough to swallow ... Airports are among the safest places on earth these days.' N. D. Schwartz, 'The Infinity Pool of Executive Pay', *International Herald Tribune*, 6 April 2013.

84. M. Flinders, 'Down and Out in Bloemfontein', *OUP Blog*, 8 January 2014, at blog.oup.com.

85. Personal correspondence, John Hague, Whittlesey, Peterborough, 29 May 2013.

86. P. Torija, 'Do Politicians Serve the One Percent? Evidence in OECD Countries', Working Paper, Department of International Politics, City University, London, 2013, p.18, at ideas. repec.org.

87. R. Brand, 'Russell Brand on Parliament', *Guardian*, 24 May 2013.

88. R. O'Farrell, 'Irish Inequality During the 20th Century', Progressive Economy Blog, 23 September 2010, at progressive-economy.ie.

89. The tax is 0.18 per cent a year on the value of property below €1 million and 0.25 per cent on the portion of any value above that: Ryan, N. 'Revenue will use this system to spot homes undervalued for Property Tax', *The Journal*, 10 March 2014, at thejournal.ie.

90. 'IT1 – Tax Credits, Reliefs and Rates for the Tax Years 2013 and 2014', 'Domicile Levy' and 'Capital Gains Tax', all at revenue.ie.

91. T. McDonnell, 'Wealth Tax: Options for Its Implementation in the Republic of Ireland', National Economic Research Institute Paper No. 6, September 2013, at progressive-economy.ie.

92. T. Picketty, 'Should We Make the Richest Pay to Meet Fiscal Adjustment Needs?', in S. Princen and G. Mouree, 'The Role of Tax Policy in Times of Fiscal Consolidation', Economic Papers 502, August 2013, Brussels, European Commission, at piketty. pse.ens.fr.

93. In January 2014, 'The German central bank raised the idea of an emergency "capital levy" in its monthly report'. See zerohedge. com. See also A. Evans-Pritchard, 'Wealth Tax to Pay for EU Bail-Outs', *Telegraph*, 14 April 2013.

94. McDonnell, 'Wealth Tax', p. 21.

95. A. B. Atkinson and S. Morelli, 'Chartbook of Economic Inequality: 25 Countries 1911–2010', INET Research Note 15, New York, Institute for New Economic Thinking, 2012, pp. 23, 49, at ineteconomics.org.

96. N. Dejevsky, 'Buy-to-Let, Not Help to Buy, Is the Real Scourge of Generation Rent', *Financial Times*, 25 October 2013.

97. Skandia, 'Millionaire Monitor+: A Survey of Millionaires and Equivalent Wealthy Individuals across Skandia's Wealth Management Territories', Southampton, Skandia, p. 6, at www2.skandia.co.uk. They were asked for the various sources of their wealth. In the UK, 74 per cent said employment, 57 per cent investments, 41 per cent inheritance, 15 per cent their own businesses, 15 per cent marriage, 7 per cent a sporting career, 7 per cent a lottery or gambling, and 4 per cent a divorce settlement.

98. S. Wood, 'Ed Miliband's Mansion Tax Policy Threatens Britain's Historic Homes' (letter), *Telegraph*, 20 February 2013.

99. D. Gibson and C. Perot, 'It's the Inequality, Stupid', *Plutocracy Now*, March/April 2011, at motherjones.com.

100. E. N. Wolff, 'The Asset Price Meltdown and the Wealth of the Middle Class', Occasional Paper, New York University, 2012, Table 4, p. 60, atappam.confex.com.

101. Oxfam, 'A Tale of Two Britains', press release, Oxfam, 2014, at thenextrecession.files.wordpress.com.

102. TUC, 'Top 10 Per Cent Now More than 500 Times Wealthier than Bottom 10 Per Cent', 12 July 2012, at tuc.org.uk.

103. J. Lugo-Ocando, *Poor News: Global Journalism and the Reporting of World Poverty* (London: Pluto Press, 2014). Many of today's rich in the UK come from families whose original riches can be traced back to slave ownership or violence; others are recent arrivals from other countries, with dubious stories concerning how they made their money.

104. N. Shaxson, *Treasure Islands*.

105. It is of course an old campaign. Winston Churchill even supported a land value tax – perhaps because, although born at Blenheim Palace, he never owned it or had a chance of owning such a property. See C. Joseph, 'Duke's Dissolute Son Kicks Heroin Habit … and Wins Back His Birth-Right – the Keys to Blenheim Palace – in Amazing Tale of Redemption', *Daily Mail*, 18 November 2012.

106. Capgemini and RBC, 'World Wealth Report', 2013, Fig. 23, p. 37.
107. G. Monbiot, 'Europe's €50bn Bung that Enriches Landowners and Kills Wildlife', *Guardian*, 26 November 2012.
108. ECB, 'The Eurosystem Household Finance and Consumption Survey, Results from the First Wave', Statistics Paper No.2, European Central Bank, 2013, Table 2.3, p. 32, at ecb. europa.eu.
109. C. Jones, 'Did QE Only Boost the Price of Warhols?' *Financial Times*, 18 October 2013.
110. L. Warwick-Ching, 'Classic Cars Geared to Top Alternative Sector', *Financial Times*, 6 September 2013.
111. Ibid.
112. K. Watkins, 'God, Mammon and the Debate on Inequality', Overseas Development Institute Blog, 21 January 2014, at odi. org.uk.
113. Staff Reporter, 'UK Planning Fast-Track Passport Lanes For Rich Travellers', *Huffington Post*, 18 September 2012, at huffingtonpost.com.

5. Health

1. L. Else, 'Of Wealth and Health: Special Report on Inequality', *New Scientist*, 28 July 2012, p. 45.
2. Y. Sugiura, Y. S. Ju, J. Yasuoka and M. Jimba, 'Rapid Increase in Japanese Life Expectancy after World War II', *Bioscience Trends* 4: 1 (2010), at ncbi.nlm.nih.gov.
3. N. R. Nowatzki, 'Wealth Inequality and Health: A Political Economy Perspective', *International Journal of Health Services* 42: 3 (2012), at mspace.lib.umanitoba.ca.
4. T. McVeigh, 'Inequality "Costs Britain £39bn a Year"', *Observer*, 16 March 2014.
5. Figures for 2005–08 had shown no difference by income in the prevalence of antidepressant usage in the US, but the rate for all persons over twelve years was 13.6 per cent for non-Hispanic whites, 3.9 per cent for non-Hispanic blacks, and 2.3 per cent for Mexican Americans, which might partly reflect access to health-care. See L. A. Pratt, D. J. Brody and Q. Gu, 'Antidepressant Use in Persons Aged 12 and Over: United States, 2005–2008', NCHS Data Brief Number 76, October 2011, atcdc.gov.

6. S. Boseley, M. Chalabi and M. Rice-Oxley, 'Antidepressant Use on the Rise in Rich Countries, OECD Finds', *Guardian*, 20 November 2013.

7. H. Mulholland, 'David Cameron Axes Equality Assessments in War on "Red Tape"', *Guardian*, 19 November 2012.

8. D. Dorling, 'In Place of Fear: Narrowing Health Inequalities', Centre for Labour and Social Studies (CLASS), 21 May 2013, at dannydorling.org.

9. R. Jones, 'End of Life and Financial Risk in GP Commissioning', *British Journal of Healthcare Management* 18: 7 (2012), at hcaf. biz.

10. C. J. Conover, 'The Health Spending 1 Percent: Healthcare Fact of the Week', American Enterprise Institute, 22 November 2011, at aei-ideas.org. The Medical Expenditure Panel Survey, which was used to produce the graph of US medical expenditure in this source, produces figures for what households actually spent (mostly on insurance), not what their medical treatment cost, which will be higher.

11. Such as through supporting the advertising of fatty foods to children. It is London companies owned by the 1 per cent that buy this advertising; and, in the UK, it is in London that there is the greatest concentration of poverty in the UK, and where children are at greatest risk of obesity at both ages five and ten. See A. Baker, J. Fitzpatrick et al., 'Capital Concerns: Comparing London's Health Challenges with England's Largest Cities', London, London Health Observatory, 2012, p. 9, at lho.org.uk.

12. D. Blane and G. Watt, 'GP Experience of the Impact of Austerity on Patients and General Practices in Very Deprived Areas', Glasgow, General Practice and Primary Care, Institute of Health and Wellbeing, University of Glasgow, 2012, at gla.ac.uk.

13. BBC, 'Life Expectancy Rises Again, ONS Says', BBC News, 19 October 2011, at bbc.co.uk.

14. D. Dorling, *Unequal Health: The Scandal of Our Times* (Bristol: Policy Press, 2013).

15. CPAG, 'The Cuts: What They Mean for Families at Risk of Poverty', Child Poverty Action Group, 2012, at cpag.org.uk. For an update, see CPAG, 'Welfare Reform: What It Means to Families at Risk of Poverty', 20 May 2013, at cpag.org.uk.

16. Comment by John Ashton, posted 8 September 2013, 6:18 p.m., under S. Lind, 'Public Health England Admits Winter Death

Spike Was Due to Flu and Cold Weather', *Pulse Today*, 20 August 2013, at pulsetoday.co.uk.

17. 'This is not the whole story. Tom Hennell is one of the best health service statistical analysts in the country and he doesn't buy this explanation and nor does the remarkable professor Martin McKee.' See online comment by John Ashton, endnote above, and further information in: D. West, 'Mortality Rates among Older People Show Unexpected Rise', *Health Service Journal*, 26 July 2013, pp. 6–7.

18. D. MacKenzie, 'Pattern Behind the Shutdown', *New Scientist*, 12 October 2013, pp. 8–9.

19. D. R. Williams and C. Collins, 'US Socioeconomic and Racial Differences in Health: Patterns and Explanations', *Annual Review of Sociology* 21 (1995), pp. 349–86, Table 1, p. 365, at links.jstor.org.

20. Ibid.

21. C. Greenhalgh, 'Why Does Market Capitalism Fail to Deliver a Sustainable Environment and Greater Equality of Incomes?', *Cambridge Journal of Economics* 29 (2005).

22. K. Smith, 'Long-Term Decline in Calorie Purchases Despite Increase in Calories from Eating Out, Snacks and Soft Drinks', press release quoting Kate Smith, a research economist at the IFS, on ESRC funded research, 4 November 2013, at ifs.org.uk.

23. Social Mobility and Child Poverty Commission, 'State of the Nation 2013: Social Mobility and Child Poverty in Great Britain, October 2013', London, Stationery Office, para. 33, at gov.uk.

24. Personal communication, David Gordon, December 2013, commenting on a pernicious and persistent myth (sometimes spread by leader writers on the *Daily Mail*).

25. P. Gregg, J. Waldfogel and E. Washbrook, 'Expenditure Patterns Post-Welfare Reform in the UK: Are Low-Income Families Starting to Catch Up?', Centre for Analysis of Social Exclusion Working Paper 99, 2005, London, LSE, at sticerd.lse.ac.uk.

26. See Greenhalgh, 'Why Does Market Capitalism Fail to Deliver a Sustainable Environment and Greater Equality of Incomes?', p. 1,101 for a more nuanced discussion of how the very rich come to see themselves as time poor, because they cannot buy more time, and how this then begins to warp their priorities and behaviour.

27. P. Crawshaw, 'Public Health Policy and the Behavioural Turn: The Case of Social Marketing', *Critical Social Policy* 33: 4 (2013), at csp.sagepub.com.

28. M. Pember Reeves, *Round About a Pound a Week* (London: G. Bell & Sons, 2013).

29. A. Gregory, 'North and South Health Divide: Chilling Study Reveals Premature Death is "Postcode Lottery"', *Mirror*, 11 June 2013.

30. L. Johnston, L. Miles and C. N. Macrae, 'Why Are You Smiling at Me? Social Functions of Enjoyment and Non-Enjoyment Smiles', *British Journal of Social Psychology* 49: 1 (2010), at ncbi.nlm.nih.gov.

31. C. Darwin, *The Expression of the Emotions in Man and Animals* (London: HarperCollins, 1998 [1872]).

32. D. Goleman, 'Rich People Just Care Less', *New York Times*, 5 October 2013, at opinionator.blogs.nytimes.com.

33. Occasionally there are accounts of shame, when the poor are forced to talk to the rich. For a review of a book that includes many examples, see M. Savage, *Review: A Phenomenology of Working-Class Experience*, Simon J. Charlesworth' (Cambridge University Press, 1999), at socresonline.org.uk.

34. S. T. Fiske, 'Look Twice: How Prejudiced Are You?', Greater Good Science Centre press release, University of California, Berkeley, 2008, at greatergood.berkeley.edu.

35. 'Social death is the condition under which some people can be condemned to civil death, while the rest of us fail to care or even to notice. It is the condition under which entire groups of people may be exposed to disproportionate state violence, neglect, and/ or exploitation, without provoking the concern or support of other members of the community. Social death is both a condition of civil death and one of its effects; they amplify one another in a vicious circle that is difficult to interrupt.' From Lisa Guenther's blog on the California prison hunger strikes, written on 6 August 2013, at 08.15, at crimeandjustice.org.uk.

36. Lisa Guenther is an associate professor of philosophy at Vanderbilt University. Located in Nashville, Vanderbilt was built thanks to a gift of a million dollars from a member of the incredibly wealthy Vanderbilt family in 1873. Nearly a century and a half later, their investment is helping to define the problems of a return to the inequalities of their times.

37. R. Walker, G. Bantebya Kyomuhendo et al., 'Poverty in Global Perspective: Is Shame a Common Denominator?' *Journal of Social Policy* 42 (2013).

38. P. Townsend, *Poverty in the United Kingdom* (Harmondsworth: Penguin, 1979). A. Sen, 'Poor, Relatively Speaking', Oxford Economic Papers 35 (1983).

39. Goleman, 'Rich People Just Care Less'.

40. M. Goodwin, 'Why the "Immigration Debate" Is Getting Us Nowhere', *New Statesman*, 27 November 2013.

41. B. Guerin, 'Demography and Inequality: How Europe's Changing Population Will Impact on Income Inequality', report by Rand Europe, April 2013, at rand.org.

42. Z. Minton Beddoes, 'For Richer, for Poorer – Special Report: The World Economy', *Economist*, 13 October 2012.

43. G. Wyler, 'US Women Are Dying Younger Than Their Mothers, and No One Knows Why', *Atlantic*, 7 October 2013.

44. D. Stuckler and M. McKee, 'Why Are Death Rates Rising in People Aged Over 85?', Better Health For All – The Blog of the Faculty of Public Health, 23 August 2013, at betterhealth forall.org.

45. BBC, 'Southern Cross Set to Shut Down and Stop Running Homes', BBC News, 11 July 2011, at bbc.co.uk.

46. J. L. Fernandez, T. Snell and G. Wistow, 'Changes in the Patterns of Social Care Provision in England: 2005/6 to 2012/13', Personal Social Services Research Unit, PSSRU Discussion Paper 2867, December 2013, at pssru.ac.uk.

47. ONS, 'Period Expectations of Life, Principal Projections Based on Historical Mortality Rates from 1981 to 2012', 11 December 2013, at ons.gov.uk.

48. N. Triggle, 'Many Vulnerable People Denied Care, Says Age UK', BBC News, 6 March 2014, at bbc.co.uk.

49. D. Campbell, 'Age UK Sounds Alarm Over Cuts to Care for Older People', *Guardian*, 5 March 2014.

50. N. Pratley, 'Barclays' So-Called Pay for Performance Is a Distortion of Capitalism', *Guardian*, 5 March 2014.

51. D. Dorling, 'Why Are the Old Dying Before Their Time? How Austerity Has Affected Mortality Rates', *New Statesman*, 7 February 2014.

52. A. Gollner, *The Book of Immortality: The Science, Belief, and Magic Behind Living Forever* (Canada: Doubleday, 2013),

quoted in the online weekly 'Too much' on excess and inequality, at toomuchonline.org, 9 September 2013.

53. You have to enter the realm of science fiction to see where such behaviour would eventually lead: G. Egan, *Permutation City* (London: Gollancz, 2008).

54. A. Aittomäkia, P. Martikainenb, O. Rahkonena, E. Lahelmaa, 'Household Income and Health Problems During a Period of Labour-Market Change and Widening Income Inequalities – A Study Among the Finnish Population Between 1987 and 2007', *Social Science and Medicine* 100 (2014), at sciencedirect.com.

55. A. Hartocollis, 'With Affordable Care Act, Cancelled Policies for New York Professionals', *New York Times*, 13 December 2013.

56. R. Guillén, 'We Slept and Now We Have Woken. Square Occupied', *Le Monde Diplomatique*, 12 July 2011, at mondediplo.com.

57. B. Kavousii, 'Spanish Locksmiths Refuse to Help Evict Homeowners Any Longer', *Huffington Post*, 23 January 2014, at huffingtonpost.com.

58. Details can be found at studentfinance.direct.gov.uk.

59. R. H. Tawney, *The School Leaving Age and Juvenile Unemployment* (London: Workers' Educational Association, 1934), p. 29.

60. A. Kershaw, 'Fewer Teenagers Staying On for Post-16 Education', *Independent*, 28 June 2012.

61. P. Ainley, '"Lost" Generation' (letter), *Guardian*, 22 January 2014.

62. N. Groves, 'Student Suicides Rise during Recession Years', *Guardian*, 30 November 2012.

63. By the Boston Consulting Group, reported in R. Neate, 'China and India Swell Ranks of Millionaires in Global Rich List', *Guardian*, 31 May 2012.

64. R. B. Reich, 'The American Right Focuses on Poverty, Not Inequality, to Avoid Blame', *Observer*, 23 February 2014.

65. L. Elliott, 'IMF Eyes Tax Potential of the World's Super-Rich', *Guardian*, 13 October 2013.

66. P. Krugman, 'The Long Run History of Taxes on the Rich', *New York Times*, 12 July 2012.

67. S. Fothergill, 'Welfare-to-Work Isn't Working', *People, Place and Policy* 7: 2 (2013), at extra.shu.ac.uk.

68. BBC, 'Southern Cross Set to Shut Down'.

69. C. Jeffery, 'Jugaad Neoliberalism' (letter), *Guardian*, 9 October 2012.

70. OECD, 'Crisis Squeezes Income and Puts Pressure on Inequality and Poverty', New Results from the OECD Income Distribution Database, Paris, OECD report, 2013, at oecd.org.

71. P. Collinson, 'Pension Schemes Have Fewer Members than Any Time since Records Began', *Guardian*, 16 July 2013.

72. M. Morrissey and N. Sabadish, 'Retirement Inequality Chartbook: How the 401(k) Revolution Created a Few Big Winners and Many Losers', Economic Policy Institute, September 2013, at epi.org.

73. And also a debtor, who wrote these words in the year before his death at age sixty-five. This quotation taken from Essay XV of *Seditions and Troubles* (London: Everyman, 1962), p. 46. See also 'Spreading the Muck', *Economist*, 17 May 2007.

74. Z. Williams, 'Achieving a Social State: What Can We Learn from Beveridge's Giant Evils?', *Think Piece*, London, Centre for Labour and Social Studies, February 2013, p. 6.

75. R. Seymour, 'How Food Insecurity Keeps the Workforce Cowed', *Guardian*, 23 August 2012.

76. I am grateful to Kevin Albertson of the Department of Accounting, Finance and Economics, Manchester Metropolitan University Business School, for some of these suggestions. Personal communication, September 2012.

77. It is estimated that four local jobs are lost for every job created in a large supermarket. This is not hard to calculate, as the till take per employee is about four times higher. D. Craig, 'Why Can Stupid Journalists Not Understand that Supermarkets Destroy Jobs?', *Snouts in the Trough Blog*, 20 March 2012, at snouts-in-the-trough.com.

78. J. Kay, 'Higher Pay Boosts Economics and Politics', *Financial Times*, 2 October 2012.

79. Only eight prosecutions have ever taken place for failure to pay the minimum wage. J. O'Leary, 'Is the Government Failing to Enforce the Minimum Wage?', *Full Fact*, 6 March 2013, at full-fact.org.

80. Simultaneously the 1 per cent get away with most of their crimes, or have done thus far: 'The real test will be the government's willingness to indict or obtain a guilty plea from a major bank. If the Barclays agreement is any indication, it will have plenty of opportunities. None of the other banks implicated can take credit for being the first to come forward, since Barclays has

already claimed that prize.' See J. B. Stewart, 'Calculated Deal in a Rate-Rigging Inquiry', *New York Times*, 13 July 2012.

81. H. G. Rufrancos, M. Power, K. E. Pickett and R. Wilkinson, 'Income Inequality and Crime: A Review and Explanation of the Time–Series Evidence', *Social Criminology*, 1: 1 (29 August 2013), relying in turn on B. Reilly and R. Witt, 'Domestic Burglaries and the Real Price of Audio-Visual Goods: Some Time Series Evidence for Britain', *Economic Letters* 100 (2008), at econpapers.repec.org.

82. BBC, 'Burglaries in Wales up 20 Per Cent in Year, Despite Falling Crime', BBC News, 8 March 2012, at bbc.co.uk.

83. 'In egalitarian countries the cultural activity is high, in highly stratified countries it is low.' T. Szlendak and A. Karwacki, 'Do the Swedes Really Aspire to Sense and the Portuguese to Status? Cultural Activity and Income Gap in the Member States of the European Union', *International Sociology*, 27: 6 March 2012. The online version of this article can be found at iss.sagepub.com.

84. B. Olinsky and S. Post, 'Middle-Out Mobility: Regions with Larger Middle Classes Have More Economic Mobility', Centre for American Progress Report, 4 September 2013, at american-progress.org.

85. A. Petri, 'The Most Ludicrous Hitler Comparison, Ever', *Washington Post*, 21 March 2014.

86. R. Urwin, 'We're So Mean to Those Poor Billionaires', *Evening Standard*, 20 March 2014, p. 15.

Conclusion

1. J. Schalansky, *Pocket Atlas of Remote Islands: Fifty Islands I Have Not Visited and Never Will* (London: Particular Books, 2012), p. 76 (although she should have said mutinies rather than revolutions perhaps).

2. M. Taussig, *Beauty and the Beast* (Chicago: University of Chicago Press, 2012), pp. 11, 152.

3. G. Dines, 'Downton Abbey and House of Cards: Dramas that Live in the World of the 1 Per Cent', *Guardian*, 20 February 2014.

4. N. Powdthavee and A. J. Oswald, 'Does Money Make People Right-Wing and Inegalitarian? A Longitudinal Study of Lottery

Winners', Warwick University Working Paper, 2014, at ideas. repec.org.

5. C. Davies, 'Lottery Millionaires Each Fund Six Jobs a Year, Study Shows', *Guardian*, 22 October 2012.

6. M. Robinson and J. Stevens, 'Couple Who Scooped £148 Million Lottery Jackpot to Divorce Just Over a Year Since Their Win', *Daily Mail*, 20 November 2013.

7. Ibid., quoting from the *Sun* (which is now behind a paywall).

8. R. Pendlebury, 'Spent, Spent, Spent – Pools Winner Now Living on £87 a Week', *Daily Mail*, 22 April 2007.

9. Think of pop stars who die young in the US, such as Michael Jackson or Whitney Houston. And of the more extreme stories of how so many unknowns will do almost anything for money. In 2002 Fox TV in the United States aired the show *Who Wants to Marry a Multi-Millionaire?* Some fifty women competed to marry a man they could not see. All they knew about him was that he was rich. The man turned out to be Rick Rockwell. He married the contestant from California. She, Darva Conger, got some money and a big ring, and had the marriage annulled within a few weeks. Then she posed for *Playboy* magazine. Neither Darva or Rick appear particularly happy: R. Palazzolo, 'Darva Conger and Rick Rockwell Reunite', ABC News, 21 February 2001, at abcnews.go.com.

10. Centre for Policy Studies, 'The 2013 Margaret Thatcher Lecture – Boris Johnson', 27 November 2013, at cps.org.uk.

11. For National Insurance, the rate falls from 12 per cent or 9 per cent self-employed to only 2 per cent above an upper threshold. See J. Browne and B. Roantree, 'A Survey of the UK Tax System', IFS Briefing Note BN09, London, Institute for Fiscal Studies, at ifs.org.uk.

12. ONS, 'The Effects of Taxes and Benefits on Household Income, 2011/12', London, Office for National Statistics, 2013, at ons.gov.uk.

13. M. West, 'Britain's Banks Show They Have Learned Nothing as Figures Reveal Top Bankers' Salaries Soared by More than a THIRD in 2012', *Daily Mail*, 29 November 2013, at thisismoney.co.uk.

14. EBA, '2012 Report on the Data Collection Exercise for High Earners', London, European Banking Authority, 2013, at eba.europa.eu.

15. J. Norman, 'The Co-op Bank Calamity Proved One Thing: What Matters is Good Ownership', *Telegraph*, 4 December 2013.

16. J. Moore, 'RBS Settles £5.7bn Debt, but We're Still £20bn Under Water', *Independent*, 5 May 2012.

17. The City of London is home to the Livery company, the Worshipful Company of International Bankers. P. Latham, *The State and Local Government: Towards a New Basis for 'Local Democracy' and the Defeat of Big Business Control* (Croydon: Manifesto Press, 2011), p. 87.

18. K. Roose, 'One-Percent Jokes and Plutocrats in Drag: What I Saw When I Crashed a Wall Street Secret Society', *New York*, 18 February 2014.

19. J. Nye, 'Inside Wall Street's Most Secret Society: The Billionaire Banker Fraternity where Cross-Dressing New Members Make Jokes about Hillary Clinton and Drunkenly Mock the Financial Crisis', *Daily Mail*, 18 February 2014.

20. The 'most expensive schooling, the right connections, the financial backing [can produce a] sense of entitlement'. See D. Exley, 'Attacking the Evidence that Excessive Inequality Prevents Social Mobility Doesn't Stand Up to Scrutiny', *Equality Trust Blog*, 29 November 2013, at equalitytrust.org.uk.

21. It does not include the effect of the small section of society that continues to get wage rises, and the large section whose wages are frozen or reduced, nor the added effects of inflation. J. Cribb, A. Hood, R. Joyce and D. Phillips, 'Living Standards, Poverty and Inequality in the UK: 2013', Institute for Fiscal Studies Report R81, June 2013, p. 48, at ifs.org.uk. This relies in turn on M. Brewer, J. Browne, A. Hood, R. Joyce and L. Sibieta, 'The short- and medium-term Impacts of the recession on the UK income distribution', *Fiscal Studies*, 34, 2013.

22. D. Stuckler and S. Basu, *The Body Economic: Eight Experiments in Economic Recovery, from Iceland to Greece* (London: Allen Lane, 2013).

23. Figures from Table 5.1, 3.6 and 3.5 of Cribb et al., 'Living Standards, Poverty and Inequality in the UK: 2013'.

24. Office of the Children's Commissioner, 'A Child Rights Impact Assessment of Budget Decisions – Including the 2013 Budget, and the Cumulative Impact of Tax-Benefit Reforms and Reductions in Spending on Public Services 2010–2015', June 2013, p. 38, at childrenscommissioner.gov.uk.

25. Social Mobility and Child Poverty Commission, 'State of the Nation 2013', London, Stationery Office, 2013, p. 180, at gov.uk.

26. IFS, 'Elderly See Incomes Rise, Whilst Young Adults See Large Falls', London, Institute of Fiscal Studies, 2013, at ifs.org.uk.

27. J. Suk, A. Pharris and J. Semenza, 'Health Inequalities, the Financial Crisis, and Infectious Disease in Europe', Stockholm, European Centre for Disease Prevention and Control, 2013, Figure 1, p. 3, at ecdc.europa.eu.

28. D. Attenborough, 'Population Cannot Go On Increasing', BBC News, 16 December 2013, at bbc.co.uk.

29. T. Dávid-Barrett and R. I. M. Dunbar, 'Social Elites Can Emerge Naturally When Interaction in Networks is Restricted', _Behavioral Ecology_ 25: 1 (2014), at oxfordjournals.org.

30. T. Piketty, E. Saez and S. Stantcheva, 'Taxing the 1%: Why the Top Tax Rate Could Be Over 80 Per Cent', Vox: Research-Based Policy Analysis and Commentary from Leading Economists, 8 December 2011, at voxeu.org/index.php?q=node/7402.

31. M. Luke and J. Mukuno, 'Why Do Leonardo DiCaprio and Richard Branson Lecture Us About Carbon Consumption While Plotting Trips to Space?' _Wall Street Journal_, 7 January 2014, at online.wsj.com.

32. L. Dam, 'Elvin Wyly Speaks at Occupy Vancouver', _UBC Geographer_ 7: 3 (November 2011), at geog.ubc.ca.

33. J. V. Beaverstock and J. R. Faulconbridge, 'Wealth Segmentation and the Mobilities of the Super-Rich: A Conceptual Framework', GaWC Research Bulletin 422 (2013), at lboro.ac.uk.

34. E. Saez, 'The Evolution of Top Incomes in the United States (Updated with 2012 Preliminary Estimates)', University of California, Berkeley, press release, 3 September 2013, at elsa.berkeley.edu.

35. E. N. Wolff, 'The Asset Price Meltdown and the Wealth of the Middle Class', New York University Working Paper, 26 August 2012, at confex.com.

36. S. Gilani, 'Income Inequality Is What's Destroying America', _Forbes Magazine_, 27 September 2013.

37. As Shah Gilani did in _Forbes_ (see endnote above) after saying that the middle class of the US 'will increasingly slip into poverty and the backbone of America's increasingly brittle skeleton will turn to dust.' See: 'About Shah Gilani', at capitalwaveforecast.com: 'Gilani studied economics and psychology at the University

of California, Los Angeles. He now lives in Florida and is a managing member of a private equity company.'

38. 'In February 2008, Gilani advised his blog followers to "sell everything and short everything or stay 100 per cent in cash." On 27 March 2009, in a lead story for *Money Morning*, Gilani said the market had bottomed and told investors to jump back into stocks.' Ibid.

39. S. Greenhouse, 'Here's a Memo From the Boss: Vote This Way', *New York Times*, 26 October 2013.

40. C. Freeland, 'Why the Superrich Really Hate Obama', *New York Times*, 12 July 2012.

41. M. Gilens and B. I. Page, 'Testing Theories of American Politics: Elites, Interest Groups, and Average Citizens' forthcoming in Autumn 2014 in *Perspectives on Politics*, pre-publication version available at http://folk.uio.no/sigurdkn/usa_oligarchy_empirical. pdf in April 2014.

42. Which continues: '"It doesn't make me feel personally uncomfortable because I like each of the individuals concerned, but it's ridiculous", Mr Gove said. "I don't know where you can find some such similar situation in a developed economy."' G. Parker and H. Warrell, 'Gove Takes Aim at Cameron's Etonians', *Financial Times*, 14 March 2014.

43. P. Wintour, 'Ed Miliband Attacks Coalition's Growth Strategy in which Rich Will Gain Most', *Guardian*, 17 March 2014.

44. 'He was later widely reported as saying that Labour would "tax the rich until the pips squeak", which Healey denied.' Denis Healey, at en.wikipedia.org.

45. Apparently income inequality has been falling worldwide since the year 2000. Figure 3 in B. Milanovic, 'Global Income Inequality by the Numbers: in History and Now', Policy Research Working Paper 6259, November 2012, World Bank, at elibrary.worldbank.org.

46. CROP, 'Mobilizing Critical Research for Preventing and Eradicating Poverty', Policy Brief, January 2013, Bergen, Centre For Research on Poverty.

47. U. Elbaek and N. Lawson, 'The Bridge: How the Politics of the Future Will Link the Vertical to the Horizontal', London, *Compass*, at compassonline.org.uk.

48. H. Dalton, 'The Measurement of the Inequality of Incomes', *Economics Journal* 30: 119 (September 1920), at jstor.org.

49. World Bank, 'Where is the Wealth of Nations? Measuring Capital for the 21st Century', Washington, DC, World Bank, 2006, at web.worldbank.org.

50. J. B. Stewart, 'Calculated Deal in a Rate-Rigging Inquiry', *New York Times*, 13 July 2012.

51. E. Logutenkova, 'UBS, Barclays Dodge $4.3 Billion EU Fines for Rate Rigging', *Bloomberg News*, 4 December 2013, at bloomberg.com.

52. T. Piketty, *Capital in the Twenty-First Century* (Cambridge, MA: Harvard University Press), pp. 515–17.

53. Ipsos MORI, 'General Concern About the Economy Continues to Fall as Concern Shifts to Poverty/Inequality and the Personal Economy', *Economist/Ipsos MORI*, 29 November 2013, at ipsos-mori.com.

54. P. Diamond, 'Labour's Economic Path to Power', *Policy Network*, 2 December 2013, at policy-network.net.

55. C. James, 'A Prediction That's a Safe Bet', BBC News, 2 January 2009, at news.bbc.co.uk. For Clive James's astute observations on the free market, see the quote on page 88.

56. E. Rolfes, 'Clive James on Turning His "Last Time on Earth" into a Writing Wellspring', PBS *Newshour*, 3 December 2013, at pbs.org.

57. A. Cockburn, *A Colossal Wreck: A Road Trip through Political Scandal, Corruption and American Culture* (London: Verso, 2013), p. 566.

58. One of the most famous payouts was to Mike Ovitz, the former president of the Walt Disney Company, who may have been awarded as much as $140 million on his departure. Images of him on his luxury yacht can be found at hollywoodreporter. com – where, of Michael and his friend, it is said: 'Both Ovitz and Tamara are nothing if not deeply litigious. Tamara battled her own mother in court. They are two of the most ruthless people ever when it comes to business, so they are perfect for each other.' Why, when we can see how the 1 per cent behave when their private lives are revealed, do we not recognise them for what they are? Could it be because most of us are just not that ruthless?

Afterword

1. C. James, 'A Prediction That's a Safe Bet', BBC News Magazine, 2 January 2015, at bbc.co.uk.
2. Z. Williams, 'Labour's Leader Is Not the Problem. The Party's Missing Soul Is', *Guardian*, 11 May 2015.
3. B. Gidding, 'Analysing the Results: Labour's Love Lost', Campaign for Nuclear Disarmament Blog, 14 May 2015, at cnduk.org.
4. R. Winson, 'Five Ways to Deal with a Full-Blown Conservative Government', Centre for Labour and Social Studies (CLASS), 8 May 2015 at classonline.org.uk.
5. L. Elliot, 'London House Prices "Could Double in the Next 15 Years to £1m"', *Guardian*, 14 May 2015.
6. J. Geddes, 'Trudeau Warns the Rich to Watch Out, Again: If We Don't Deliver Fairness, Canadians Will Eventually Entertain More Radical Options', *Maclean's*, 11 May 2015.
7. J. Pring, 'Greens Demand IDS Apology for "Misleading" Voters on Benefit Deaths', Disability News Service, 6 May 2015.
8. J. Pring, 'DWP Told to Publish ESA Deaths Report, after Two-Year Delay', Disability News Service, 6 May 2015; video is on YouTube under the title 'UK Benefit Sanctions the Black Triangle'.
9. The list as of 21 October 2014 can be found here: blacktriangle campaign.org/2014/10/21/uk-welfare-reform-deaths-updated-list-october-21st-2014. It begins with Terry McGarvey, died age forty-eight: 'Dangerously ill from polycythaemia, Terry asked for an ambulance to be called during his Work Capability Assessment. He knew that he wasn't well enough to attend his WCA but feared that his benefits would be stopped if he did not. He died the following day.'
10. D. Dorling, 'Why Are the Old Dying before Their Time? How Austerity Has Affected Mortality Rates', *New Statesman*, 7 February 2015.
11. A. Grice, 'Nick Clegg Rocked as "Depressed" MP Sarah Teather Quits over Welfare and Immigration Policies', *Independent*, 8 September 2013.
12. DWP, 'Benefit Cap Quarterly Statistics: GB Households Capped to February 2015', London: Department for Work and Pensions, at gov.uk.

13. Should you wish to know what that is, see: minimumincome. org.uk.

14. D. Webster, 'Benefit Sanctions: Britain's Secret Penal System', Centre for Crime and Justice Studies, 26 January 2015.

15. J. Armstrong, 'Couple in Court for Stealing Food from Tesco Bins Had Just £8 a Week to Live On', *Mirror*, 12 May 2015.

16. G. Whitham, 'Child Poverty in 2012: It Shouldn't Happen Here, London', Save the Children, at savethechildren.org.

17. All the sources for these statistics come from the Campaign for a Fair Deal for Women, itself founded by eleven women's organisations: fairdealforwomen.com/asks/economy; see also, fawcettsociety.org.uk/2013/02/benefits; fawcettsociety.org.uk/ 2014/08/new-research-low-paid-women-firmly-shut-recovery.

18. C. Beatty and S. Fothergill, 'Annex A of the Welfare Reform Committee 1st Report, 2015 (Session 4): The Cumulative Impact of Welfare Reform on Households in Scotland', Scottish Parliament, 2 March 2015, at shu.ac.uk.

19. Professor David Gordon quoted in P. Butler, 'UK Living Standards Fell for All but the Richest under Coalition', *Guardian*, 5 May 2015.

20. 'Sunday Times Rich List: Britain's Richest Double Their Wealth in 10 Years', *Guardian*, 26 April 2015.

21. D. Dorling, *Injustice: Why Social Inequality Persists*, (Bristol: Policy Press, 2011).

22. 'David Cameron: Civility and Social Progress', *Daily Telegraph*, 24 April 2007.

23. 'We have come to such conclusion before and we'll be come to them again and in between there is battle for hearts, minds and love.' 1 Corinthians 13: 4–8.

Index